BARE

A cabaret dancer's life

Tessa Skola

Darling Jenny

With love,

Tessa x

Published by Tessa Skola

ISBN 978-0-9567788-1-9

Dedicated to

My Beloved Mother, Husband
and Dancers Everywhere.

My love and gratitude to

Penrose Halson, Robert Smith, Jeff Hudson, Phillip Kerr,
Jane Thynne,Joyce Johnson, Marjorie Barrie, Kathyrn Stimson,
Judy Douglas-Boyd, Gaby Alexander, Maurice Poole, Maria McCarthy,
Angela Kelly, J.J., Ken Dyer, White Heat and Backlash.

www.tessaskola.com

CONTENTS

PROLOGUE

THE CURTAIN STARES BACK

'Five minutes please!'

The intercom crackles backstage and there is a sudden explosion of movement. A last stampede for the loo. Half-eaten takeaways left — ketchup dripping. Noses blown, aspirin swallowed, gum spat out, and secretly-smoked cigarettes flushed away. Final checks made in front of the mirrors: pubic hair neat, Tampax string inserted, perfume. Nothing left to chance. Hair solid with spray, wigs pinned securely, corn plasters in place. Just one thing left. Shoes on, straps pulled as tight as possible.

Everything carried out at breakneck speed. Everyone moving as one blur.

Everyone except me.

Three minutes.

I've been ready for half an hour. I've checked, double-checked and checked again every part of my costume. My hair is perfect, my make-up just so and my shoes would require a surgeon to cut them off.

I know the routines inside out and I can't wait to get started.

So why am I so nervous? Why am I not running and chatting with the other girls as they pile towards the edge of the stage? Why am I ignoring the friendly, flirting smiles of the male dancers?

Because I can't make out a single word any of them are saying.

Because they are the professionals. They are the performers who have done it all before, twice a night, for months or years. And because tonight, for the first time, I will be joining them.

One minute.

I stand there, exactly on my mark on the darkened stage. Tense. More anxious than I have ever been in my life. My arms are raised in position, my legs poised. My grin is fixed and my eyes focus directly ahead.

The curtain stares back.

I can feel every beat of my heart and almost hear the blood pulsing around my body. Every inch of my skin tingles with excitement. It is the longest ten seconds of my life.

I've waited a long time for this chance. I've trained until I was black and blue, broken and bent. I've been abused and bullied, threatened and abandoned. There were so many times when I thought I couldn't go on, so many nights when I nearly walked away.

Then the music starts, the curtain swings open and four hundred faces at London's legendary Windmill Theatre stare at my body bathed in the spotlight.

And I know it was all worthwhile.

*****

In twenty-five years of being a cabaret dancer in some of the most glamorous venues in the world I never lost that thrill of standing behind the curtain. I would probably feel exactly the same now. Just waiting to go onstage, knowing that no two performances are ever the same is so tantalising. It's unlike anything else I've ever experienced. For the next ten or twenty or however many minutes – time has no meaning on stage – you really feel you have the world at your feet. It doesn't matter if you're tired, ill or in the peak of health. The moment the announcer makes his introduction, the second the music strikes up and that heavy velvet screen sweeps back, you are in another world. A world where the only thing that matters is the show. Where your body switches to automatic pilot and it would take a bomb to wake you up.

A world where you think, 'This is what I was born to do!'

And it all starts with that curtain. Of course, there's so much more going on in your head.

'Will my headdress stay on tonight?'

'Have I tightened my shoes properly?'

And most important of all, 'Is the stage clean?'

I don't want to sound like a diva – far from it – but a single feather on the stage left over from the previous act's maribou boa is more than enough to ruin the performance. One slip on that and it could be a twisted ankle or worse. It's such a thin line between the premature end to your show – and to your career. And just knowing it's there is almost worse. Focusing on anything external breaks the spell of the dance when the very thing you're aiming for is complete loss in the moment.

When I'm on stage I don't think about the ache in my foot. I don't even think about breathing. I don't notice the exertion or worry about the next step in the routine. My body just takes over and I'm transported completely to another world.

It's how I imagine being under a spell might feel: or in the grip of a powerful hypnotic suggestion. I've known nights when I've come off stage and collapsed in a heap, aware only then that I'd pulled a muscle in my thigh. I remember performing in Bodo, Norway, when I was shocked to be grabbed by another artiste mid-dance.

She was screaming.

'Tess, we've got to get out!'

'Why?' I asked, confused and suddenly aware that I was out of breath. Coming out of a performance ahead of schedule is utterly disorientating, like trying to dismount a merry-go-round while it's still in full cycle.

'The fire alarm! Everyone else is going.'

I peered into the darkness. Apart from a crush around the exit, the club was empty. I don't know how long the bell had been ringing but I'd been oblivious.

And yet, even if I'm immersed in a complex routine, when the night is going well I feel a powerful connection with my audience. I can almost touch their energy and it pushes me to new levels. The right response from a crowd really can make the difference between a good show and a spectacular one. I always give one hundred per cent but somehow the right mood from the right audience seems to squeeze out that little bit more. The kicks go that fraction higher, the smile is more natural, the lifts make me feel I can fly.

I'd like to say that every night was perfect, that every performance was met with a wave of appreciation that propelled me to greater heights. But that hasn't always been the case. I've toured the world as a solo performer several times over and there have been moments I want to forget – if I'm honest, there are entire countries that I wish I'd never set foot in.

All the full houses in the South of France that accorded me rapturous applause, whistles and cries of 'Encore!' can't erase completely the memories of the hell-holes in Greece, all those venues unfit for public performance and club bosses who treated their acts worse than they treated their unwanted dogs. All the lifelong friends I made along the way, and the several who showed me kindness in so many ways, only highlight the level of callousness meted out by so many others.

It's impossible to count the times I've stepped blinking towards my audience and found an almost empty room. The show has to go on, they say. The customers might arrive any moment, give it your all. But it's hard. I only need one pair of eyes to be fixed my way, just one couple who want to make a connection with me and I can do my work. A single fan is more valuable than a dozen disinterested drinkers. But without anyone I may as well be singing in the shower: it's like dancing in clogs.

But working with the Moulin Rouge girls in Japan, winning some of the most cherished contracts in the business to perform at the Nairobi Casino and, of course, appearing at the historic Windmill Theatre, imagining the shows of Mrs Henderson and the stars who had trod the same boards before me – people like Peter Sellers, Tony Hancock, Bruce Forsyth and Tommy Cooper – makes up for all that. That was my dream and I achieved that in style.

But I encountered so much that I didn't bank on: the dark side to the industry.

The things I've endured in pursuit of my dream to dance make me shudder as I look back. Whenever I'm introduced to new people, they always ask the same questions – what did I eat? Why didn't I travel with a group? Was I ever scared being alone? Did I have many lovers around the world? They want to know how dancers cope during their period, how we get our work, how much rehearsal we do – all the mundane details of this other life that seems so glamorous and so completely alien to them. I will always answer any question honestly, but nobody has ever asked about the down side. Those moments I've genuinely feared for my life, the physical assaults *and worse*. I've never told anyone this side of my story before.

So why did I do it? Why did I travel round the world dancing, often topless, sometimes nude?

It's simple: because dancing is all I've ever wanted to do.

And why did I do it on my own?

Because that's the only way I know – the only way I've ever known. I didn't have any money. I didn't have a father. I needed to work and, more importantly, I *needed* to dance.

It's all I've ever wanted to do. And I remember exactly when that started…

CHAPTER ONE

WHY DID SHE CALL ME CATHERINE?

The Cornish sea port of Fowey has a rich and varied history. Once home to Daphne du Maurier, it's become a must-see destination for the thousands of literary fans who make the annual pilgrimage along the area's scribble-like country lanes to find it. And not only has it has seen off invasions from the Spanish, French and Romans, it has also launched the voyages of Drake, Raleigh and Frobisher.

History for a three-year-old, however, means very little. Fowey was my home. It was where I paddled in the sea and scrambled along the beach. I was a tomboy, even at that age, more interested in running and climbing than playing with other girls. Around strangers I was shy and meek and I certainly didn't like being indoors. But when my mother took me to Fowey Working Men's Institute on the quay one evening my life was changed forever. To this day I can remember being led sullenly up the dark, narrow staircase, becoming increasingly aware of the sound of music growing louder with every step.

Where is it coming from?

Suddenly intrigued, I pushed past my mother and ran towards the main hall. I couldn't believe what I saw.

People were dancing.

I had heard music before, on the radio and Grampy's piano, but nothing like this. This was live. The sound was so rich, the volume so loud – and it seemed to be all around me like the air itself. And all those men and women holding one another close or spinning together around the room seemed transported to another world. It was enchanting to see.

I was drawn in instantly. Before my mother had even got my coat off I ran into the middle of the throng. I'm sure there were a few smiles as I tried to copy what the adults were doing but I can only remember one thing – what it felt like to dance myself. I don't recall seeing anything else. I don't even know what the music was. I just remember how my body reacted to the sounds and how it made me happy inside.

Mum says I went from the shyest girl in the village to the biggest show-off in the space of two minutes.

Keen to capitalise on my enthusiasm for a more 'girly' pursuit, Mum signed me up for local ballet classes the following week. I absolutely loved them. I realised then it wasn't just the music that had enraptured me. Dancing itself was the hook and it always would be for the rest of my life. That's how I was able to perform topless, aged seventeen, at The Windmill and even nude in places like Finland and Australia. The most important thing for me was to dance. In fact, it was the only thing I cared about. To this day it has been the rock in my life, the one thing that has kept me going when I could so easily have given up. It has been my salvation on many occasions.

As I made my first enthusiastic attempts at pliés and arabesques, I didn't appreciate it was filling a large gap in my life even then.

There was nothing I loved more than reliving each lesson for my captive audience at home. We lived at the time with my grandparents – Gran and Grampy – who were forced to witness every technique I'd learned a dozen times.

'She's certainly got a beat,' Gran told Mum.

'You'll be a star one day,' Grampy promised. 'You mark my words.'

Gran was an amateur actress and Grampy played the most beautiful jazz piano so I relished every compliment they paid. My mother, of course, applauded everything I did – even when she'd seen it for the hundredth time that afternoon. To be part of such a supportive family meant everything.

Their real show of support came when I was six, however, and I was enrolled in a more advanced class at the Cornwall School of Dancing above a bingo hall in St Austell, about half an hour away by car. Financially my mother could barely afford it – she juggled jobs cleaning holiday homes and working at the Penlee Hotel, run by the actress Shirley Eaton's family, to scrape together my fees. Then there were the other costs. We had a standard uniform of black leotard, pink ballet tights, leather ballet shoes with elastic sewn across the instep and a black hair band to keep our hair back, which all needed to be paid for. Somehow, though, Mum managed it.

Logistically the class posed tremendous problems too. If Grampy, as the only driver, couldn't get home from his job at the Midland Bank on time then one of our neighbours had to be called upon to take me. Looking back, it really was a tremendous inconvenience to so many people, but nobody complained or moaned. We weren't that type of family.

In fact, we weren't conventional at all. This was pointed out to me one day in St Austell as I waited with another girl to be taken home. It started with the most innocent of questions.

'Is your daddy picking you up?' she asked.

'I haven't got a daddy,' I replied.

I'll never forget the next words she said to me.

'Oh, you poor thing.'

That little girl seemed genuinely sad for me and I honestly didn't know why. I had Mummy and Gran and Grampy and that was it. I didn't really know what a daddy was. I just knew I didn't have one. I never considered myself as missing anything: but of course I was.

My mother, Doreen, was born to a family in Lambeth, London, just before the war. Her parents already had four boys and they couldn't afford another mouth to feed, especially once the war began, so she was evacuated down to Launceston and adopted by Gran and Grampy, who couldn't have any children of their own. They moved to Fowey some years later and gave her a blissful childhood. Of course, she always knew that her real family had given her up and one day, in her late teens, she made the journey back to Lambeth to meet them.

It was a disaster.

Imagine the feelings in her stomach as she stepped off the Underground. Nervous, excited and confused. Why was she, the child, making the effort to see them? Why hadn't they come to find her?

I think she regrets ever going. It was an awkward meeting. 'We were like strangers to each other,' she says, 'which, of course, we were. I didn't know them and they didn't know me.'

When she walked out of that little London house she knew she would never see them again.

For a while Mum moved to Bath and trained in nursery care, cooking and housekeeping. Then she made a decision that would alter her life. Aged twenty six, she replied to an advertisement to work as cook for Lord and Lady George at Government House – in Adelaide, Australia.

It's obvious looking back years later that I inherited my wanderlust and spirit of adventure from my mother. But so many other qualities I know I took from a man she met over there.

Adelaide, like much of Australia, had a large Latvian population, many of whom had fled Riga after the war. My father, Dainis Skola, was one of those. Like a lot of Latvians who despised the Russian occupation of their country, my father, still a boy, cheered when the German army took over.

'How could things get any worse?' he said.

But one night, in a forest just outside Riga, he witnessed SS soldiers executing Jewish families. He gasped – he couldn't help it. And of course he was heard.

Daddy turned and fled as fast as his teenage legs would carry him. Suddenly he felt himself fall over but he didn't know why. He hadn't tripped. He'd run through these woods hundreds of times. He was as surefooted as a cat, even in moonlight. Then he realised.

He'd been shot in the thigh.

He was bleeding and in terrible pain. His heart was racing and the adrenaline seemed to push even more blood out of his body. But at least he was alive.

Somehow Daddy got back to his family and they made a terrible decision. They buried the family silver and fled their home. They made it to Dresden and were herded into a Displaced Persons camp where they lived and worked until the end of the war. Grandfather never made it, though. Like so many prisoners desperate for relief from the horrors of their lives, he experimented with alcoholic drinks made from the fuels he had access to at the aeroplane base where he worked. One of these concoctions took his life.

Daddy was terribly damaged by these experiences. Aged fourteen, he and his brother, Viktor, and their mother, Jo, were shipped to Australia. He couldn't hold down a job and he threw himself on the mercy of alcohol. Viktor says, in fact, that Daddy's life didn't really begin until he set eyes on my mother years later.

Doreen and Dainis made a perfect couple. They were so in love and in 1958 got married without telling Gran or Grampy. To this day Daddy has always been the only man for Mum. But love wasn't enough. When Mum discovered she was pregnant with me she took a new look at her marriage. Dainis was wonderful in so many ways but every month that they were together seemed to bring fresh problems.

One day they argued, Daddy drunk of course, and he cut his wrist right in front of her.

'If you ever leave me I'll kill myself!' he said.

She knew it was the alcohol talking but by then it was only ever the alcohol talking. She also knew that he would never change, not even fatherhood could make that happen.

So the next day she packed a suitcase and boarded a ship for Southampton. Even though every fibre of her body told her that she was doing the right thing, I don't think Mum has ever got over the decision to escape. She loved that man so much – in fact she has never loved a man again – but she gave him up for the sake of her unborn baby.

For me.

And she never saw him again.

******

Waiting for Grampy outside the Cornwall School of Dance, aged six, I didn't know any of this. Every Christmas I'd receive a card from my grandmother in Australia, Jo, with a ten-dollar bill inside but it didn't really register as significant. She was just a name.

As far as I was concerned, Grampy was the father figure in my life. He was the one I would watch *The Black and White Minstrel Show* with and recreate the backing dancers' movements for. He was the one who ferried me around and played games with me in the garden.

Under the tutelage of our brilliant teacher, Irene Luke, I excelled at the Cornwall School. Irene practised the rigorous style of the Russian ballets – the Cecchetti system – as opposed to the standard Royal Academy of Dancing syllabus, and I really responded to this incredibly physical discipline. You can always tell a dancer who has studied Cecchetti by their muscular legs because it's all about strength and speed – both qualities I possessed thanks to a childhood of boyish adventures.

It was all a far cry from the Tessa everyone knew at my junior school. There I reverted to my demure and quiet self, slow to learn and even slower to attract a teacher's attention through daring to ask a question. So imagine the shock of our headmistress, Miss Hunkin, when she spied me running through some movements for a few of my friends. I still smile reading her shocked report to my mother: 'I was amazed to see this little mite confidently taking the other children through all the steps, completely oblivious to anyone else around, let alone me. In her absorption she had become a completely different child. It was obvious that beyond the quiet, shy exterior there lay a real talent.'

At home, which was now a flat near the waterfront so Mum could work as housekeeper opposite, I began to put on shows with school friends. The square hall was the perfect size for a stage and it saw dozens of little plays and dances performed, each one more colourful and extravagant than the last. I loved entertaining and the thrill of choosing the perfect costume for dressing up was as important to me as the music. When I got to see professionals do it, it was even better.

Summer holidays were spent in Torquay, where I learned to swim in the hilltop pool, jumping in at the deep end with all the boys. But it was the evenings that I looked forward to. The Princess Theatre often hosted a ballet during the tourist season and Mum would take me as many times as she could afford. I remember being so entranced by the performers that as soon as the interval arrived I leapt into the aisle and began my own rendition of what I'd seen. After the show I continued in the foyer – much to the embarrassment of my mother.

One night Mummy took me to the Spa Ballroom. I was too young to go in but the manager let me peep through the door curtain. It was such a wondrous sight, I gasped. The glitterball cast technicolour stars around the darkened hall, picking out the beautiful dresses, bare shoulders and hairstyles of the swirling couples. The heat from the room was incredible and as for the pulsating live music – I was immediately transported back to Fowey Working Men's Institute, aged three.

Suddenly I felt a pat on my shoulder and it was time to go.

'Just a bit longer,' I pleaded, my gaze not leaving the ballroom.

The manager chuckled at Mum. 'Another two minutes shouldn't do any harm.'

I couldn't bear to leave that doorway. It was like my wardrobe into Narnia. I was witnessing another world: a shining, alive, mesmeric world that called out to me. A world that I knew I had to be a part of.

Every penny of pocket money or gifts that came my way I ploughed into buying ballet music. I soon had a marvellous collection of LPs and played them constantly, choreographing my own dances. It was a film, however, that I really became obsessed with – Michael Powell's *The Red Shoes*, and, in particular, Moira Shearer's captivating portrayal of Vicky.

The movie captured in vivid colour the hard work and manic drive required to become a ballerina, and I determined to learn its lessons.

Aged eight, I passed my Grade 1 exam with Honours and a year later Irene Luke advised my mother that we should be thinking about taking my dance education further. It turned out Irene wasn't the only person thinking along those lines. Mum had started helping out an eccentric old lady called Murchie who lived with her Scottish companion, Kirsty, in a rambling house above Readymoney beach. I liked going to visit them because their place was heavy with atmosphere and filled with Murchie's collection of telescopes. One weekend I arrived with Mum as usual and Murchie greeted us waving a piece of paper.

Before we had even reached the door, Murchie said, 'Well, it's decided, she has to go to the Royal.'

'Morning, Murchie,' Mum said, quite used to the old lady's ways. 'What's this then?'

'Ah, young Tessa,' Murchie said. 'We've told Moira Shearer all about you and she's quite adamant you need to apply to the Royal Ballet School.'

I was knocked back.

Moira Shearer? *The* Moira Shearer? My idol from *The Red Shoes*?

'What's all this about, Murchie?' Mum asked.

That's when we were shown the piece of paper. It really was a letter from the great ballerina herself.

'Well,' Murchie explained, 'Kirsty and I wrote to her. We said that there's this delightful child in the village who's always dancing in the streets, full of talent, and asked what advice she could give. She's just written back.'

I studied that letter for what seemed like hours. I couldn't believe my heroine had asked about me! It was incredible. I'm just sad that I never really thanked Murchie and Kirsty enough for thinking of me like that. Sadly, it's too late now.

The Royal Ballet ran a school in Richmond Park, London, called White Lodge, for the ten-to-sixteen age group and Irene Luke told us that the entrance exam would have to be taken in Bristol; that was the nearest one. As soon as we made an application I was told to bring three black-and-white photographs each featuring a different position.

'That seems quite a fuss for a nine-year-old,' Gran said.

In fact it was just the tip of the iceberg.

For a little girl who'd been cocooned in the sleepy confines of Cornwall all her life, travelling to a city like Bristol seemed like an adventure – an exciting but scary adventure. When Mum and I arrived we immediately felt isolated. Everyone else seemed so confident. Just walking into the waiting room was a sharp introduction to the harsh, competitive world of ballet. Boys and girls looked aloof and preened to perfection. They didn't even look like children any more. The parents were even worse, fussing and issuing commands – clearly more nervous than their sons and daughters. By contrast Mum and I observed quietly from the corner. She would never dream of fussing over me in that way and I would never expect it. We'd done our best and that would have to be good enough.

'Just enjoy the dancing as you always do,' Mum assured me.

But I very nearly didn't get the chance.

One by one the boys and girls were summoned into the performance hall. Each time I sighed with relief that it wasn't me – but the wait was excruciating.

With just half a dozen people left in the room the organiser came out again and called, 'Catherine Skola.'

Once more I relaxed as I waited for the next girl to get up. But no one moved. Suddenly I felt a nudge in my side.

'Go on then,' Mum said. 'What are you waiting for?'

'But the lady called "Catherine",' I said.

'That's you, silly. Now get going.'

I don't know how I managed to complete the audition but once again my ability to lose myself in dance kicked in. As soon as I'd finished, though, I needed answers.

'Why did she call me Catherine?'

Mum smiled, 'Because that's your name.' And apparently it is. She relayed how Grampy's sister, Auntie Dot, had tutted when she'd learned I was to be called Tessa.

'Tessa is not a name,' she said and for some reason Mum was persuaded and I was christened Catherine. But Mum regretted it instantly and she has never called me anything but Tess all my life.

Auntie Dot highly disapproved of my career as a dancer which only encouraged me, but her reaction was one that I would have to get used to throughout my life as people frowned on my choice of work.

I passed the audition in Bristol but that wasn't the end of it. Next I travelled to Penzance to work one-to-one with a teacher there, for technique and improvisation. Again I passed this stage – and in return was awarded a scholarship to White Lodge. No one else from Cornwall had ever earned a grant to the Royal Ballet!

But I still had one more hurdle – an audition at White Lodge itself.

It was just before Christmas when Mum and I travelled up to London. I had butterflies in my stomach about so many things but the tranquillity of Richmond Park soon calmed me – until I saw the majestic old Georgian building where I was due to perform.

If the other stages had been nerve-racking, this was traumatic. I was handed a number to pin to my leotard and told to wait. I was used to that by then. Ten stern-faced teachers sat behind a long table, calling us over one by one. As usual I was barely capable of walking when my name was said, but as soon as I started performing I became a different person.

At the end they said, 'Congratulations. Your dancing is of a high enough standard. You just need to pass the medical tomorrow.'

I hadn't really paid that part of the test any thought – I'd been too worried about the audition. But we returned the next day and the doctor at White Lodge took measurements from every part of my body. Once again we were told to wait and it was several hours later before a lady came out to see us. She didn't look at me at all, just spoke directly to Mum. I knew then it was bad news.

'Mrs Skola, I'm afraid we can't offer your daughter a place.'

My tears started before she'd even finished speaking. Apparently, while my head and body were the perfect shape right then, according to their forecasts I would not develop the required physique for a member of the Royal Ballet. One shoulder, they said, had a slight bow. It was not noticeable then but it would become so.

And for that I was rejected.

I was crushed. All that hard work, all my dreams smashed to the floor. To be accepted for your dancing but not for the shape of your body is a harsh decision. No nine-year-old should endure that level of disappointment but in the ballet world it was commonplace. Looking back, I probably got off more lightly than most of the other rejected children – I doubt their parents were as understanding. It was part and parcel of gleaning the cream of the crop.

Long-limbed and tall I would never be – not a Kirov model. I would grow up to be more like Lynn Seymour; muscular, strong and a rebel.

Mummy was amazing. She did her best to take my mind off it and when my thoughts did wander, she assured me it was for the best.

'Tomorrow we'll visit Brooking's and you'll get a place there instead,' she said.

The Nesta Brooking School of Ballet was another highly-respected school in central London and we had already made back-up plans to go there. Once more I wasn't very confident when we arrived, but this time I was judged only on my dancing ability and the teacher sat down and spoke with me to find out more about me and my ambitions.

And I was accepted.

Our train journey home was so much nicer than the journey up. I was in such a good mood that I didn't notice Mum seemed less enthusiastic. Eventually she admitted how much she was dreading being separated from me. Looking back, perhaps it reminded her of being abandoned by her own parents.

'And I don't know what Gran and Grampy are going to do without you under their heels all the time,' she added.

I was sad for a second but then my happiness bubbled over again. 'I shall have so many new dances to perform for Grampy every time I come home,' I beamed. 'I can't wait to show him.'

Unfortunately I would never get the chance.

Even as we made our train journey from London, Grampy was being declared dead at the wheel of his car. Another driver had collided with him on the way home from work and he'd stood no chance. When I found out I broke down uncontrollably. Mum and Gran did their best to console each other but the tears flowed between them too. It was the worst day of my life and the following weeks did not make the loss any less painful. I can still picture his Christmas presents, unopened under the tree.

As well as being the best grandfather a girl could want, Grampy had been the only father figure I had ever known. I wouldn't appreciate how important his loss would be until years later.

All I knew was that it was the worst possible time to be leaving home for London.

CHAPTER TWO

GO TO THE DOGS

On my first trip to London I had been full of wonder at everything the city had to offer. The marvellous shops, the diverse architecture and even the crush of people moving as one from street to street all seemed so exotic to a little girl from the coast. The trepidation I felt at auditioning for the famous White Lodge and then Brooking's, however, had kept my emotions in check. But I knew at the time that if I was lucky enough to win a place I would really look forward to coming back and experiencing everything properly.

When the time came, though, it was the last thing I felt like doing.

Grampy's absence affected me every day. There were reminders of him everywhere I looked. I'd be running down the street, then suddenly pass a bench where the pair of us had loved to sit, or a park where he'd pushed me on a swing. Today those images just stir the fondest warmth in my memory. But at ten years old every memento was painful. I only felt loss.

I was too wrapped up in my own emotions to notice anyone else's but Mum and Gran saw to it that I focused on my adventures ahead: that must have been so hard for them.

Compared to losing Grampy, saying goodbye to my schoolmates was straightforward for me. I also had the advantage of knowing what I wanted to do with my life – and of having taken the first step to achieving it. I doubt whether a single other person in my year had even half an idea of what they wanted to be when they grew up.

A mixture of excitement and nerves carried me through my final morning in Fowey. Mum had booked a hotel near Brooking's and we were travelling up a couple of days early in order to acclimatise. Just as we were about to leave for the train station there was a knock at the door. It was Gran. I had been expecting her but my tears still welled up as soon as she stepped in. I gave her a twirl in my smart travelling outfit and she smiled at Mum.

'How grown-up she looks,' Gran said. 'Grampy would have been so proud.'

The morning before term started Mum and I visited Freed, the ballet-shoemaker in St Martin's Lane, Covent Garden, to buy the required kit. It was an olive green, gilded corner shop with plush carpets and high-backed chairs. Mats and floor mirrors allowed customers to see how their feet looked *en pointe*. The walls were a treasure trove of signed photographs from ballet stars all over the world, with Beryl Grey and Margot Fonteyn taking pride of place.

Dance outfits were available in every colour imaginable but our shopping list was very specific. Brooking's requested sleeveless black leotards, a black crossover cardigan and pink tights with full feet and back seam. The most important part of the costume, however, came only in one colour. Freed's pointe shoes were pink, square-toed and far more supportive than other multi-coloured brands. That was most important as I would be spending more than twenty hours per week strapped into them by pink ribbons that tied round my ankles.

Two hours later we left the shop laden with olive and gold bags. As usual, it didn't occur to me to wonder how many sacrifices Mum had made to scrape the money together. She seemed to be as excited as I was with our purchases though.

The laughter stopped once we reached the building where I would be boarding. Brooking's girls from outside London were required to lodge at a grand property in St John's Wood called Littlehouse and, while I was nervous about being separated from my family, I was sure I would feel better once I settled in and met the other students. As soon as we were introduced to Miss Rice, the Irish housekeeper, however, any promise of a friendly welcome and enjoying my new "life" in this elegant house disappeared. Miss Rice was big-boned, drably dressed and unsmiling as she showed us to the bedroom I would share with four other junior girls; four seniors slept upstairs.

Even Mum seemed cowed by Miss Rice's presence and I'm sure that was intentional. It seemed that as soon as I'd stepped foot inside Littlehouse I had become one of her girls. She couldn't wait for Mum to leave, yet wouldn't give us any privacy for our goodbyes. Miss Rice stood steadfast in the room, intruding on our last moments together, almost daring us to cry. It was a symbolic moment. She'd taken over responsibility for me and the time for emotions and tenderness had gone.

I wanted to watch Mum walk away until she was a dot in the distance but as soon as she'd left the room, Miss Rice slammed the door.

That was the moment I realised that I really was on my own. In several hours' time my mother would be back in Cornwall with Gran.

A sudden nightmare flashed into my mind.

What if Mummy forgot about me like her parents had forgotten about her?

We had made the reverse journey compared to the one she had endured as a child; me coming to London, her leaving it. But the effect was still the same. A girl thrust out into the world, away from every comfort she has ever known.

The parallels loomed large in my overactive imagination but Miss Rice was not the kind, I soon learned, to humour dreamers.

'Dinner is at seven,' she snapped.

I nodded, suddenly aware I was back in Littlehouse.

'Don't be late.'

The house itself reflected the Irishwoman's personality. It was dull and dark, as if scared of fun. The entrance walls were adorned with portraits of past students who'd all been through what I was about to endure. Rules were many and rigid: calls home or received had to be booked, only one allowed each week unless there were exceptional circumstances. Meal times and chores were both set to a strict timetable.

That night's supper gave me the chance to meet the rest of the girls. Another junior, Jackie, also from Cornwall, had been there for a year.

As we all sat down to eat, instinctively in silence, Miss Rice served our meal. I don't remember what it was even though she had a very limited repertoire due to Miss Brooking's insistence on a strict diet of wholefoods and a spoonful of cider vinegar a day, but I do remember the sensation of her eyes on me as I took each mouthful. She watched like a hawk to ensure every last scrap disappeared. Talking to other girls that night, I learned they all felt the same scrutiny. Somehow she was able to monitor all nine of us at once.

The next morning I was ready with my fellow students to take the tube to Baker Street. As soon as we were out of Ricey's sight – the seniors' nickname for her had already filtered down – everyone reverted to normal behaviour. The frostiness I'd encountered from everyone else at Littlehouse had been purely down to fear of the housekeeper's wrath. Once introductions were made properly I was quickly at ease in their company. For the first time since Mum had left, I felt the weight lift from my shoulders. Here were girls like me in the same boat, striving for the same goals.

My relief was short-lived. As soon as we entered Marylebone High Street and were in sight of the red brick building that housed a Robert Dyas store on the ground floor and the Brooking School on two floors above, the atmosphere in our group altered. Emotional shutters were pulled down and the rest of the girls began to walk with more considered, upright steps. The seniors led. Instinctively I followed suit.

If the air of intimidation cast by Miss Rice had been unfriendly, the welcome offered by Nesta Brooking and her partner Eleanor Hudson was positively hostile. Their style was closer to that of an army sergeant major than a dance instructor, all bristling severity and no obvious love for children. Even though it was the first day for some of us they made no attempt to ingratiate themselves.

I was terrified just looking at them. They were like sisters in their sixties, although I would later discover they were lesbians. Each was short and round with a sturdy stride and small, puffy hands. From the first time I saw them until the last, they were dressed in slacks, smocks and slippers - and a scowl. Very rarely did either smile, and certainly not on that day.

'The seniors will show you where to go,' Brooking barked. 'Changed and in the studio in ten minutes.'

As at Littlehouse, the school was divided into areas for juniors and seniors. The lower floor housed school classrooms because we still had to receive an academic education. A corridor separating the studio area served as our changing room. A bench ran along each wall with a row of hooks, marked with each student's name. It was sparse, like Littlehouse. It was not quite what I expected.

'Is this it?' asked another new girl.

I didn't dare do anything more than shrug in case I was heard, but I thought, 'Irene Luke's school was better equipped than this.'

We filed into the junior studio for our first session with Miss Brooking, everyone as nervous as they were uncomfortable, even the long-term students. I wasn't the only one desperately self-conscious in my new ballet outfit and having my hair parted in the middle and scraped up into a high bun with a net, as ordered: no fringes or ponytails.

As soon as Miss Brooking ran us through a few steps I began to relax. That familiar feeling of being transformed through my body's movements started to take over and I felt myself smile for the first time since Mum had left.

'Very good, Skola,' Miss Brooking called out and I glowed inside. After barely an hour in her company I could sense that compliments were hard won.

But that was when I noticed that my dancing really was a lot better than one or two of the others. A couple in particular seemed too overweight to carry off moves with any grace and another had almost no ability whatsoever.

How on earth had they secured a place?

Later I learned it was for one simple reason: their parents were prepared to pay and Brooking and Hudson were happy to take their money. The school cost £75 a term with another £95 on top for lodgings at Littlehouse. A private ballet lesson was £1.25. I'm sure they would have preferred only the finest dancers because the school had an excellent reputation to maintain, but a paying student was better than no student at all.

Lunch was at twelve-thirty. There was no canteen so everyone sat cross-legged on the studio floor munching sandwiches in near silence. At one o'clock we were taken by the teachers on the educational side of the school, followed by another two hours of ballet. By the end of my first day as a Brooking's student I was almost too tired to be lonely.

Almost, but not quite.

Miss Rice seemed hell-bent on filling every moment with distractions. We were all instructed in how to wash our leotards and tights in Lux Flakes. I'd never washed anything before – Mum or Gran had always done that. Even before I'd finished scrubbing, I noticed a reaction on my skin.

Ricey took one look at my reddened arm and sniffed. 'This is the powder Miss Brooking insists upon.'

'But…'

'No buts,' she said and left the room.

A second later another girl sneezed. I'm sure it was the powder but it didn't matter. It was best never to complain about or question anything; just shut up and do.

Homework was next, followed by dinner, then half an hour to prepare lunch for the following day. Finally we were allowed upstairs to bed. Even though there were four other girls in the room, for the first time that day I felt like there weren't eyes fixed on me. I allowed myself a minute to think about home, and, of course, I cried. I wasn't the only one. There were sniffles from all round the room.

I thought about what Mum would say if I spoke to her. She'd tell me to cheer up and to work hard. She'd say she loved me, of course, and that she was missing me. But mainly she'd say, 'If you want to achieve your dream then you have to work hard.'

Was my dream worth that feeling of loneliness though?

The next few weeks seemed to follow very slowly. Miss Rice's rules were rigid at the boarding house and I never looked forward to returning there. Weekends were the worst. Most of the boarders disappeared back to their parents on Saturday afternoon. Living so far from home, there was no chance of me disappearing. At least my new friend Jackie was in the same position. We could play in the garden and were even allowed to watch television. *Little House on the Prairie* was a favourite programme – despite its name reminding us of our own living quarters.

On Saturday mornings everyone attended a morning ballet lesson together – juniors and seniors – taken by Miss Brooking in the top studio. Some of the older girls were exceptional performers but it was the boys who caught my eye; watching them held a fascination for most girls. Their jockstraps were a thing of humour for us but we were all in admiration of the way they worked with, guided and supported a ballerina during duet work. Purely from a dancing point of view I couldn't help imagining myself in the boys' arms. But even though I was so young, I'm sure I was developing feelings that went beyond ballet as well.

Classes would begin at the barre, a beam fixed waist-height around the walls to aid balance. Turning left or right I'd face the back of another student. Only the confident or late-comers stood on the end – that position was too exposed. The pianist played set pieces and we would perform our rehearsed steps centre-studio, beginning with allegro (quick movements), then pirouettes, followed by leaps across the room and then, my favourite, adage (slow, graceful balances and extensions). Every instruction was in French, as classical training dictates.

'Poor lines!'

'More expression!'

The personal torture of whichever dancer had earned the rebuke was on display for the whole room, but the rest of us just kept our eyes straight ahead. No one ever responded or questioned. We finished by presenting a long curtsey, dripping in sweat, then filing out of the studio, either quite pleased with our performance or feeling a failure. There was no in-between and Miss Brooking let us know on which side of the divide we fell.

During my first few days at the school I had found it odd when no one talked as we got changed but it quickly became habit. There was nothing to say. I knew how everyone else was feeling and they knew exactly what was on my mind. Some days I was the girl sniffling quietly under the coats, trying to pull myself together before going to maths or walking home, and I would feel the supportive pats on the back from the others. But everything was conducted in silence.

Miss Brooking was never slow with a harsh word or a barked order. In fact I had never met anyone with a worse temper. Everyday things seemed to be the bane of her life. How girls dressed, walked, spoke or didn't speak were some of her favourite bugbears and she would punish anyone for transgressing her unwritten and often inconsistent expectations. I was as likely to upset her mood as anyone if we passed in the corridor. We had to darn the top of our pointe shoes with pink wool to prolong their wear and I was not good at sewing. My attempts were always criticised.

However, in the studio I'm sure I had an easier ride, in the early days at least. For all her faults Brooking really did recognise and want to encourage good dancing and I think she honestly saw something worth developing in me. Her greatest act of generosity came towards the end of my first term.

'Skola, is there anything you can use from this?' she asked me one day.

She was holding a large box which I recognised as the "lost property" collection. It swelled with tops, socks and ribbons from the previous weeks because no one ever dared to claim anything. It was safer to buy a new leotard than admit to Miss Brooking that you'd lost one.

Nesta Brooking was hard to like even when she was being nice. I couldn't relax fully in her company knowing she was only an untied ribbon or a stumbled pas de deux away from fury. Even though my first term passed without incident compared to the treatment of some of the other girls, I still felt a tremendous sense of relief when the day came for me to catch the train home. I would only have a fortnight back in Cornwall but I would have settled for a day. The opportunity to escape from the claustrophobic atmosphere of Brooking's and Littlehouse seemed like heaven.

Every mile the train put between us and Paddington saw my spirits soar. By the time we pulled into Par station and I saw Mum's smiling face I had completely put Brooking's behind me. It's not that I didn't want to tell my family how hard things were – I just didn't want to spoil my time with them. It was a trait that I would find hard to shake even as an adult.

The following term was harder than the first, both in workload and attention from Miss Brooking. Whatever initial fondness she had felt for me vanished one Sunday when she announced we were all to be confirmed at our local church.

'I don't want to be confirmed,' I told her.

'All Brooking's girls are confirmed,' she insisted. For her that was the matter closed.

I didn't say anything else but I refused to join the line of young dancers blessed by the vicar that day. I don't think Miss Brooking ever forgave me. It was as if it reflected badly on her.

She seemed to be pushing us all harder than ever in the studio as well and was rarely satisfied. Lessons were conducted via shouted instruction and criticism was doled out freely. Her approach to teaching was like a surgeon's to resetting a fractured bone. First she needed to break us before we could be improved.

And it worked. We were so desperate to please her that the shouting and the insults became just another part of the day. We took the put-downs like praise and only grew stronger with the ritual humiliation.

We even began to accept physical abuse as part of everyday life.

I don't know if she had been holding back until we'd settled in, but there was a definite change in Miss Brooking's teaching technique towards the end of my first year – and not for the better. With the entire class holding a pose, she walked down the line, tapping her cane on the floor. Feeling her eyes settle on me for a second longer than normal, I felt my supporting leg wobble. It was the slightest movement but it was enough to rile Miss Brooking.

'Maintain your poise, Skola!' she shouted. And as she did so she swung her heavy wooden cane against the side of my calf.

The pain seared through me like an electric charge. I don't know if she'd intended to hit flesh not bone, but I was so skinny anyway there wasn't much difference.

The one thing I knew I mustn't do was react. Miss Brooking was waiting for that. Nothing would have given her more pleasure at that moment than making an example out of me.

'Don't cry,' I told myself over and over. 'Don't cry.'

After what seemed like the longest few seconds she stepped away and I felt a huge weight lift from my shoulders. I couldn't believe she had hit me. No one had ever touched me like that in my entire life.

Later that night I was still shocked by the assault. The other girls were sympathetic but they all knew it could have been them. I was said to be one of the best new dancers – if I'd attracted Miss Brooking's wrath then they could too. As soon as I reached my bedroom I pulled out my writing paper and began a letter.

> *Dear Mummy,*
> *I had the most awful day. Miss Brooking hit me with her cane. I didn't cry but I really wanted to. She said I'd ignored her instructions but I hadn't. Is she allowed to hit me, Mummy? I've got a large bruise on my leg and it still hurts.*

Then I stopped. I read what I'd written once more then tore it up. There was no way I could send that letter. It would break Mum's heart. There was nothing she could do. She wouldn't want to worry Gran with the news so she would just store it up herself and get upset. I just wished Grampy was around. She could have told him. He would have known what to do. But Grampy wasn't there.

And Daddy was on the other side of the world.

For the first time in my life I felt emptiness and bewilderment that he wasn't around. Even though I didn't know him, it seemed that just having a father would make things better. *Wouldn't it?*

Miss Brooking's new trick with her cane became a regular feature of our classes. I probably escaped with fewer whacks because I generally managed to perform everything she asked. But I was standing next to another girl when the teacher suddenly threw a stool across the studio and it collided first into her then into me. Pain, I realised, was now a daily part of our routine.

I can't forgive Miss Brooking for training us into such submissive obedience and taking away some of our spirit but I have to admit her methods had results – and I wasn't the only person to think so. One day there was a buzz around Littlehouse as I ate my breakfast.

'What's going on?' I asked.

'There are talent scouts in today,' Jackie explained. 'One of the seniors told me.'

'Talent scouts for what?'

'I don't know.' She giggled. 'Does it matter though?'

Having strangers in the room while we ran through our paces could have been inhibiting and in fact a lot of the girls failed to meet their own standards. I was the opposite. Somehow the presence of an audience scrutinising me pushed my performance to a higher level. I was in my element.

It was just like that moment of being three and losing myself at the Fowey Working Men's Institute. I danced without a care in the world. It was just me and the music.

Of course, it helped that Miss Brooking was in a good mood. She was tremendously sociable whenever outsiders came to visit – especially those who could spread the word about her work.

At the end of the session I was called over to meet our guests.

'Hello, Tessa,' a tall blonde woman said. 'How would you like to dance on television?'

On television!

I was speechless. Miss Brooking was never lost for words, however.

'She'd love to, wouldn't you, dear? Brooking's girls are always ready to perform.'

A week later I was escorted to a studio on the outskirts of London and asked to do a little dance with a couple of other girls. Performing someone else's steps has never been easy for me – I prefer to choreograph myself – but I picked up the routine very quickly. At the end, the director came over to us and said, 'Congratulations, girls. You have just danced for the new Lyon's Maid commercial.'

I appeared in quite a few things while I was at Brooking's. As well as adverts for chewing gum, soap and other household goods I even won a part in *Candid Camera* – the number one television show at the time – and a small role in the film of *Alice in Wonderland*, starring a young Fiona Fullerton. On each occasion I thrived in front of the camera where others faltered.

I also began to be chosen for demonstrations, choreographic competitions and whenever a teacher in training required a pupil. I realized then that I would never want to teach dancing.

I couldn't wait to put down my experience in letters to Mum and Gran. The girls back at Littlehouse were also keen to hear of my time mingling with the stars. But however proud Miss Brooking was that her school was so well represented, she was ever quick with a dismissive comment as soon as she saw me after a performance.

'I hope you didn't let the school down,' she sneered. 'We have a reputation to uphold, you know, and we don't want you getting too big for your boots.'

By contrast, I lost count of the number of times she made us watch the old black-and-white film, *Mandy*, featuring a previous Brooking's girl. I like to think that after I left the school she began to acknowledge the talent of more recent pupils – but somehow I doubt it. We were a new breed, not like the "wonderful students" from a decade ago.

The gruelling exertions of the ballet classes, combined with the unrelenting sniping, took their toll. It's what was termed "the hard grind". It started here and wouldn't stop until the dancing stopped. After the first year at Brooking's I returned to Cornwall a thinner, quieter version of the girl who had left. But I was a much improved dancer: there was no denying that.

Once again I didn't tell Mum or Gran about the intimidation or the beatings. How could I?

Looking back, that was a terrible decision for an eleven-year-old girl to have to make. Would it have been any different if I'd had a paternal influence to confide in? I don't know, but things would have been different in one way at least because I remember thinking, 'Mum has enough on her mind just paying for me to attend Brooking's. I don't want to add to her problems when she's already doing so much for me.'

Cornwall in summer meant swimming, running and climbing and other outdoor pursuits, although Miss Brooking forbade horse riding due to the use of different muscles. But it also meant eating and relaxing – two pastimes that were never indulged at Brooking's. But dancing was never far away from my thoughts and when a lady called Rosita opened a boutique in Fowey I was inspired once again.

Rosita was an ex-flamenco dancer from Spain who'd studied ballet then graduated to classical Spanish dance at the Barcelona Opera

House. Everyone in the town told her about me and eventually we met. I instantly liked her and soon she was a regular audience member for the little dance shows I put on in our home. She was also happy to share all her memories of the dance world. I pored over hundreds of her photos, firing question after question. Mostly Rosita answered shyly, not wanting to make herself seem too successful: there was just one exception.

'Is this...?' I asked as I studied one picture of her on stage in Europe with a striking blonde woman next to her.

Rosita nodded. 'I worked with her.'

I couldn't believe my ears.

'You worked with Ingrid Bergman!'

She smiled and told me all about it. It had been a short step from classical ballet to touring the world on the burgeoning cabaret circuit. She'd seen countries I had never heard of – and worked with some of the biggest names in entertainment. It sounded so glamorous but Rosita said there was a lot of hard work involved – and some aggravation.

'In some clubs we would dance our hearts out over the din of plates and chatter.' she told me. 'There'd be chairs scraping, people moving about but it didn't matter. You have to carry on no matter what happens. Never break the spell, your expression or the standard of your performance. Always be professional.'

There was one thing that no amount of professionalism had prepared her for, though. Certain clubs insisted that all dance troupes mingle with the audience afterwards to encourage them to buy drinks. I was too young to appreciate what this meant but it didn't sound nice.

'We lost lots of contracts by refusing to do this,' Rosita said. 'But that's not what dancing is about. Never forget that, young Tessa.'

I didn't fully appreciate what she was telling me but soon enough her advice would haunt me every day.

*****

By coincidence my second year at Brooking's began with the introduction of flamenco onto the syllabus. I was in my element among the foot-stamping, swirling movements and the solid beat of the castanets, just as Rosita had promised I would be. The teacher was Miss Cogan, a stocky, fiery woman with thick-rimmed black glasses and masses of black hair. There was something else about her that I couldn't put my finger on at first. Then I realised: she was 'sexy'. Her passion for the dance lit up her entire body and it made everyone watching fall in love with her. I was thrilled when she took me under her wing for extra practice.

Where ballet is regimented, cerebral and artificial, flamenco thrives on energy and the heart. But you can't excel at the latter without a solid grounding in the other discipline. Succeeding at ballet, however, takes its physical toll and every minute was given to transforming our bodies in some very unkind ways. It was only the fact that we had young, supple figures that allowed many of the techniques to be physically possible. Pupils' legs were pushed by a teacher into ever more extreme splits as they lay on the floor. Our lives were about practice and repetition, honing the same exercises over and over again, regularly working on highlighted 'bad habits' during our own break times. I remember one girl walking around on tip-toes for half an hour at a time to improve her insteps. A boy, Raj, had his feet manipulated daily to increase his point. I had to stand on ping-pong balls to open my rolling ankles, as prescribed by Miss Brooking.

At eleven I passed Grades 2 and 3 with Honours and from classes in soft leather shoes I now progressed to wearing pointes all the time. The treasured Freed's glossy pink shoes were soon scuffed and grey. It was a daily assault on the feet, cramped and distorted to produce the exquisite arch required. It took weeks to acclimatise to wearing them. My toes didn't actually touch the ground when up on the pointe block. The toe joints were supported by a cast made from layers of hessian and glue which held the foot in a rock-hard grip. It was impossible to stand on your toes without pointe shoes but wearing them made normal walking feel like climbing uphill. You could only progress with feet turned out; "at ten-to-two" we would joke, referring to a clockface. To stop blistering and bleeding we washed our feet in surgical spirit and wrapped lambswool around our toes. Dancers' feet are their worst feature next to lank, thin hair.

As we matured, and our fashion sense developed, everyone started investing in new clothes and jewellery. This could only be worn in our own time – and even then only out of sight of Misses Hudson and Brooking. One hint of a high heel and we were handed additional chores: extra sewing or cleaning of the studio floor. Jewellery was simply confiscated, never to be seen again. It wasn't enough that they dominated our school days with abuse and violence – they terrorised every minute they could.

But still I made progress. The following year I passed Grade 4 with Highly Commended and gained a place in Scholars, a series of classes for top students from various schools, culminating in a theatre performance. Weekends were suddenly taken up with rehearsals – but being away from Brooking's made the effort worthwhile.

With every month that passed the pressure increased; and with the greater training demands came harsher words and harder whacks. Yes, I was improving all the time. But at what cost? When I arrived in London I had been a carefree dance obsessive. My lessons seemed designed to strip any joy from the one thing in my life that gave me any pleasure. Every night, exhausted in my narrow bed, I cried myself to sleep with the same thought: 'It's the teacher I hate, not the dancing.' But in my mind the two were beginning to merge.

Ironically, as I fought to maintain my love for ballet, I found salvation of sorts in more academic pursuits. At first, our schooling was an inconvenience to all of us – we all wanted to dance for a living, so why did we need to learn about Shakespeare and the square of the hypotenuse? With the arrival of a new headmistress, however, I discovered an unlikely ally.

Penrose Colyer arrived in comical circumstances. When she'd replied to the advert, she thought it was for an "autistic" school. It actually said "artistic", but by then it was too late. While her predecessors had let themselves be dictated to by the school's overbearing owners, Miss Colyer immediately distanced herself from their methods. She became a friendly refuge for all the dancers, especially those who suffered most at the tongue – and cane – of Miss Brooking. And, for reasons I was yet to deduce, I definitely seemed to be singled out. Thanks to the new head's kindness I actually found myself enjoying academic study for the first time and I now knew I always had a friend to confide in.

But Miss Colyer couldn't be around all the time. At weekends and evenings and during the dance work itself I was on my own. It didn't matter that I was surrounded by other girls and boys – we were *all* on our own. Either by accident or design Miss Brooking destroyed any sense of community. I could be in a room of twenty dancers who were all working through the same problems as me, and yet feel absolutely alone.

I needed help. I was crying out for someone or something to take away the pain and fear and desperation. And then one day I found it.

Alcohol.

The tabloids these days are full of stories of underage drinking and young teens drunk on "alcopops". I read those reports and think, *'These poor kids are often drinking out of boredom. They do it for a laugh.'*

I never had that luxury. I was drinking because I was scared, because I was worn down by the harshness of my life at Brooking's. I was drinking to escape.

Acquiring wine or spirits wasn't as easy for a child then as it appears to be now, although it wasn't impossible. Once we'd reached thirteen years of age, Brooking's allowed us to go out after Saturday class. Carnaby Street, with its 1960s feel and flea market, was a regular draw. Michelle, an American student, pretty, with blonde hair and a wide smile, also introduced us to the delights of The Great American Disaster – one of London's earliest fast food bistros. These were the happier times, but made so much better when older boys could be influenced to buy us a drink.

I knew from my first sip that I had a taste for it.

Not having access to alcohol every day probably saved me, although I could never have attended lessons while drinking because when I did find a supply, I drank and drank until either the bottle was empty or I couldn't physically take any more. I felt sick the next day, of course, but that memory always faded. The one that stuck, however, was the bliss of sinking into that place where I wasn't scared of Miss Brooking anymore. The realisation, as another glass disappeared, that I didn't care about the school.

I didn't care about anything.

Like so much else, I tried to keep my new-found obsession secret from Mum – but she quickly found out for herself. On my next trip home we were invited to meet the new vicar of Fowey at a reception thrown at a neighbour's house. I was the only young girl in the room and was quickly ignored by the adults. But I didn't mind, because that meant nobody noticed me helping myself to the bottles of sherry on offer.

Even though I was so far from Brooking's, the school was always at the front of my mind. Dancing, Littlehouse, Miss Brooking – everything was jumbled together and I could no longer differentiate between good and bad memories.

Not sober, anyway.

But I remember that first glass of sherry pushing my London life back into my brain. I actually felt free of the school's influence for the first time since I'd been back, so of course I had another glass. And another. And another.

I drank quickly, worried about being stopped, and not allowing the effects of each subsequent measure to take its toll before embarking on the next. I proudly counted fourteen glasses in total .

The next thing I remember is being woken up by the terrific noise of someone shouting and screaming.

'Go away! Leave me alone! It's not my fault!'

It was an awful sound. Someone was obviously in a lot of trouble.

Then I realised the person shouting was me.

I had passed out and been found by the daughter of the house, ranting and crying, completely drunk. She laid me on her bed and I woke with her holding my hand, soothing me.

Still, though, I didn't confide to Mum or Gran what had driven me to drink. They both thought it was my first taste of alcohol and I'd been naïve. I don't know what Mum would have done if she'd thought I genuinely had a problem. After all, she had left Australia and her husband because he had been an alcoholic. How on earth would she react if she saw me in danger of treading the same path?

I didn't learn my lesson. After one weekend back in London I was offered the chance to stay at a girlfriend's house on Saturday night. I would have grabbed that opportunity even if there weren't the promise of a party as well. That night I drank to my usual extreme levels and I continued the next day. Finally it was time to return to Littlehouse.

Standing at South Kensington station I remember the sense of dread swarming over my body. Even in my inebriated state the fear was rising. Suddenly I heard a voice.

'Are you all right?'

It was a man – a builder, judging by the state of his clothes. We started talking and soon we were travelling on the tube together. But we didn't go to Littlehouse. We went to his flat.

I think he sensed an opportunity. He couldn't have known I was only fourteen and a virgin. I was not at all sexual as I was too far gone. He undressed and lay on the bed but I didn't know quite what to do. When he asked my age he got angry and said I should leave. He just let me walk out, unsteady, with no money, in that state. But at least he didn't touch me. Somehow I staggered back to the boarding house, relieved at my narrow escape. But it was a stupid thing to do. I was lucky; that same scenario could have ended very differently. In a few years I would discover to my cost just how fortunate I had been.

There was no denying my new-found interest in boys. That summer Mum somehow found the money to take us both to Majorca. I'd never flown before and the whole experience was so exciting. In those days tourists dressed for travel the way they might for church. The Sunday best was always worn and, as someone who adored dressing up, I was no different.

But once we had settled into our hotel it was my other interests which surfaced. I loved the swimming and sunbathing and I was naturally proud of my lean, dancer's physique, but it was the figures of the local boys who caught my eye. Once I'd been introduced to some of the region's sangria I wanted to do nothing more than party with my new friends. The fact I had dark hair and a strong tan probably made me look Spanish to them.

That holiday was a marvellous tonic for me. It reminded me that life didn't need to be as hard as Brooking's made it. But it also helped me appreciate that it was the school I disliked, because one night my love for dancing was reignited with a fury.

Tito's nightclub had a reputation for the best shows so Mum and I decided we would try to get in. Perhaps if I stood as tall as possible, they wouldn't notice I was underage: and it worked. When the show started I thought I had gone to heaven. Music sounded and half a dozen girls in little more than silver boots and g-strings dazzled their way onto the stage and started to dance as though their lives depended on it. The colour was sensational and the flamenco moves just suited the atmosphere so perfectly. For two hours I watched transfixed, utterly absorbed by these hypnotic performers.

'I wish that was me,' I thought.

For the first time in months I thought about my lessons at school without a pit in my stomach.

'If that's what I need to endure to be like Rosita or Miss Cogan then so be it. This is what I want to do.'

And I wanted to start that night! Mum still reminds me how she heard a commotion in the courtyard soon after the show had ended and discovered me leading a procession of drunken tourists through a chaotic flamenco conga! And of course I was drunker than anyone.

While sangria fuelled a lot of flirting with the Spanish boys, it was back in Cornwall that my interest in the opposite sex reached its natural conclusion. I'd met a lad called Quentin at a funfair. He was obviously smitten with me and I liked him. After months at Brooking's, being told I was no good every day, I think I would have responded to kind words from anyone. Over the course of the summer we got closer. So much so that my mother suspected what was on my mind.

'I can't stop you sleeping with this boy,' she said calmly, 'but I do want you to be safe. You can use the upstairs room here.' And, ever practical, she added, 'You'll need to lay a towel down on the bed first'.

Considering we were close enough to talk about that sort of thing, why on earth didn't I trust Mum with my problems at school?

As it turned out, her precautions weren't required: and, as usual, alcohol was involved. Quentin used to pick me up on his little moped but he was always late. That infuriated me so I would have a drink of Gran's gin while I waited. By the time he arrived one night I was completely sozzled. Quentin didn't have much in the way of conversation but we had a real physical connection and that night we got even closer. I don't think much was said but we parked along the beach by a shelter and I lay on the bench. He knelt over me and the next thing I knew we were making love.

I didn't have any expectations but I was somehow disappointed. Quentin didn't move at all and I didn't know what to do either.

Is this it?

I was still wondering when Quentin climbed off. Before I could pull down my skirt I heard a click and suddenly my body was bathed in torchlight.

'What on earth are you doing?' I shouted.

Quentin didn't answer, but by the way he was examining me I soon guessed. He wanted to know I was a virgin, I think, in the only way his teenage mind could conceive. But there was no tell-tale blood. Years of over-stretching every part of my body for five hours a day had robbed him of that satisfaction.

I saw Quentin again but whatever chemistry we'd had had disappeared.

No sooner was I back at school than my holiday was forgotten and my misery reinstated. Miss Brooking's first words to me were typical.

'You've put on weight, Skola. You need to be careful.'

Are there any words crueller for a fourteen-year-old who is so conscious of the changes in her body?

I was crushed. Was I fat? Had I over-indulged during the summer? I could barely get through the morning's lesson because I was thinking so much about her words. At midday I looked at my sandwich then put it back in the bag. I felt sick with hunger all afternoon but back at Littlehouse I did the same. As soon as Ricey turned away I scooped as much supper as I could into a handkerchief in my lap. Then I excused myself to go to the toilet and got rid of it all.

I cried myself to sleep that night, upset and hungry.

The next day I ate an apple for breakfast – and nothing else all day. I made up for it with plenty of water but, after I'd done the same thing three days' running, I was really beginning to suffer. I lost concentration in English and could barely lift a foot in the studio that afternoon. Still I fasted, though. A full week went by and, strangely, the pain of starvation stopped. But I was still so weak and my dancing was beginning to suffer.

'Move your arms, Skola!' Miss Brooking screamed. 'They're like coat hangers.'

A full two weeks since I'd last eaten properly my body gave up. I was in a maths class and feeling incredibly tired. Suddenly it seemed like someone had extinguished all light. I awoke a second later and burst into tears. Clumsily I rushed out of the room in tears. A few moments later the classroom door opened again and Michelle came out. I barely had strength to lift my head up but I saw she was holding something.

It was a Mars Bar!

Ravenously I fell on that piece of chocolate. I should have savoured it but I couldn't and it was gone in seconds, every mouthful healing me.

Speaking later, Michelle said that she had guessed my problem. She pointed out that I wasn't the only one driven to starving myself and as soon as she told me the signs I realised many of the girls ate artificially small diets. Two girls, she confided, were almost certainly anorexic.

After a few days and a series of proper meals, I felt like a new person in the studio. I must have danced better, too. Even Miss Brooking noticed.

'You're looking slimmer, Skola. Look how much more gracefully you move.'

Whether she was right or wrong I swore never to let her words affect me like that again.

After that episode I think I grew a bit stronger. The following weekend I went to stay again at a friend's house in Knightsbridge. On the Sunday afternoon, however, instead of returning to Littlehouse I went to Paddington instead. Six hours later Gran got the shock of her life when I appeared in the garden.

I wish I could say my family understood when I poured out my problems to them, but they didn't. Because I had bottled so much up they had no idea of the relentless suffering and bullying that had been going on for so many years. Of course they both tried to console me in their own ways, but they just assumed I was fabricating the details and making a fuss about nothing.

'You'll feel better after a good night's sleep,' Gran assured me.

'You can't throw all your hard work away after one little problem,' Mum agreed.

The next morning I was horrified to be put back on the train to Paddington.

'You have no idea what Miss Brooking will do to me now!' I cried.

Mum looked genuinely worried but obviously thought I was over-reacting like any teenager.

'She'll understand,' she said. 'I'll explain it to her.'

I was physically quaking when I saw Miss Brooking the following day. She stood an inch from me in the studio and I felt her cold, milky eyes examine me. I braced myself for the pain.

But it didn't come.

'We'll have to watch you very carefully, Skola, from now on,' she said. And that was it. She just moved on.

From the way the veins in her temples were raised as she spoke I'm sure she wanted to hurt me but something was obviously holding her back. Later I realised that not only had Mum spoken to her but also to Penrose Colyer, the academic head. Miss Brooking was like all bullies. She knew when to pick her fights.

Despite her words she didn't watch me very carefully. In fact, outside of class, she did her utmost to ignore me for the next year. I was completely frozen out of shows and demonstrations. When the casting agents called I was not allowed to audition.

The enforced solitude allowed me to study towards my O-levels. Miss Colyer was able to take more care of me but she could see the treatment I received was wearing me down. Foremost in my mind was the realisation that I no longer wanted to concentrate so much on ballet. It was time I transferred to flamenco full time. But before I could do that I had to tell Miss Brooking. I sweated with nerves every time I even thought about it.

I swear, sometimes, that woman had a sixth sense. Just as she was always able to appear at Littlehouse when we were most disruptive, or walk into the studio while someone was misbehaving, I sometimes felt she could predict what I was going to say. While I was trying to steel myself to tell her about my switch, she began to compliment my dancing once more.

'You are becoming a beautiful ballerina, Skola,' she said one day. 'I think it's time you started training with the seniors.'

What an honour! For a few hours I was so grateful for the recognition that any thought of opting out of the discipline slipped my mind. In fact I let a few weeks slide by, which allowed me to experience working with the older girls, before I finally confronted my nemesis.

'Miss Brooking,' I stuttered, 'I'd like to switch from ballet to flamenco next term. I think it suits me more and I would like to audition for the school in Madrid that Miss Cogan recommends.'

I'd said it! Breathless I waited for her response. Once more I felt those shark-like eyes penetrate into me. Then, without saying a word, she turned her back on me and left the room.

She didn't speak to me again for another four weeks.

I was obviously in the doghouse, though. Another teacher informed me I was not ready to take my Intermediate exam – even though I was more than capable. And overnight my chores at Littlehouse and the school seemed to double. Worst of all, I was banned from further flamenco classes. I didn't think it was possible, but I was the most unhappy I had ever been.

The next time Miss Brooking spoke directly to me was during a class. She suddenly interrupted the session and said, 'Skola, in the changing room – now.'

The whole studio hushed and I followed her, heart pounding. I thought I was going to wet myself.

What have I done? I wondered.

As soon as we were alone Miss Brooking stepped towards me.

'Skola,' she hissed, 'you are the most disruptive, irresponsible child in the school. In fact, you are sub-human. You are too close to your mother. And your father is a bastard.'

My father is a what? How dare she.

I knew she wanted a reaction. The whole episode was so staged she must have been plotting it for days. But I refused to give her the satisfaction.

I will not cry, I will not cry.

Somehow I followed her back into the studio and completed the class. But that was it for me. I'd had enough. The following Saturday, rather than rehearse for our forthcoming show at the Barbican with the students from the Royal Ballet, I just caught the tube and without even realising how I'd got there, I found myself in Leicester Square. I lost track of how many times I walked around the same small area, weaving in and out of tourists, almost trying to lose myself among them. Eventually I sat down against a shop wall and just stared unblinking ahead.

I must have been there hours. Then I was aware of someone standing over me.

'Hello, young lady,' a tall man wearing a dinner suit and a bow tie said casually. 'Are you waiting for someone?'

I shook my head.

'How would you like to make some money today?'

I didn't know what to say. So he continued, 'Do you think you can talk to men in a room? You look the friendly sort.'

I think I must have said "yes" because the next thing I heard was him saying, 'Right, I just need to get some cash and speak to a few friends. You wait here. I'll be right back.'

As soon as he was out of sight, all the common sense that seemed to have deserted me five minutes earlier came flooding back. That man wasn't going to fetch money.

Run! I thought. But where to? I saw a telephone box and dashed into it. The operator connected me to the number I wanted and the next person I heard said, 'Hello, this is the Samaritans. How can I help you?'

It was the only thing I could think of. I'd just read Monica Dickens' book, *Befriending: The American Samaritans,* for an English project, so I knew how they helped strangers in distress all over the world. I prayed they could help me.

The man I was speaking to gave his name as "Paul 621". He was very nice so I told him about running away from the school and my encounter with the smartly-dressed man. 'I don't know what else to do,' I sobbed.

'Don't do anything,' Paul 621 said. 'Where are you?'

'Outside the Empire Ballroom, Leicester Square.'

'Stay exactly where you are and we'll come to you. You're going to be all right.'

I did as I was told and stood by the theatre. My heart was racing. Who would reach me first – the stranger or my guardian angels?

It was the latter. A young man and a young woman approached me and said, 'Are you Tessa? I'm Paul 621.' Without saying a word I just fell into the woman's arms.

That couple drove me to Paddington Station and paid for a ticket to Cornwall, where Mum had recently moved back in with Gran. All the way they comforted me and listened. They didn't offer opinions or judgement, just the warmest feelings of support. Thirty-five years later I'll never forget them.

Home was the only place I wanted to be but I was worried how Mum would react when she saw I'd run away again. I needn't have worried. By the time I arrived Paul 621 had explained everything and she held me like never before.

'I'm sorry,' she said. 'I'm so sorry.'

She knew then I hadn't been making things up. The next day she spoke to Miss Brooking, who said I was causing trouble and telling lies to get attention. Mum then called Penrose Colyer who gave a different view. 'Things are far from happy at the school,' she confided. 'I don't want to say anything slanderous so I shall only say that Tessa was in no way being selfish or difficult'.

What should we do? Mum said it was up to me – 'whatever makes you happy, darling' – but at Penrose's suggestion I was persuaded to finish the term and then leave. After all, she reasoned, the fees had already been paid and I was due to appear with the Royal Ballet in a number of prestigious shows, including a night at the Barbican's Golden Lane Theatre.

So, with a very heavy heart, once again I returned to London.

Stepping into the top studio to face Miss Brooking's wrath the following day was one of the hardest things I have ever had to do. I was steeled by the knowledge that the end was in sight. *Just a few more weeks to endure,* I assured myself. The atmosphere in the room was foul. My friends were all sympathetic but for their own sakes none of them dared be seen to take my side. Miss Hudson was there and she just shook her head as though in shame. Her partner blanked me completely. *What is she up to?* I wondered.

That night, I found out.

Littlehouse had just finished supper when there was a noise in the hallway. My heart sank when I saw Miss Brooking arrive and beckon me from the door.

The second we were alone she cuffed me around the back of the head.

'Upstairs!' she spat, pushing me violently forwards.

I sprinted up two at a time and waited, breathless, for my overweight tormentor to join me at the top. I was visibly shaking. This made her smile weirdly.

'Look at this bathroom floor,' she said and as soon as I glanced down I felt another punch on the side of my head. The force knocked me straight to my knees and I started retching.

'Don't you dare be sick!' she yelled, storming away. Moments later she reappeared. 'While you're down there, you may as well clean the floor,' and she kicked a metal bucket and a cloth at my head and walked back downstairs. I had to stay in the small top bedroom in solitary confinement until breakfast.

At school she acted as though nothing happened but her violence had taken one more thing from me – I no longer felt safe at Littlehouse.

The only thing that carried me through those last painful few weeks was looking forward to performing with the Royal Ballet. It was hard work but how many teenage dancers got that opportunity?

The final performance took place on the last night of term – and both Jackie and I were booked onto the overnight train to Cornwall.

The Golden Lane Theatre was a warren of studios and dressing rooms on several floors. We had a day of dress rehearsals on the big and slightly sloping stage and that night I packed my case and spent my last night at Littlehouse. The next morning I said farewell to Ricey then Jackie and I lugged our cases to the theatre. It was surreal to think that what seemed like a lifetime of horror was going to end in a few hours.

But first I had to give the performance of my classical life.

The show went without a hitch. I was thrilled to be in such a huge theatre with the Royal Ballet and I'm convinced I danced better than I ever had before. Afterwards all the dancers were bubbling over with adrenaline backstage when suddenly a hush fell on the room as Nesta Brooking and Eleanor Hudson entered.

'What a performance!' they gushed and rushed over. I couldn't help smile in anticipation – but they both waddled past me and went straight to Jackie. 'You were tremendous.'

'The best on the stage.'

Jackie had been very good but we both knew this act of affection was purely for my benefit. I didn't mind. I was happy to be ignored – which once again I'm sure Miss Brooking sensed and determined to ruin.

'As for you, Skola,' she turned to me. 'Go to the dogs.'

I was fourteen and those were her last words to me. For a moment I was crushed but then I felt a tremendous sense of relief. I was free of her. Free of her school.

And ready to begin the rest of my life.

CHAPTER THREE

AND ALWAYS LOOK GORGEOUS

Even though I left Brooking's ahead of schedule, it still took my ballet education up to eleven years. Had it been worth it? As I sat at home with Mum and Gran I didn't think so. I was haunted by nightmares for years to come. I was convinced I'd be scarred for life and I'd walked out before I could take my O-levels.

Once again my guardian angel at Brooking's stepped in. Penrose recommended a special boarding school that was the antithesis of Brooking's, called Monkton Wyld in Dorset, and I went there to take my exams. It was a Hogwarts-style house which took in children from eight to eighteen. Most had their own social worker or were from famous families but needed extra care due to their unusual backgrounds. Where ballet school had been regimented, this was relaxed and I settled in well. At the end of my year there Mum was confident enough that I had mended to make a big decision for herself.

In 1970 the film *Midnight Cowboy* picked up the Academy Award for Best Picture as well as scooping the Best Director Oscar for John Schlesinger. Seven years later Schlesinger had also achieved acclaim for *Sunday Bloody Sunday* and *Marathon Man* and was preparing for one of his most ambitious projects yet – the war film *Yanks*. Tackling a love story set in World War II would require precise planning down to the last detail. But Schlesinger had something else to contend with that he hadn't predicted.

Me.

At the end of 1976 Mum applied for the post of live-in housekeeper at an address in Kensington. She decided we both needed a change of scenery after a hard few years and, more importantly, my future dancing career would benefit from being in the capital. She went for an interview with the owner, who turned out to be Schlesinger. She was offered the job there and then so had to mention she had a daughter in tow.

'One more person here won't make a bit of difference', he laughed.

Within a week of moving into 10 Victoria Road we knew exactly what he meant. It was a large house which JRS – as John was called – used as both a home and his business centre and it was never quiet. Far from it, in fact. Phones rang endlessly, couriers and messengers dropped off and picked up twenty-four hours a day, and there was a constant stream of visitors for auditions, screenings or other meetings. And it didn't seem to matter whether JRS was there or not. People came and went and Mum ran around after them.

The house itself was a white, Mediterranean-looking corner building with a roof garden, striking in its own way on the outside but like opening a sumptuous box of chocolates once you stepped through the front door. Designed in typically bold fashion by David Hicks, who counted Windsor Castle and the Prince of Wales among his other clients, the chocolate mousse and lime green interior's carpeted walls and thick drapes cushioned the sound of laughter, music and film projections, while pine candles, lit every day, created a sense of well-being, like floating in a different space. Here anything seemed possible. The lounges were lined with collections of Lalique and erotic figurines but it was the downstairs loo, covered with stills from his films, which held most fascination for guests. I never tired of peeping inside John's black suede office because among all the clutter on his desk was the shining figure of Oscar himself, used as a paperweight.

John's humour and impeccable taste were just two of the qualities I quickly learned to admire. He was a ball of energy, handsome in his fifties, and brilliantly funny and charming. Like most artistic people he could be bad-tempered and demanding but the dark times never lasted. He was only ever a moment away from laughter. As a teenage girl in the throes of my own sexual development I found him incredibly attractive. The fact that he was gay didn't bother me – in fact I think it added to his allure.

In some ways Number 10 wasn't that dissimilar from living at Littlehouse. Everyone around me was highly creative, sacrificing a normal life for a chance at expressing themselves on stage or screen. But there was one vital difference. Whereas Nesta Brooking ruled by fear and seemed threatened by any spirit in her charge, John couldn't be happier to help his friends – and for them to succeed.

Apart from Mum there was a secretary, Valerie, two cleaners, a gardener and Ray the chauffeur. Ray was like an uncle to me, in his forties with a youthful attitude. He had previously worked for Led Zeppelin and I never tired of hearing his behind-the-scenes stories and about touring the world. That was my dream and he encouraged me to pursue it all the more. Like the majority of the men who passed through Number 10, Ray was gay, but that didn't matter to me. On the contrary, it was affectionate paternal company I craved – the very thing I hadn't known since Grampy died.

Mum and I lived in a basement flat which had a separate street entrance but was also linked to the main house. She quickly discovered that being so close meant there was no time off. It didn't matter what time of day or night it was, JRS or one of his guests wouldn't think twice about knocking on our door for help with something or other. Considering the amount of stimulants consumed in the house it is amazing anyone slept at all. Guests would stagger down for breakfast any time between seven in the morning and four in the afternoon, in between mouthfuls of uppers and downers, then disappear back to their rooms. I remember the American actress Brenda Vaccaro wandering into the orange lacquer kitchen once.

'Doreen, have you seen my grass?'

Grass? Mum didn't know what she meant so said, 'No, sorry.' Clearing up half an hour later, she discovered an unused cigarette. Without thinking, she lit it – and was high all day! I couldn't stop laughing when I realised what had happened.

'Mum, you've smoked Brenda Vaccaro's marijuana!'

She still can't live it down to this day.

Vaccaro was best known for her role as Shirley in *Midnight Cowboy* but many of Number 10's other overnight visitors were considerably more famous. One guest room was known as 'The York Suite' because the actor, Michael, and his wife stayed so frequently, but within days of moving in I also helped Mum serve breakfast to Burgess Meredith, Angela Lansbury and Placido Domingo. Even though I had some experience of dancing in adverts and on stage, it really was another world where film stars wandered around in their dressing gowns while you were pouring a cup of coffee.

It was a sign of JRS's hospitality that a lot of his visitors arrived with no intention of staying over. Then their host's charm offensive would start.

'Don't be silly, you must stay over. It's no trouble – Doreen will have a room ready in five minutes. And if you need anything, just knock on her door.'

So they did.

Our flat was treated like an all-night supermarket.

'Doreen, do you have a toothbrush?'

'Headache tablets?'

One morning there was a knock at the door and I opened it. Richard Gere was standing there in his boxer shorts.

'Hi, I was told I could get some shaving foam here....'

It's a surreal introduction to one of the world's perennial heart-throbs but one that no sixteen-year-old will ever forget!

Everything at Number 10 happened at top speed. Everyone worked to incredibly tight deadlines. On our third day John flew into the kitchen looking for Ray, who was preoccupied with a problem and deep in conversation with us.

'Right, I want suits collected from Tommy Nutter, film reels from Wardour Street, photo proofs from David Bailey and then a meeting at The Ritz, so come back for me about two o'clock,' he ordered. Still without pausing for breath he added, 'Michael will call about a photo collection so I need those back here ASAP.'

Ray leapt to attention.

'Right away, sir,' he said.

Then, as JRS bolted out the door, still issuing instructions to his secretary, Ray stared blankly at us, 'What did he say?'

Everyone chipped in. John was incredibly trusting and after just a few weeks he came down again, this time to see me.

'Tessa, we're all on a shoot. Valerie will be back at four. You're in charge of the phones.'

And that was it; he was off again.

No sooner had the whole party disappeared than the phone rang. I sprinted into Valerie's office and timorously answered.

A familiar but sinister voice drawled down the receiver.

'Hello, is Coral Browne there?'

'I don't know, sir. Who is she?'

The deep voice gave a chuckle.

'She's a world-famous actress, my dear, and she's also my wife.'

The voice belonged to Vincent Price, star of so many horror films. And yes, his wife was there – somewhere. Over the next few months I met Vincent many times and was never prepared for the incredible aura that surrounded him – or his rather flat feet!

Mum quickly learned to prepare for the unexpected – like Oscar winners wandering in to ask for stain removal tips or pop stars desperate for a particular recipe. Her main role was to make sure everything was ready – at short notice – for any meeting, dinner party or event. I helped choose menus and served some of the dishes. I was a little nervous but never so in awe that I made a fool of myself: although at one dinner party for twenty, I nearly dropped the bottle of wine I was to pour when I saw Elton John seated at the head of the table! It was the most splendid gathering of musical talent, including Freddie Mercury, Paul McCartney and the composer Marvin Hamlisch – who, at the time, was just completing the score to that year's Bond movie, *The Spy Who Loved Me*.

I'm not sure Mum recognised any of them because she was certainly unfazed. The only thing that troubled her the whole evening was worrying about the state of the upstairs bathroom. Someone kept throwing up, missing the pan and causing a vile stench. Fortunately, the din of conversation drowned out the echoes of retching filtering down the stairs.

JRS bustled in and on hearing the sound effects mouthed, 'Bulimia – not your cooking'.

Having had my own brush with eating disorders I knew someone was seriously suffering, yet the party continued well into the night with all guests delighted.

Dinner gatherings were sedate compared to the behaviour at JRS's bigger parties. At first I thought John must actively seek out the most raucous, flamboyant people possible. Then I realised they all sought him out. These were the actors and the directors and producers, singers, designers and models that were all desperate to be seen with him. Drugs were plentiful and sex was never far from anyone's thoughts. I'd never seen so many beautiful people in one place – and I probably haven't since.

But beneath the beauty, there was definitely a sinister side to so many of the visitors. John confided to me that the industry is full of people out to get what they can.

'A lot of these people only like me because I'm successful, because they think I can do something for them.'

'So why do you invite them?' I asked.

'Because they're my best friends!'

He was only half joking. When JRS started out he was desperately poor and worked hard to meet the right people. He was acutely aware that the movie industry operated on a "who you know" policy. He forgave friends their superficiality because he knew they needed it to survive.

John was incredibly generous to those he liked, although not everyone treated him with respect. After a day spent helping Mum get ready for her first big event, I watched gingerly from the sidelines as the stunningly dressed party-goers hit dazzling new levels of debauchery. There was a greed to so many of them. At John's request, I had set dozens of bowls around the house containing the exclusive Bond Street Sobranie brand of cigarettes. I was shocked to see how many people literally scooped handfuls of the multi-coloured packets into their pockets or handbags. The next morning Mum reported that dozens of bottles of vintage champagnes and wines had gone missing. There were even half a dozen towels stolen from the guest rooms!

Unfortunately John's sexuality was responsible for a lot of the worst behaviour. The London gay scene in the late 1970s was incredibly experimental and even dangerous, and many of the actors and pop stars arrived with rent boys they'd just picked up. I could spot them instantly – always the handsome but awkward young men hanging around older, more successful and usually more intelligent partners. Their eyes would light up as soon as they stepped inside John's palace.

'You may as well put price tags on everything,' Ray told me. 'That's all they're seeing.'

The only time theft didn't happen, it seemed, was when John's family was staying. His father, Dr Schlesinger, viewed the whole scene with detachment; but nothing escaped his scrutiny and the guests knew it.

Always with a smile for me he would enquire, 'And how's "We never closed"?' (A nickname he used owing to my contract at the Windmill!)

Drugs were such an important part of the lives of most visitors to Number 10 for different reasons. Some people took them to be part of the "in scene"; others because they needed new highs all the time. I met some users who saw tablets as a replacement for food. In the entertainment business looks are all-important, especially for women and gay men.

As I knew from my own experience with Nesta Brooking.

I never had any interest in experimenting with pills or potions. My drug of choice at Brooking's had only ever been alcohol; that's what I used to escape from the tortures of my life there. It was no different, I realised, from John's friends whom I witnessed losing themselves in cocaine and worse to dampen the pain of professional rejection.

But while my reasons for drinking may have gone away – my taste for it hadn't.

I never drank at home – not secretly, anyway; I wasn't one of those drinkers. But if anyone offered me a glass of something, I never said 'no'. Not to the first glass, not to the second, in fact not to any of them. I drank until I blacked out. Then as soon as I recovered I would drag myself to my bed. The house was so big and Mum was so busy and so tired that she never noticed.

I always ended the night in my own bed but there was nothing I wouldn't get up to before that point. I was in an awkward position socially, because as the housekeeper's daughter, I wasn't part of the glamorous set – I was staff. And yet I was sixteen, I was dressing more and more provocatively, inspired by the overtly gay fashions around me, and I had my own experience of working for years to pursue my artistic dream. Some of the visitors to Number 10 sensed my empathy immediately and tried to seduce me as an equal. Others were fragile egos, desperate to bed me to flatter their own esteem. And then there were the ones who chased me for their own unpleasant amusement.

One night I overheard a conversation between two well-known men.

'You can't touch her, she's the cook's daughter.'

'That's *why* I'm going to touch her. I need a bit of rough.'

I was offended, of course. But I was drunk; and I was theirs.

There was a fourth group, however, who viewed me differently. Because I had the ear of JRS, they thought, I was a catch. Anyone who could influence the great director was worth spending time with. Straight men and gay men made plays for me and I found it very hard to say 'no'. Everyone in the house used their bodies as calling cards – and I had soon built up a nice collection.

With the obsession at Number 10 on physical appearance I suppose it's natural that sex would be so high on everyone's agenda. Sex drove the house. Deals were done on the strength of it, surgery was undertaken because of it. Everywhere you looked there were hints of it.

John spent half the year in New York where the gay/disco world led the way and so the house was filled with magazines like *After Dark* with its adverts for strip shows, blatantly gay models with enormous bulges, topless shots of actresses and plastic surgeons' addresses. I watched my first porn videos at that house – mostly featuring men with men – and one day, helping Mum clean a bedroom, I found an enema kit.

Gay relationships intrigued me. Partner swapping and continual conquests were normal but some couples stayed and played together exclusively. JRS and his partner, Michael, had an open relationship but were there for one another until the end. In fact, John's film, *Sunday Bloody Sunday*, starring Peter Finch, was partly autobiographical.

A lot of the men I met were bisexual. Really, I think, they were heterosexual, but when you view sex as a means of greasing a business transaction, as so many of them did, I guess it paid to be more flexible.

I had several brief relationships with guests, who'd sneak down to the flat either while Mum was working or already in bed. I was also taken out quite regularly by celebrities and other important figures. Some were regular visitors, others were John's "flavour of the month", never to be invited back to Number 10. Lorenzo, a mysterious arms dealer, took me to Regine's on Kensington High Street, all gold palm trees and mirrors, while the Playboy Club on Park Lane and Annabel's in Berkeley Square were other popular haunts. I remember going to Tramp on Jermyn Street with some of the guys from Led Zeppelin, the young actor and pop star Paul Nicholas, and Lorna Luft. I remember wearing cowboy boots and the evening getting very wild. In the car on the way home Paul was kissing someone else.

'What about me?' I asked.

We were all so far gone that I was invited to join in. Paul came back to my room but once he learned I was only sixteen he couldn't get his clothes back on quickly enough.

With sexual abandon in the air, it wasn't unusual for my "date" for the evening to get high and pick up somebody else and continue the party elsewhere. I never minded at the time – that was how we all lived. But the next day would tell a different story. I would wake up, crushed at being passed over. When I was sober the sense of abandonment was strong. Yes, I was having an incredible time and I was following my body's desires to the maximum. But I wanted more than flings and one-night stands with men who would use me and throw me away. I wanted to be held in someone's arms.

I wanted love.

Drinking hid the agony of rejection and, even better, gave me the confidence to hunt down my next conquest for the night. But it also allowed men to take advantage of my affection – and worse.

One night I was with friends at a club and I met a man who was going on to another party in Windsor. Recklessly I agreed to go with him. As soon as we arrived my escort disappeared, so I did what I always did in those circumstances: I drank. A short while later I was talking to another guest and he suggested we go upstairs. The house was being decorated so we ended up in the bedroom where all the coats were being kept. My new friend put his arms around my neck warmly, kissed my neck then pushed me gently back onto the pile of suede and cashmere jackets – which is when I passed out.

I don't know how long I was asleep. When I came round I felt like a patient regaining consciousness on the operating table. I could see and I could hear but I couldn't move.

I was aware that a man was standing over me pulling up his trousers. It wasn't my date and it wasn't the man who had brought me upstairs.

No!

I wanted to scream, to fight him off. But I couldn't even cry.

I was numb.

Suddenly I heard a commotion. Another chap had entered the room. Casually the man towering over me started to unzip his trousers.

What was happening?

Suddenly a man pushed him out of the way and helped me sit up.

'Can you hear me?' my saviour was shouting. 'Are you all right?'

Eventually I came out of my living coma. I collapsed into the man's arms and cried and cried. He took me into the bathroom and helped me wash. The very thought of what had occurred made me feel so dirty. All the while he kept repeating, 'It's all right, it's all right,' without judgement or blame.

When he drove me home a short while later I learned my rescuer was an actor. The next day I arranged for him to come for an interview at Number 10. I never met him again but years later I was pleased to see him in a prime-time soap opera. I'll never forget his kindness.

*****

Many people at JRS's house were there because they thought they could benefit but most of them were genuinely happy to help others out if they could.

'Speak to Noel,' John advised. 'When he's finished with you we'll see what we can do.'

Noel Davis was an actor and an agent who stayed for long spells at Number 10. He was acid-tongued and a great joker but he knew the business inside out. He explained all aspects of the acting profession and went out of his way to coach me on how to present myself and talk to the camera. He was often scathing but he knew exactly what he wanted and what I desperately wanted as well.

One day he called round with a photographer.

'I wanted a second opinion,' Noel announced. 'Come and stand over here, Tess.'

For an hour he had me posing in different positions in different lights. At the end he nodded emphatically.

'I thought so. Your best side is your right. Don't ever let me see you leading with your left. We won't want Vaseline on the lens - yet!' The cheek! This was a well-used Hollywood trick for softening the features of ageing actors.

In his own way he was a brutal as Nesta Brooking. The difference was that he cared about me and about what I was trying to achieve. More importantly, he had nothing to gain from helping me.

At Noel's suggestion I attended a modelling course at the Lucie Clayton School on Gloucester Road where I learned to walk with an umbrella and eat quail eggs. I then joined the Carnaby People modelling agency in Soho. Although not tall enough for fashion magazines I could do catwalk dancing and commercials. Noel helped me get my black-and-white photographs needed for my 'Z card', which contained all my details. Five hundred were printed and posted to potential employers.

My first modelling job came more quickly than I thought. The photographer who shot my promotional pictures hired me to model rings. It was only my hands but it was a start. I was a paid model!

At Noel's recommendation I started reading *The Stage* newspaper and *Screen International* as well as *Spotlight*, the annual directory for theatrical agents and photographers.

'You never know where your next job will come from,' he advised. 'But one thing you should never say is "no". Don't turn anything down.'

I soon acquired a holdall, ready at a moment's notice for auditions or stand-ins, full of make-up, jewellery, hair pieces, gloves, every colour of socks, tights, shoes, and a changing robe – anything that might be needed to complete a "look". From commission to leaving the house, I could be ready in minutes.

For my second job I was employed to advertise skateboards, the new craze in Britain. But it was my next job that got me really excited.

'Mum!' I cried, throwing the phone into its cradle and rushing up from the flat. 'I've got a part in a film!'

The film in question was only *Confessions Of A Plumber's Mate*, one of a series of 70s romps, but I had a speaking part. That's all that mattered.

Unfortunately I also had a sporting part, despite my Z card not listing any skills in that area. My character was required to play tennis in one scene and, having never picked up a racquet before, I didn't hit the ball once – not even when it was thrown from six inches away!

I was far more comfortable taking my clothes off for a shower scene. In the script, my character stumbles upon the plumber already in the shower – and prepares to pounce on him. Fortunately the director yelled, 'Cut!' before anything else happened.

I was paid £36 a day and I had a great time working with the likes of Elaine Paige and Suzy Kendall at the start of their careers. It was a stepping stone in the right direction, I was sure of that.

I earned twice as much modelling for Biba, followed by swimwear collections, posing by the pool. I didn't mind being naked and most work required me to wear a bikini or bath towel. More interesting shoots involved being sprayed in gold paint to advertise mechanics' grease and wound in tape to sell office equipment. To this day I can still hear Noel Davis's words – 'Don't say "no" to anything'.

JRS suggested I do a few odd jobs for him to get my face seen by other people so I grasped every opportunity to deliver or collect scripts or help out on shoots.

I enjoyed the modelling and acting but there was something missing. I needed to get back into dancing. The wounds from Brooking's were still open but the desire was coming back as strong as it had been once before.

I typed my first CV and posted it with photos to all the dance agents advertised in *The Stage*. Trends Management contacted me and I was sent for my first dance audition since those ballet days.

Can I still do it? I wondered, unsure if the demons of Littlehouse would affect my performance. But although it was a difficult routine with hundreds of applicants, split into groups and whittled down, I was accepted in the final twenty.

I can do it!

The next stage of the audition was trickier. I had to attend an interview.

By the time I arrived at the typical narrow, old building in Soho there was already a queue of girls winding up the stairs. I gave my name then had a Polaroid taken of my face. Finally I was introduced to the casting directors.

Without looking up, one asked, 'What experience have you had dancing with a group?'

I paused. 'Er, nothing since ballet school but...'

It was too late. I had blown my chance. Eavesdropping on the next candidate's answers as I put on my coat, I realised the trick. Tell the interviewers what they want to hear: embellish, fabricate, lie. How else do beginners get anywhere?

For my next interview, this time for an ad for Wrigley's gum, I remembered the advice of one of my co-stars on *Plumber's Mate*: 'Never be late – and always look gorgeous.'

I took my CV in a zip briefcase, wore a bright red dress, made an entrance and was gorgeousness itself. I acted as if I was someone different, a cut above the rest, with all the experience in the world.

And I got the job.

Other work followed. I was chosen for dance scenes in popular dramas like *Rumpole of the Bailey* and *The Goodies*. Then I received an offer that made me think. The choreographer Dougie Squires offered me twenty-one weeks in pantomime and two months in Bahrain as part of his well-known dance troupe *Second Generation*.

Dancing and travelling is exactly what I want to do with my life, I thought. *In fact, it's all I've wanted to do since I was a child.*

I seriously considered the offer but turned it down.

'It is what I want to do, Mr Squires, but as a solo performer, on my own terms. I do not want to work with a group yet. '

He wished me well but with reservations.

'Tessa, do you know how many – or should I say, how few – girls make it as a solo dance act? Hardly any. Are you sure about this?'

'I'm sure,' I said.

But what had I let myself in for?

I regretted my decision almost immediately. My new modelling agent, Mr Gordon, made all the right noises but very little came of it. My first contract from him was four days stepping off aeroplanes at Biggin Hill and dining at the Dorchester for the Harrods catalogue. It sounded too good to be true and it was – I was cancelled with twenty-four hours' notice. The next three jobs also mysteriously fell through.

Gordon looked and sounded professional. A smooth-talking, hefty man, balding, with a ponytail, he claimed all the right connections but all his jobs either disappeared or involved dirty photographers with wandering hands. Another photographer in Chinatown, supposedly doing test shots for *The Sun* newspaper, opened my eyes in new ways.

I was sitting, topless, in his dingy studio, regretting ever coming through the door, when the photographer said, 'Lovely. Now, if you'll just excuse me for a minute, I always have to have a wank before I begin.'

What do you say to that?

'That's okay,' was all I could think of. It was so matter-of-fact I sat stunned on my stool as he took the photos, fast and professional. Apart from that he was very pleasant – but I wouldn't shake his hand on leaving.

When I was sent to be interviewed at a suite in the Inter-Continental and discovered a sole photographer who asked me to undress, I'd had enough of Gordon's agency and quit. I realised he was playing at being in the business but he treated his models like prostitutes, hoping they'd do him favours.

I cursed myself for being so naïve. Once again I'd allowed myself to fall for the words of the elder man. My subconscious quest for a father figure had run aground again. Unfortunately, I would soon meet agents who made Gordon look the perfect professional.

With no other avenues open to me, John Schlesinger offered me a small role in his new film, *Yanks*. I played the girlfriend of one of the GIs which required learning lines and new skills – although fortunately not tennis. It was incredible to be on a proper film shoot, noticing the attention to every detail. The set for one pub scene was one hundred per cent authentic for the period, down to the matchboxes on the bar.

Several of us were coached for hours by a skilled choreographer in the moves of the "hokey cokey" to ensure we were all synchronised. I even had thorough guidance on how to kiss my onscreen boyfriend. The tilt of the head, the eyes (open or shut), the mouth, the tongue – everything was worked out in minute detail beforehand. I remember thinking, *I do know how to kiss, John – if anyone should know that it's you!*

'And action!' he yelled. We completed dozens of takes. John was a perfectionist and kept looking for different nuances. It really was an exclusive view into another world, that of the serious film-maker. During the days I was onset I didn't see John eat, drink or sleep. The only thing he cared about was his film.

And I was amazed at how easily I adapted to the film world, too. Although shy, I had an ease in front of the camera. I completely forgot there were sixty or so people in the same vast studio. As soon as John yelled, 'Action!' I was ready to go and I only had eyes – and mouth – for my co-star. I even found the waiting and rehearsing a lot easier than some of the more experienced extras. Perhaps the relentless drills at Brooking's were having some positive effect at last?

My greatest thrill was sharing John's limo back to Number 10 after each punishing day at Pinewood Studios. How many young actors had that privilege?! But even then he was full of words of advice.

'Working on a movie is like a long, dark tunnel and suddenly you see a light at the end,' he promised.

I was paid £16.20 for days that could last twenty-one hours but it was worth it. What's more, because of my ballet schooling, I didn't even mind the gruelling schedule. I had endured worse just a few years earlier – and I was a lot happier doing this.

When things are going well for you other opportunities seem to arise. No sooner had I finished on *Yanks* than I achieved my first solo dance employment. It wasn't what I had imagined for myself, but it was certainly a start.

I found Mrs Berry's advertisement in the back pages of *The Stage*. She was looking for dancers to perform in central London pubs and clubs. She had a stern look, a definite Mrs Danvers character, but as soon as I introduced myself at my audition in Finchley her face broke into a warm, mumsy smile.

The ad said that dancers would have to appear in bikinis so I'd purchased a flattering two-piece and boots from Marbles Market on Kensington High Street which sold way-out gear and smelled of pot. I edged the tiny outfit with sequins then worked on picking the right accompaniment. When I danced to Stevie Wonder's *I Wish* that day, everyone stopped to watch and applaud.

Mrs Berry took me on immediately and I was delighted. As I made my way to my first venue the following night, I began to have strong reservations.

'I'm sixteen years old. What am I doing dancing alone, in a bikini, in a pub full of men?'

But as soon as I arrived at the Hog and Hound in Mayfair I relaxed. I watched another girl do her routine and win a decent, respectful response from the drinkers. Nobody touched her and nobody heckled. She was simply a girl in a costume dancing nicely.

I was booked for two shows a day, at lunch time or six in the evening. Little did I know that I'd never experience a job in such a hassle-free environment again, where I was also respected and paid so promptly after each spot.

Most pubs were in Mayfair but one, in North London, had a boxers' training ring adjoined. It was there I met Denzil, a young black man training to be a heavyweight. I never drank when I was performing so Denzil saw the side of me that I wanted him to. He was gentle and encouraging when he wasn't in the ring and we dated for a few months before he was sent up North. I gained confidence with him and approached discos along Oxford Street to see about weekend shows. Soon I was choreographing different routines for an audience of five hundred people at Jacqueline's in the West End. I couldn't have been happier.

Three months later I became a resident lunchtime dancer at the Copacabana, a disco in Earls Court, where the well-known DJ, Steve Walsh, played brilliant jazz funk. I loved being part of the black club scene: it appealed to me just as much as the gay world, but in a different way. I created successful routines with snake-like moves and robotics to tracks by the Brothers Johnson and Kool and the Gang and enjoyed watching the punters, dressed in suits and trilbies, join in with their natural, perfect moves.

On my nights off I reverted to my binge-drinking ways. I spent most evenings out and weeks went by without seeing Mum to talk to. She was so busy, and I was out so often, we passed like ships in the night.

Then, as it would so many times in the future, it went wrong. I'd just finished my stint at the Copacabana when one of the bar girls came over.

'The boss wants to see you before you leave, Tess.'

'Thanks,' I said, but I wondered what he wanted. Ten minutes later I found out.

'Let me get you a drink,' he said. 'I'd like to discuss your future shows.'

For once alarm bells started to go off in my head.

'I don't drink,' I lied. 'Can I have an orange juice?'

No sooner had I taken a few sips than I started to get dizzy. I could see his lips moving but I could only make out intermittent words.

'I like you…need to co-operate…a long future…'

I fixed him a glare.

'You've put something in this!'

'No, I haven't. Come here. Sit on my knee.'

I felt him cuddling me and I remember struggling to uncoil myself. But I was giggling. Whatever he'd put in my drink was making me mad.

'You know you like me,' he said. 'It's easy. You want to keep your job, don't you?'

I felt a sudden panic, then anger. As he turned to put his glass down, I leapt from the room, stumbling up the stairs. Luckily the main entrance was unlocked. I ran out into harsh daylight, straight into a taxi and home. Somehow I managed to stagger into my bedroom before passing out. I woke with the worst hangover I'd ever had – ten hours later.

I'd held so much back from Mum in the past but I couldn't this time. She'd watched me sleep through one of the noisiest dinner parties of the year and knew there was something wrong. We sat and talked in the soothing low-level kitchen light, comforted by the warmth and lingering smells, as the house went quiet.

I was safe but unemployed – and determined to make better judgements where men were concerned.

My next brush with a boyfriend was just what the doctor ordered. I knew nothing about most of the men I went out with and they didn't care to know more about me. No one gave out their home numbers and I didn't pretend my dates were anything more than what they were. Then Larry came into my life. We met at one of the clubs along Praed Street – hip places, where a good night out meant dressing up and dancing, full of black guys, in trilbies, suits and shiny shoes - the best movers.

Larry was tall, slim, with a close-clipped afro and moustache, and came from Nassau. He was easy to talk to, and seemed to be interested in me and my family. *I'm not used to this,* I thought.

Larry enjoyed the good things in life and paid for everything. He was well-dressed and always smoked a cigar. He owned a Ferrari but often asked me to order a limousine to meet him in the West End for dinner. The city opened up for me with Larry. Instead of feeling like an outsider, I now truly belonged.

And for the first time in my life I felt I was falling in love.

In hindsight there were lots of things I didn't know about Larry. For example, one night he introduced his work partner, Errol Brown.

'Work partner?' I said, confused. 'Errol Brown is in Hot Chocolate.'

Larry laughed. 'So am I! I'm Larry Ferguson.'

I shouldn't have felt guilty. Larry had purposely disguised his life. 'I wanted you to take me for myself, first,' he explained. 'It's too easy for girls to fall for the pop star, not the person.'

I'd fallen head over heels for both. I went on tour with the band, appeared with them on *Top Of The Pops*, met their producer, Mickie Most, and accompanied Larry to all sorts of record business functions. I had honestly never been happier with another person. Mum adored him as well.

'You're a changed person these days,' she told me. 'He must be doing something right.'

Unfortunately I wasn't the only girl who felt like that. One day I received an anonymous phone call. The female voice just said one thing: 'You're not the only one, you know.'

Larry tried to deny it at first, and I tried to be accepting of the sexual pressures of a famous musician, but our relationship never truly recovered. Other men had taken advantage of me or actually scared me: but what Larry did was worse.

He broke my heart.

I honestly didn't know where to turn and, of course, alcohol provided a consoling diversion. But every morning I woke up, hung-over, with the same tears. 'What's the point? When is something going to work out for me?'

Then, like a magic moment when everything falls into place, my luck changed. *The Stage* carried a full-page advert for a show called Rip Off and I knew it was my chance. They were looking for solo dancers. Best of all, the show was at the legendary Windmill Theatre, the country's greatest cabaret venue.

Two weeks after sending my CV I received the call. They wanted me to audition. I've never understood how I can feel more anxious dancing for a handful of people than for a packed auditorium, but I shook as I took my mark on that famous old stage in front of the sharp-eyed choreographers, Milovan and Gerard, who were watching from the darkness in front of me.

Music struck up, the lights flared and I began my routine. It felt thrilling to perform up on stage rather than the usual floor level. I was on a natural high with energy and ease that I'd not felt for some time.

This was my moment.

But would it be enough to impress the critical gaze of the men in darkness?

Suddenly a voice called out.

'Stop! Enough, enough!'

I shuddered panting to a halt. *What have I done wrong?* I wondered. *I did the best I could.*

The choreographers walked to the foot of the stage.

'We've seen enough,' the one called Gerard said. 'That was amazing.'

'Very impressive,' Milovan chipped in.

'We would like to offer you a contract to join us here – for a year. What do you think?'

A year's contract at the historic Windmill Theatre? I was seventeen years old and honestly felt my life was just beginning.

CHAPTER FOUR

HE THINKS I'M A MAN

The Windmill Theatre on Great Windmill Street, Soho, is one of the theatrical world's most famous addresses. Built on the site of an actual windmill from the reign of Charles II, it started life as the Palais de Luxe cinema in 1909 before being converted by Laura Henderson into a theatre in 1930. After a series of unsuccessful shows, Mrs Henderson took inspiration from the Folies Bergères and Moulin Rouge in Paris and staged the UK's first revues to include naked performers. In a stroke of impertinent genius she convinced the national censor of the time, the Lord Chamberlain, that if classical nudes in the British Museum were not obscene, then neither were her girls if they stood still.

'I have to agree, Mrs Henderson,' Lord Cromer acceded. 'But if they move, it's rude – and I will close you down.'

After the proprietor's death in 1944 the theatre took a more general turn, hosting variety performances and famously acquiring the quote after the war - "We never closed".

Comedy legends and even Mrs Henderson's *tableaux vivants* – living statues – were a far cry from the all-writhing, all-dancing shows planned for the theatre by the man who bought it in 1974. Paul Raymond had amassed a fortune from top-shelf magazines and now was branching out into live entertainment. To compete with the forest of strip joints and private clubs that were springing up all over Soho, he envisaged his venues pushing the boundaries of dance, theatre – and sex.

And in 1977 I became part of it.

At seventeen, I was the youngest performer at the Windmill but the choreographers, Gerard and Milovan, saw something in my dancing that exceeded my years.

'You move like a twenty-five-year-old,' Gerard cooed. 'It's like you've been on the stage for years.'

Maybe some good did come out of Brooking's then.

I arrived for my first rehearsal, immaculately dressed as usual, and knocked on the stage door at the Archer Street entrance. The caretaker let me in and directed me to the dressing rooms. There were too many faces to take in. I just slipped into my regular rehearsal clothes – leotard, tights and leg warmers – and tried not to stand out. Gradually, though, some of the older dancers came over to say hello. It was a hot day, the start of a stifling summer, and they were dressed in loose T-shirts and shorts.

'Milovan and Gerard are pussy cats,' one dancer advised. 'As long as you try your best they're fine.'

Watching how relaxed everyone else seemed to be was what helped me the most.

If they're not worried then why should I be?

Even so, it was the first time I had been in such a professional environment. The Golden Lane Theatre had been intimidating – but this time I was being paid. I had as much right to be here as anyone else.

We filed onto the stage and took our marks. I took the chance to look around.

It's incredible, I thought. *Absolutely perfect.*

The stage was a dancer's dream: good grip, flat, and flanked by heavy black curtains that swished satisfactorily side to side. Harsh overhead lights threatened to blind me and the contrast they created between the stage and the dark auditorium was just what I had hoped for. The illusion of being in a separate world on stage was complete. I could dance with abandon and not worry about the faces just yards from me: it was heaven.

After two weeks of running through our paces I turned up for my first dress rehearsal. Perhaps dress rehearsal is the wrong phrase – *undress rehearsal* might be more accurate. Despite some stunning headpieces, footwear and accessories, I was shocked to see so much flesh on display as the acts ran through their numbers. But the biggest surprise was yet to come.

'Okay, Tessa, these are yours.' Carlos, the head of costume, handed me a clutch of sequinned garments. 'Try them on for size. Any problems, let me know.'

Try them on for size? The dresses looked like they wouldn't cover a child. I picked them up one at a time and studied the labels, "Second dance", "Finale". They were so small: there must be some mistake.

Then it all became clear.

Tessa, how could you be so naïve! I knew it was a nude show – that, after all, is what the Windmill was famous for the world over – but I didn't think that *I* would have to dance naked most of the time! I was a classically trained ballerina. Would I really have to move around a vast London stage wearing no more than gloves and bikini bottoms – if that?

The answer, terrifyingly, was "yes".

Considering I had performed naked in *Confessions Of A Plumber's Mate*, and modelled topless, I was surprised at my own prudishness. But there's a huge difference between appearing in front of a camera and a live theatre audience. For a start, the camera can't talk back. And you never see the film audience's reaction to your exposed physique.

The only costume that was truly discreet was a white boiler suit that dazzled purple under the ultra-violet lights, which we wore with matching visors, sleek, auburn, bobbed wigs and custom-made boots. Even so, that was only worn for the first sixty seconds before being whipped off.

Even though the auditorium was empty I still felt incredibly self-conscious as I peeled off my clothes for the first time. I was completely used to having my body scrutinised for extraneous ounces of weight but not like this. Even at the Copacabana I wore a bikini. For the first time in my life I was suddenly standing on a public stage wearing just a glittering thong.

Gerard picked up on my nervousness immediately.

'Are you all right Tessa. Something on your mind?'

'I'm fine,' I called back. 'Just a bit chilly!'

The other girls laughed. It was eighty degrees outside and more in the theatre. Whatever was troubling me, it wasn't the heat!

There were twenty in our cast including six men and we all shared the dressing rooms on the third floor – a winding staircase or lift took us down to the stage level. The "seniors" had the narrow dressing room, its window offering a view of the neon windmill which stood out above the lights of Shaftesbury Avenue. I had a space in the larger room, shared with a whole bag of characters including Maxwell Caulfield, before he found fame playing Miles Colby in the *Dynasty* spin-off *The Colbys*, and Paul "Banana", a black dancer named on account of his impressive main feature. An Australian called Ron earned his nickname of "head boy" by dint of being oldest, but he certainly didn't look his forty years. Then there was Gavin, a rugby-playing ex-bricklayer; Gary, who was gay and adorable; and Terry, easily the best dancer, tall and handsome. When I saw him years later as male lead at the Lido, Paris, I was not surprised. He was always going to make it to the top.

Of the women, Paula was a model, married to a member of Manfred Mann, Mary was a ski instructor in her former life, and Gillian had a perfect hourglass figure, with incredible breasts and a tiny waist, but at the cost of twenty laxatives a day. I never saw her eat. Rough, blonde, sexy and a friend for life, Shelley was twenty-one, and her husband had just left her to run a bar in Bangkok.

And then there was Anne. Another Australian, she had trained as a nurse but found herself in London, on the West End stage, performing to strangers in her birthday suit. The second I laid eyes on Anne, my heart skipped. I'd never experienced that with a woman before but I knew exactly what it meant. It wasn't just her dark beauty, but her smile, her sparkling eyes, it was everything about her. When she took me under her wing in those first few weeks I knew she would live up to my expectations. But did she know how I felt? *And where would it lead?*

Any performer will tell you that there is no comparison between a dress rehearsal and opening night. You can go over every step, every breath, every detail a thousand times but absolutely nothing prepares you for standing on a stage behind a curtain and listening as the auditorium buzzes with life. On the other side of that heavy, velvet cloth is your audience. They've paid to see you. They deserve to have the night of their lives.

Acts had to arrive at Archer Street by six-thirty for the first show at eight o'clock – the second show was at ten and we would finish at midnight. On that first night I set off on the half-hour journey from Kensington at four – I was leaving nothing to chance.

Mum gave me the biggest hug as I left, 'Break a leg, darling. I'll be cheering.'

You might not when you see what I'm wearing, I thought. But I said, 'Keep your fingers crossed for me – and bring an open mind!'

At my space in the dressing room the make-up was lined up, all supplied by the Windmill. We all had to wear prescribed shades or face a fine: dark lip-liner, bright lipstick and glitter for fuller lips, eyelashes and body make-up. Absolutely no sunbathing lines or bruises were permitted – everyone had to look just so. Wigs stood on the polystyrene heads waiting to transform us into outrageous idols. Nervously I rearranged everything then began the slow process of getting ready. It was more than an hour before the first person joined me.

'Just got here, Tess?' Mary joked, looking at my half-finished make-up.

We laughed then settled into silence. As the rest of the cast burst in it was as much as I could do to say "hello". Any more threatened to ruin my concentration – and if that happened the nerves would take over.

As the warning voice of Mark, the stage manager, burst over the tannoy the whole troupe crackled into life. Last minute adjustments were made.

A buzzer sounded.

'First act to the stage.'

I looked at myself once more in my mirror, mouthed a silent "good luck", then dashed silently for the lift. Around me girls gossiped, men laughed, Gary farted.

Suddenly it was showtime. Six of us were standing, tits and teeth to the cheering audience, in our white boiler suits. The lights did their magic and we moved to the beat. We formed a line with legs apart, heads turning on cue and then faced away one by one. As we spun round, the letters on our backs spelled out, one by one, R-I-P-O-F-F. This produced the second cheer of the night.

The biggest was yet to come. We threw the visors aside and walked towards the front edge of the stage. Adrenaline coursed through my body. Suddenly, as one, we stopped. *Dead still.* Watching the first few rows of the audience, wide-eyed, I could sense a level of expectation to match our own. What next? Slowly my hand moved to the zip just beneath my chin. Mary did the same. And Shelley. And Anne. And Paula. And Gillian. All of us moving as one, unzipping our suits, peeling them off, and stepping out to reveal our glittering, perfect bodies.

Our glittering, naked bodies.

It was an incredible transformation. Not only did I feel unawkward in my exposure, because everyone on stage was in the same state of undress, but a sense of empowerment surrounded me. I was dancing the steps I'd trained for so many years to be able to achieve, in front of an audience paying for the experience – my dream was coming true. I just happened to be nude.

The first act ended and the aura of the stage was shattered as soon we reached the lift.

'Whose bra is this?' Mark demanded. 'It's a bloody health hazard leaving it down here.'

I couldn't get back to my mirror quickly enough.

Time for tea and relaxation and reminiscences.

'That was brilliant!' I gushed.

'*You* were brilliant,' Anne insisted. 'I couldn't take my eyes off you.'

I blushed. 'You were terrific, too.' I didn't know what else to say.

The atmosphere was so different even though we were only halfway through. We'd met the crowd; met them and wowed them. They held no surprises for us tonight. In ten minutes' time I'd be giving them more of what they wanted. I couldn't wait.

Then I remembered one member of the audience in particular. My mother was sitting up in the gods like any normal proud parent. *What on earth was she thinking? I* wondered. *Is this really what she paid for all those Brooking's lessons to achieve?*

Our show consisted of twelve acts with incredible stage sets including motor bikes and giant props. A stiletto shoe that you could dance on, a huge roulette table and a boat deck complete with steering wheel all took the audience's breath away. The attention to detail in the costumes was just as thorough. Fantasy turned into reality with leather, studs, feathers, silk – fetish meets beauty meets in-your-face sleaze. There was something for everyone.

Well, almost everyone. I cringed to think how my mother was responding to the *Shell* performance – a girl bathing in soapy water, masturbating to a frothy climax – or the *Lesbian* – a young girl walks by a stand-up photo booth and sees the back of a sailor in a white uniform and cap. On brushing past, "he" turns round to reveal a "she" and a love affair ensues. But neither of those pieces would prepare her for *The Cage* – choreographed group sex between guards in black and their ethereal captives in pale chiffon – or *Bikers* – a virtual rape scene set to heavy metal.

At least it's so beautifully danced, I thought. *Mummy will enjoy that.*

The second half was as thrilling as the first. Every muscle flexed to kick or spin or stretch to my maximum. It was opening night and every single performer operated at optimum power right to the end. Then the curtain closed and we formed a line to take a bow for the *Circus* finale, arrayed in afro wigs, black lace-up boots, red basques and chokers, with whips thrown over shoulders. We left the stage to raucous celebration and congratulations from Mark.

'Half an hour break and we do it all again,' he added.

The natural reaction after the curtain closed was to start unclipping the wigs, they got very hot and itchy. We'd look like mannequins with bald stocking heads and huge eyes, running up the stairs.

It's amazing to remember how quickly I got into my stride. After two shows on opening night I was suddenly an old hand. Walking to the theatre the next day I was thrilled to be going to work – and knowing that I belonged. After so many years of training and being made to feel inadequate I was testing my body's capabilities to the maximum and hitting every target in front of an appreciative audience.

I didn't even mind that I was doing it nude. Yes, I would have preferred not to – but compared to not doing it at all it just wasn't an issue. I was proud of my body and I wanted to dance. I wasn't doing anything wrong on stage. This wasn't a sex show. It was a cabaret in the West End of London. I had great lights, music, choreography and – when I was wearing anything – incredible costumes. *I couldn't be more thrilled*, I realised. And I really believed that.

All the cast worked six nights in a row with an alternate seventh day off. Every five weeks we had a whole weekend free – understudies covered everyone's part. In return I earned £108 a week, a fantastic wage then, plus paid rehearsals.

I don't recall a bad night. Yes, sometimes I didn't feel well, or I had period pains, but as soon as the curtain opened I was cured for ninety minutes. There is nothing more uplifting than performing for an appreciative audience and we saw all sorts, from stag and hen parties to weekend couples, the Monday-Friday expense account businessmen and Japanese tourists as part of their whistlestop tour of London. The dirty mac brigade, of course, accounted for a percentage of all sales. There were even nights when an entire new front row would comprise handicapped groups in their wheelchairs.

Mum, of course, told me I was really professional and stood out. She would report the good news back to Gran.

'Will you be telling her everything?'

'Well, I might let her think you're wearing a little more, but apart from that – yes!'

A month in, I received a compliment from a most unlikely source. Carl Snitcher, the Windmill's chief executive, rarely interfered with the show. I knew him by sight although not to talk to. Then one day I was handed a note by the caretaker as I arrived. It said:

Dear Miss Skola,

I am going to use this opportunity of taking what I believe to be the hitherto unprecedented step of writing to you and congratulating you on what I am told by the Stage Manager are very good performances by you – particularly bearing in mind that you have only recently joined the company.

Yours sincerely,

Carl Snitcher, Chief Executive.

The other girls couldn't believe it.

'She must be sleeping with him,' one of them joked but they knew I'd never even met him. It meant a lot that everyone was so happy for me and they were confident enough to poke fun like that. I truly felt like one of "them".

As the weeks turned into months we grew closer as a group and there were no secrets – not even from the vicar of Soho who used to call frequently with a friendly 'Everyone all right?'. Intimate details of each other's sex lives were common currency – although I confided less than most.

Pussies, pubic hair and periods were also dealt with matter-of-factly in public. The general consensus was that lots of hair looked ugly and most girls opted for a "runway", where they shaved each side, leaving a centre strip. A dancer called Ally shaved hers altogether. I preferred a tidy, heart-shaped patch. I shaved from between my cheeks, right round inside my groin, so no hairs were visible even in the tiniest g-string. It was too personal to have waxed and attempting it myself, too painful.

As with many groups, the closeness of working together made our bodies beat as one and our periods would start at the same time.

Many women have to take time off work every month but performers have to soldier on through period pains. Even with excruciating swellings, the show had to go on. High on pain killers, I would insert one or two tampons, so as not to leak, and then tuck the string up inside my lips and hope for the best – cutting it was too dangerous, in case the tampon moved up too far.

Sometimes even those precautions weren't enough. I celebrated my eighteenth birthday with my first performance of the complicated *Alien* number based on the popular film of the time. A huge rope cobweb, stretched on a metal frame, filled the entire stage right up to the overhead lighting strips. Most of the movements were acrobatic and performed hanging from the ropes, weaving in and out, to make patterns against the grid. It took weeks to learn to climb and intertwine, but made a spectacular effect, although I was covered in rope burns.

In the dance, Anne and I were aliens with weapons, dressed in sparkling green capes, headdresses and matching thigh length boots. We "captured" a man from Earth, loved him, then tortured him to death.

I started the performance at the top of the net. My first move was a theatrical high kick, before moving slowly down the net, still facing the audience, to pounce on my prey. On my second performance, I extended my leg above my head and froze.

Oh no! I thought. *Not now.*

Blood was running down my thigh.

Highly embarrassed, I climbed down the net and rushed straight off stage before my period gave the murder its full effect. Aghast, Gary and Anne carried on as a duo, wondering what was wrong, and ended up killing each other!

We had such different pussies which you couldn't fail to study when the girl next to you was performing side splits and forward bends. Ally had danced with the Lindsay Kemp contemporary company and suffered from, as she put it, a "windy pussy". She wasn't embarrassed about it – but it often got us into trouble. One night we were in a love scene and Ally was called upon to do a naked handstand. Suddenly a loud raspberry resounded around the stage and the mood was shattered. We could barely contain our laughter and everyone collapsed as the curtains closed. It was agony each time.

The boiler suit zips were notorious for getting caught in pubic hair – for those of us who had any. My little heart shape was pruned unintentionally at least once a week, bringing tears to my eyes.

But at least nobody noticed; other mistakes, however, were more public. During Paula's *Mexican Hat* solo one night, which involved her kneeling on a trolley under an enormous sombrero, the stagehand in the wings pushed her too fast. As she shot forwards I realised too late what was about to happen.

Accompanied by a blood-curdling scream she tipped straight over the edge of the stage and landed in the laps of the front row. I'll never forget the rapturous round of applause as she climbed back up.

Another night we were so engrossed in conversation with a stagehand before the opening that when the curtains drew back we flew into our positions. He wasn't so quick: suddenly a spotlight and two hundred pairs of eyes were focused on him, broom in hand. Thinking quickly, he did a twirl and swept off, much to everyone's delight. Not quite everyone's – we were all fined by Mark.

It wasn't at all glamorous backstage but the stage door was something different. Even as a seventeen-year-old troupe member I couldn't help feeling like a star every time I walked towards that dark old door. Of course, I always looked my best, immaculate in high heels, elegant clothes and manicured hands carrying my expensive looking make-up boxes. In the winter months, as the nights drew in, twinkling bulbs and signs burned in the dark, guiding the way as if for an aeroplane coming in to land. Each evening I was full of expectation; on a mission, forgetting for a moment what lay ahead, blind to the sweat and effort, another punishing episode to get through. It was definitely a life of two halves: the world outside the stage door and the other realm that only existed in that magical, historic building.

Occasionally I would arrive or leave to flowers from an admirer or autograph requests from nervous fans – something else I never expected when I was training at Brooking's!

Some of the men I spoke to were dance enthusiasts and wanted to discuss that aspect of the show. The majority, however, had been bewitched by the elaborate routines. They thought they knew me because of what I'd done on stage for an hour and a half.

'I saw you looking at me while you touched yourself,' a smartly-dressed man informed me after my second night.

I smiled and ran giggling into a taxi with Anne.

The next night two young men approached me, obviously buoyed by alcohol. 'You must have a dozen orgasms a night up there,' one said, to the other's amusement.

Once more Anne helped me out. 'Two dozen,' she chipped in. 'At least.' And again we made our escape.

If they only knew the truth, I laughed. The whole sex thing was, literally, an act. For the dancers involved the experience was not at all erotic, regardless of whether we were naked or simulating fellatio. The physical exertion of performing was far too great to enjoy the pleasures we were miming. I could feel sensual and powerful, yes, but never sexual.

Off stage it was a different matter. The powerful libido that seemed to define every actor or performer who arrived at Number 10 was equally present at the Windmill. The club absolutely forbade cast members from leaving with any fan waiting outside – there was a reputation to be upheld – but away from their control we were unstoppable. And I was one of the worst.

One of the other things Brooking's didn't prepare me for was the dazzling highs performing would give. After my opening night I didn't sleep until nine the next morning; it took me so long to come down. In fact it would be weeks before I could control the urges that overtook my mind after a show. I had my life outside the theatre and my life in it. I needed to keep some perspective; but it was a struggle.

After my debut performance I packed Mum into a taxi and headed with the rest of the cast to the Candy Box off Regent Street. Of course I drank and of course I met a man. The next night we went to Heaven, a popular gay disco under Charing Cross arches, and the night took a similar pattern. I soon discovered El Sombreros on Kensington High Street, a small basement club with an elevated dance floor. There were toilets for men and women either side of the bar which was amusing as it was a predominately gay clientele – so we used whichever loo we were nearer to, or whichever one someone we fancied was heading for! It was a cheap night out. The wine was foul but free-flowing, and shots poured as the barman wished; the short Italian waiters, balancing trays, weaved between the bodies on the dance floor. I never passed out but I took myself to the edge many times.

I'd find myself going home with someone to a bedsit in Earls Court or often miles out of the centre, followed by a long taxi ride home. I wasn't able to sleep over with anyone and that saved me from enduring a shock in the morning. However drunk, I always needed to go home. Nothing ever came from it. I wanted love, they wanted sex; ravishing at night, rubbish by dawn.

Then one night something odd happened. I was dressed in stiletto boots and a man's navy suit and, as usual, using the men's washroom at El Sombreros.

Suddenly a deep voice said, 'I've been looking for you all my life.'

I laughed quietly to myself. *He thinks I'm a man!*

I turned slowly, theatrically trying to tease out my admirer's moment of epiphany. I wanted to see the look on his face. But it was me who was shocked. He was gorgeous. He pushed me back into the cubicle and kissed me.

'Didn't you think I was a man?' I asked breathlessly.

'I've been watching you all night. Your eyelashes tell me you've come from a show.'

His name was Keith and he was an enigma. Extremely intelligent, well-spoken, he wrote poetry and read Kafka. He took me to exhibitions and subtitled films I never thought I could sit through. He was a body-builder, tanned and toned, wore fur coats, tailored suits, Italian shoes and looked like a Greek God. But he was also an accountant in Fleet Street – *and something else.*

'Where do you get the money for all these clothes?' I quizzed him one day.

'I'm a gigolo.' The way he said it he may as well have been confessing to stamp-collecting.

A gigolo? A male prostitute?

Keith's main clients were two older, wealthy women who supported his expensive tastes and he had friends in the criminal fraternity, I quickly learned.

'It doesn't change anything,' Keith assured me. 'It's just work. There's nothing to be jealous about.'

I wanted to hate him for keeping it from me but I couldn't. I loved him too much. *So what if he slept with other women?* I reasoned. *It is, as he says, only work. I'm the one he wants to be with.*

Unfortunately Keith expected of others what he couldn't give himself.

He was at my flat in Number 10 one day when the phone rang. It was the Windmill's "head boy", Ron, asking how I was after a fall I'd taken the night before. I told him I was fine. 'Don't worry – it will take more than a slip to keep me down. See you later.'

As soon as I hung up I sensed the atmosphere in the room change.

'Who was that?'

'Ron – he works on the show.'

'What did he want?'

I told him, but Keith wasn't listening.

'Are you seeing this fella?' he asked.

'Of course not!' I laughed. Then I realised he wasn't joking. Laughing, in fact, had been the worst thing I could have done. Keith's ego wouldn't let him be the butt of any jokes – and now I saw he had an insane, jealous streak. He ended our relationship there and then.

'What about you sleeping with those old women every week?' I screamed, in tears.

'I've told you – that's work!'

Then the door slammed and I never saw him again.

For days after I was a mess. The show was the only thing that held me together. The moment I stopped dancing I melted, too drained to even talk. I wanted to go out, get drunk and pass out but I didn't even have the energy for that.

That was when I realised I didn't have to look too far for help.

The moment I'd set eyes on Anne I'd felt a spark. She was one of the most striking women I'd ever met; her dark hair, brown eyes and full, red lips complementing her amazing figure and graceful dancing. When she found me in the theatre's darkened sewing room one night, slumped and crying, she put an arm around me and said, 'It's all right, it's all right' and at that moment I knew it was. Just hearing that beautiful Australian voice purring and feeling the warmth of her body against mine was enough to push Keith out of my mind.

'Thank you, Anne,' I said, and pulled her head towards mine.

I had never kissed a woman before. I've always liked the roughness of a man's face, the solidness of his cheekbones and hardness of his body. By contrast, Anne was soft and delicate, inviting and smooth – and I loved it.

We didn't make love that night but I wanted to. I thought about nothing else until three nights later she came back to Number 10 with me. I had always admired her pussy for being so neat and pretty – and that night I discovered it tasted as wonderful as it looked. Anne's soft cries as she climaxed, her hands scrabbling desperately in my hair as I lay between her legs, will stay with me forever.

*****

Life couldn't have been better. Anne and I were lovers, albeit not exclusively – if we needed the company of a man we took it – and I was five months into my first professional contract at the world-famous Windmill Theatre. I was even being raved about by Noel Davies and everyone else from Number 10 who came to watch me dance. They were incredibly supportive.

'Fantastic dancing!'

'You can tell you've had the training!'

I'd been doing it for so long I totally forgot about the nudity aspect. Thinking about it later, I realised how odd it must be for these men and women to see me serving dishes at home one minute, then stark naked on a West End stage the next. If anything, I was even more shy when I bumped into them fully clothed the next time.

But everything was working out well. Then I got a reminder that life has its own plans.

One afternoon at rehearsal, I was running through a new routine when the watching Gerard made his way down to the front.

'Tess, are you in love or something?'

'What do you mean?'

'You're looking a bit chubby, girl. Love does that to people. You need to be careful.'

Chubby.

My happiness was punctured in a second. I wasn't in Soho anymore, I wasn't a woman. I was a thirteen-year-old girl standing in the lower studio at Brooking's, being told to lose weight.

I ran off stage and cried. Anne found me, of course. 'Don't listen to him,' she soothed, 'you're the perfect size.'

But of course I wouldn't listen, not even to her. When one of the other girls offered me a miracle cure I nearly snatched her arm off.

Passing me a handful of tablets, she said, 'These are called blues. Take two and you won't want to eat for a couple of days.'

I took three and I hardly ate for a week! But I didn't sleep either. Days passed in minutes, scenes whistling by as though I were on a high speed train. I managed to dance but each number seemed over in a split second. Somehow I got to my day off and collapsed. I slept for twelve hours solid and Anne was there when I woke up.

More than thirty years later, I'm still very unhappy about what happened next. I turned up the next day as usual and Gerard came over.

'Tess, you look great. Have you lost weight?'

I mumbled that I probably had.

'Incredible,' he said. 'I think it's time you had your own solo number.'

My own number? That was what I'd been dreaming of. I was just ashamed that I'd had to starve myself to get it. I was no better a dancer this week than I was last. 'The industry stinks,' I told Anne. She agreed.

Then we laughed.

'Your own solo number though!' she squealed and I felt my spirits rise.

The *Piano* was so called because it looked like I was dancing on two black keys. I wore black heels, a one-armed, one-legged turquoise body suit with black fishnets and my hair flowing loose. Gerard choreographed complicated movements with contortions over the keys, to a jazz soundtrack, especially for me. I couldn't have been prouder – or so I thought until after my second performance when Carl Snitcher made a rare appearance backstage.

'Tessa, that was superb!' he bellowed. 'What's taken Gerard so long to give you a solo?'

As I blushed he put a hand on my shoulder and said quietly, 'But you're looking a bit tired to me. Have you been overdoing it?'

I nodded – although I knew it was the blue pills that had drained my colour.

'Listen,' he went on, 'if you need some time off just come and see me. We can't have our star getting sick!'

I felt ten feet tall hearing that. Carl's opinion meant everything. As far as we were concerned, he was the voice of the Windmill organisation.

But there was one person above even the Chief Executive.

A few weeks after my solo number had had its debut, there was a greater buzz than usual backstage. Then suddenly everyone went quiet. I was unpicking my eyelashes at the mirror and so didn't look up immediately. When I did, a long-haired man in an exquisite blue silk suit and a woman, wearing a long fur coat and a trilby, were standing in the middle of the room. There was an almost tangible aura about the pair of them.

'Mr Raymond, did you enjoy the show?' Mark asked nervously.

'Enjoy it?' Paul Raymond's droopy-looking face broke into a charming smile. 'I thought it was sensational. We both did.'

His companion, the model Fiona Richmond, nodded.

'And you,' he pointed at me, 'you were stunning.'

I felt myself burn with embarrassment.

It was a surreal moment, watching one of the richest men in London offer compliments around the room, but it meant the world to me. He owned the club that I was so proud to dance in – and he said I had been stunning.

I want to work here for the rest of my life, I decided.

*****

Unfortunately, no sooner had everything finally slotted into place, than it started to unravel. Cast members began to reach the end of their contracts and leave the show. This meant a lot of the choreography needed to be changed and I spent weeks in the theatre just rehearsing all day. People were refused days off and my leave was cancelled. I slept through Christmas Day and didn't notice. Everything felt as if it was falling apart and from never wanting to leave I suddenly couldn't wait to get out.

Anne felt the same. When her contract ended she said, 'I've had enough. I've been here four years – I'm going back to Australia.'

I never thought we'd stay lovers forever but knowing she would be on the other side of the world was a painful realisation.

Casting my net, I was offered a place in an off-shoot of Hot Gossip, featured on the *Kenny Everett* TV show, choreographed by Arlene Phillips. My Windmill contract finished in April and I prayed the dates wouldn't clash.

In the end I had time on my hands sooner than I expected.

After ten days' solid daytime rehearsals followed by two shows a night, I approached Mark.

'I haven't been paid for the last fortnight's rehearsals.'

Without even looking up from his desk, he snapped, 'Not now, Tessa.'

I was in a bad enough mood without him being rude to me. 'I haven't had a day off in a month,' I insisted. 'The least you can do is to pay me on time.'

Now he looked up. His face was red. 'If you don't like it, Tessa, you can fuck off.'

So I did.

I packed my bag, cleared my dressing table and walked out of the stage door onto Archer Street for the last time.

For a few days I revelled in catching up on my sleep. Then I started to think again about work.

When am I going to hear from Arlene Philips?

The call came soon enough – but it was bad news. The group had argued so much they'd disbanded. I wouldn't be needed.

Just when I thought my luck couldn't get any worse I received a letter. It was from a solicitor and it stated quite simply that Paul Raymond was taking me to court for breach of contract.

The first person I ran to was Noel Davies.

'Don't worry, Tess, we can fight this,' he assured me.

Fortunately I'd been at the Windmill long enough to qualify for help from Equity. Backed by the union and the Schlesinger household, I made my way to a room on Charing Cross Road in January 1979 to face charges at the Variety Artists & Entertainers' Council.

Ten men were already seated around a huge oval table by the time I walked in. I paused nervously in the doorway. There was just one place available next to the Equity rep. It may just as well have had a neon sign saying "the accused" on it. I felt so ashamed as twenty eyes bore into me.

The questions came thick and fast.

'Are you Tessa Skola?'

'Yes.'

'You live at Number 10 Victoria Road?'

'Yes.'

'You performed at the Windmill Theatre for ten months?'

'Yes.'

By the time a man said, 'You have no father and your mother works all hours,' I couldn't hold it in any longer. I crumbled into loud sobs and had to be led from the room to gather my thoughts.

When I returned the pressure only increased. The representative from Paul Raymond wanted my Equity card taken away and compensation of £700. But I, along with my advisors, fought back.

'I hadn't been paid for rehearsals for nearly two weeks, I was having to cover for missing dancers and all leave had been cancelled,' I reported calmly. 'That's without having to pick our way around rat poison backstage, and sharing costumes even though some of the cast members have had VD or worse.'

After a gruelling and tense day a verdict was delivered.

'We find in favour of Miss Tessa Skola.'

I was so relieved when I left the room that I didn't even notice Carl Snitcher standing outside.

'Congratulations, Tess. Now, when are you going to come back and join us? We can't do this show without you.'

Was I hearing right? He wanted me back?

'It's been a long day, Carl. I'll have to think about it.'

'Call me when you've made your mind up.'

'I will,' I promised, but my mind was already made up. *I'm not going back there again. Not after that ordeal.* What was he thinking of, even asking?

I was bitterly disappointed how it all ended but I stuck to my principles. Even so, I still needed work. I sent my CV to several agencies and applied for different posts. I took the first offer I received – but it wasn't what I expected. The "dancing job at a new venue in Leicester Square" turned out to be a peep show next to the Empire – a place that held chilling memories for me since I'd run away from Brooking's. It wasn't my dream job by any means but I started straight away. I selected my own music and danced in a small boxed room. Once I got going I even forgot that men's eyes pried from outside. I was paid £16 for five spots per day, three girls working on rotation every half hour. Most of the other girls were students, not dancers, just earning money to get through college. It was quite a different atmosphere, nothing like a show, but I still felt the excitement of performing and it was an ideal stop-gap.

Five weeks later one of my CVs hit the bullseye. An agency in Leeds rang me with a proposition: a three-month contract as a solo dancer in northern France, starting 1st May.

'Your flight and accommodation will be paid and the agent in France, Jo, will look after you on arrival. What do you think?'

What did I think?

'I'll take it!'

Three weeks later I stood at the port of Dover with the leather suitcase Mum had travelled with to Australia all those years ago and a little French dictionary from Gran. I had packed the minimum of summer clothes, my show tapes, shoes and bikini costumes.

I was ready for my first job as a solo dancer.

My dream was coming true.

CHAPTER FIVE

I DYED IT WITH TEA

I was three when I discovered the power of music to move me. At six Irene Luke identified something in me that, if harnessed, could be developed. But, for all the scars it left me, the teachings of the horrific Nesta Brooking, from ten to fifteen, had the greatest influence. My plaudits at the Windmill would not have been possible without her punishing tuition. By the time I left her school I really was a technically excellent dancer instilled with a discipline and unspoken set of rules of how to be truly professional.

It was the sexy Miss Cogan who introduced my body to the flamboyant, vivacious flamenco and Rosita who lit the spark that drove my passion for that most expressive of dances. But those topless cabaret girls at Tito's in Majorca – they were the ones who'd captured my imagination. They were the people I dreamed of becoming. They had the lives I wanted to lead.

And finally, aged eighteen, I was taking my first steps towards reaching that dream.

Catching my first hovercraft at Dover was exciting but the real emotion in my stomach came from the knowledge that I was doing it on my own. The furthest I'd ever travelled alone had been from Cornwall to London. Suddenly I was riding a space-age transporter to another country.

Somehow I picked my way through the signs at Calais and found the station. An hour after setting foot on French soil I found myself on a train bound for Lille, the agreed rendezvous for my "manager" Jo. My new life began there.

I can't wait.

*****

It's funny how environment can shape mood. I'd boarded the train in the brightest of spirits, but as we passed through the outskirts of Calais and into the industrial heartland of northern France I felt my mood sink. I could see my face reflected in the window against the grey backdrop and for the first time started to question my decision to come.

Why don't I go back to the Windmill?

It's not too late to call Carl Snitcher.

The peepshow would have me back tomorrow.

I took a deep breath and relaxed into my seat. The carriage smelled vaguely of chocolate. I needed to calm down. *It's only nerves. You're doing the right thing. This is all you've ever wanted.*

It wasn't the dancing that I found daunting, or even the travelling. It was just doing it on my own. I seemed to have been on my own for most of my life; as a girl on the beach, as a little dancer ferried to classes miles away, as a child playing with my grandparents while Mum worked. Even as a lone victim of Brooking's spite. It would have been nice, sometimes, to share my time with someone else.

But I'd had the chance. When Paula and Gillian had left the Windmill to tour with a troupe in a circus around Mexico, they'd invited me along.

'There's a place in the group if you want it.'

'Come on, Tess, it will be fun. You said you wanted to travel.'

'I do, girls, but I'm going to have to pass. It's not the right time for me.'

'Well, stay in touch. If you change your mind I'm sure the manager can find a spot for you.'

I would love to have gone with them but the timing was awful. I'd just been given my own solo spot in *Rip Off*, I couldn't bear to throw that away.

Those ten minutes every show – twenty minutes every night – were the highlight of my time in Archer Street. They were when I really came alive, when I got to dance as *I* wanted to dance, when the moves were written just for me and *my* talent, not for a dozen other faceless performers. I could do things most of the other girls could only dream of and in *Piano* I got a chance to showcase – to *show off* – everything I'd worked so hard to learn.

If I'm honest, I enjoyed the peep show performances as much as some of my later Windmill nights. At least then I was dancing to my own beat, in my own costume, on my own terms. Okay, there were men doing God knows what the other side of the wooden screen – I tried to ignore the movements through the little spy holes around the room – but as a performer I was in control. I could move when I wanted, stop when I wanted, smile when I wanted.

And now, travelling slowly through the Nord-Pas de Calais region at the end of the 1970s, I had the opportunity to do what I wanted in France.

Too excited to sleep yet too unimpressed by the landscape to stare out of the window for long, my eyes wandered around the carriage. It was more empty than not, and everyone else looked as thrilled as me with the scenery. I looked over to the baggage rack and my eye caught my own suitcase. Myriad thoughts – unprompted – flashed across my mind.

All those labels, I thought. *They're diary entries from Mum's life.*

And not just her life, I realised.

From her life with Dad.

Absent-mindedly I let my gaze fall on a white sticker. From my seat I could make out the words 'Southampton Docks'. That's where Mum had caught the ship that took her to the promised land of Australia. And then there were the labels from Adelaide. I walked over to the case. There were three Oz stickers, each with dates stamped on them. I scanned them quickly. There it was: the one that said, quite simply, 'April 1960.

That's when Mum left Dad for the final time: when she came back to England – for me.

Something hit me. A wave of sadness or guilt or just a feeling of lost opportunity – I don't know. I fell back into my seat. That piece of luggage had probably met my father. I hadn't. It was an odd thought. I had to smile. Was I really jealous of a suitcase?

Even so, there was so much history in that old leather and I was only just beginning to appreciate it. Dad, of course, had made the trip to Australia, hounded out of his own home by the war. My mother, on the other side of the Iron Curtain, had been forced to leave her home as well. That sense of abandonment by her parents had driven her wanderlust, I was convinced of it. She was without identity when she took that job with the Governor General in Adelaide. Thanks to meeting Dainis, she found it, I believe.

I stared harder at the case. The feeling of not knowing her own parents had eaten away at Mum all her life. But there was the sticker saying 'April 1960'. That was the date – the proof – she did to me exactly what had been done to her.

She'd condemned me to a life without knowing my father.

What must have been going through her mind? Just as her parents had sacrificed their daughter for her own safety, she was doing the same to her unborn baby. I felt the tears begin to well and tried to blink them away. *Now is not the time.* But oh, how I loved my mother so much, whatever the past.

Compared to both parents crossing the Pacific to start a new life, my twenty-minute hop across the English Channel didn't seem so significant. But to me it was. In my own way I was looking for something, just like they had been. Maybe not safety, like my father, but certainly some sense of belonging – I'm pretty sure my mother went through that. I was following my heart, I wanted to dance. But I was also looking for adventure. I was looking for thrilling new experiences. And something else.

I was looking for love.

Looking back, I think I was always looking for love. Everywhere I went. It didn't have to be France. I'd been looking all my life and a few times I thought I'd found it. Quentin and Anne had opened my eyes to new experiences and emotions. Keith and Larry had shown me what a true relationship involved, the ups and downs. Both men had made me fall in love with them, or so I thought at the time. They'd both hurt me in the end. Both walked away with someone else. Had I made bad choices or was I just unlucky? *Maybe that's just men,* I thought. But I didn't know.

And then there were all those faceless fumbles I'd let myself endure over the years. Endure or enjoy? It was what I'd wanted at the time – usually. Sometimes men had misread the signs. The memory of what nearly happened on that drunken night in Windsor still gave me nightmares.

Funnily enough, one of the men I loved more than anyone had never laid a hand on me or even pretended to fancy me. He'd never strung me along in any way. John Schlesinger was exactly the sort of man I would love to have married.

As the train pulled into the beautiful old Lille station building, I smiled. John being gay was the only drawback I could see. The fact that he was old enough to be my grandfather hadn't even occurred to me at the time. What did that say about my ambitions with men?

Love, for now, would have to wait, though. As I lugged my case down the narrow steps to platform level I took a deep breath. My career as a solo dancer was about to begin.

*****

Underneath the clock on the main concourse I saw a dark-haired man in an ill-fitting suit, with overflowing chest hair and a gold medallion around his neck. *That's him.* I gave a wave and the man revealed several missing teeth in a broad smile. *Definitely him.*

Jo, the agent, was from Argentina. He was short, skinny, with a small nose, thick lips and black oily eyes to match his hair. From my experience of London men he looked incredibly sleazy – and I was about to climb into his less than impressive car. What had I let myself in for? But as soon as he offered to carry my case I knew there was more to him than my first impression. In fact, we'd barely got going before I was already laughing.

My image of a foreign agent, based on whispers and stories from the more experienced girls at the Windmill, wasn't encouraging.

'Steer clear of their hands and you'll be all right.'

'Remember to get everything in writing – in English. And cash up front.'

While Jo looked the part, he was soft spoken and at times had a little-boy-lost feel. He worked on his own, not as part of a larger agency, which meant he had no airs and graces. He wasn't a show-off nor was he demanding. As he ran through my itinerary for the next few days – we were staying in Lille overnight then driving down to the South of France – I was overwhelmed with the feeling that I didn't want to let him down.

We drove straight to a hotel in Lille. So far I'd seen precisely nothing of the city – this wasn't what I had in mind as a traveller. When I saw my room, I was even more disappointed. I would be sharing it with Angie, a girl from Birmingham, and Bebe, Jo's sister. Both were dancers in Lille, Jo's clients, and had offered to put me up for the night. I put my bag on the small single bed and looked at Jo, standing in the doorway.

'What time will you be picking me up in the morning?' I asked.

He gave a thick, earthy laugh. 'Whenever you're ready.'

'And how will you know when that is?'

'Because I'm sleeping in this room with you!'

My heart sank.

'Don't worry,' Angie's voice called out from the other room. 'There's a spare blanket. He's going on the floor.'

That was a relief. But even so: my first night in France and I'd have a strange man on the floor in my room.

As long as he doesn't try anything…

The girls disappeared off to work and Jo and I discussed my contract at length. Then, tired, I got ready for bed and slipped under the quilt. I was aware of the door opening a few minutes later, and Jo trying to get comfortable on the floor. Then I was asleep. Nerves, excitement and the long day had taken their toll.

I awoke with a start. Eyes still shut I tried to get my bearings. The details were slow to reach my brain. *I'm in France. I'm in a hotel in Lille. And there's someone in my bed!*

I froze and kept my eyes screwed firmly shut. I was on my side and the person was behind me. I felt a small hand reach out to my hip. I still didn't know who it was. Then the unmistakeable hardness of a man pressed against me. Now I knew. It was my agent. It was Jo.

'What do you think you're doing?' I pulled myself away and sat bolt upright on the edge of the bed, quilt pulled around my neck.

In the half-light I could make out the embarrassment on Jo's face.

'I'm sorry,' he mumbled, crawling back out. 'I'm sorry.'

It took forever to get back to sleep. With every creak I heard in the hotel I thought he was climbing back in. Once I could hear Jo snoring, a new fear entered my mind. Was that the end of my contract? Is that how business was conducted in France? Had I blown it before I'd even begun?

The next morning I would find out.

By the time I woke up the others were already having breakfast. Awkwardly I stumbled out of the bedroom. The girls clearly had no idea what had happened last night – and Jo didn't mention it. But he did say there had been a change in plan. Rather than travel today, we'd be staying another night.

'Then tomorrow we'll drop off Bebe in Knokke before going south,' he explained.

'Is that on the way?'

Angie laughed. 'About as on the way as Dover is.'

She wasn't joking. The next morning the four of us finally squeezed into Jo's car and drove for ninety minutes north into Belgium. Every mile that passed was more depressing than the last. I just wanted to get started on stage. Until I had done my first performance I wouldn't know if I'd made a huge mistake coming here. *But God knows when that will be,* I sulked. *I'm further away now than when I started.*

When we entered Knokke I perked up. This small, affluent-looking Belgian town made a nice change after Lille, and as we pulled up outside the Casino club I even felt a tingle of excitement. Sleek sports cars lined the driveway outside the marble foyer and smart men and women were entering the building. This was exactly the sort of place I dreamed of performing in – and little did I know that one day I would.

'We need to get going now,' Jo said, as he unloaded Bebe's case, but she wouldn't hear of it.

'Don't rush off. Give Tessa a tour of the place, let her get a taste of how they do things over here.'

Jo wasn't convinced. 'I'd really like to look round,' I said. 'It would probably help my nerves later.'

Sighing like a husband with three overbearing wives, Jo led us all into the venue. One of the first people we saw was the Casino's owner, a short man with a kindly face who reminded me of the singer Burl Ives. The main club was buzzing with wealthy people. I was intrigued to see podiums mounted six feet above the tables, each with a topless girl dancing on top. Podiums are all the rage these days but in the 70s I'd never seen them before. How on earth would I contain my dancing on one of those? I wondered. If I did the splits my feet would shoot off both sides.

The girls were used more as glamorous background entertainment than any real attempt at a stage show, but even so they were dressed as though headlining at Drury Lane. None of the girls had a bikini line, which would have been unusual in England, and they all wore shiny g-strings, which I'd never seen before, and Latin-style flares called jambières which added movement and a swirl of colour, with matching arm ruffs and chokers. I thought everyone looked stunning. They weren't trained, I could tell, but they moved well.

Bebe saw my amazement.

'You like the costumes?'

'Oh yes, they're beautiful. Even the g-strings.'

'Come to the dressing room. I've got some spare things you can have.'

Bebe opened her case and took out some tiny, sparkling garments. 'These are for you.'

I held up a string of flesh-coloured elastic attached to a pouch the size of a pirate's eye-patch. Bebe saw my confusion. It was a g-string.

'Where do you find elastic this colour?' I asked.

She laughed. 'We don't. It's white elastic – dyed with tea!'

She gave me two costumes in sparkling purple and pink and wished me luck. I couldn't wait to try them on.

Setting off at eight o'clock, Jo, Angie and I drove overnight down the length of France. I drifted in and out of sleep, cheeks crushed against cases, and I was amazed at the number of roadside cafés serving enticing selections of hams and patisseries throughout the night. Finally we arrived on a baking, blue morning in Toulon, about forty miles along the coast from Marseilles, and I felt a lift of excitement. I was on the Côte d'Azur. It looked like a different country and it even smelled like a different country. I wound down the car window and inhaled the sea air. My adventure was really just about to begin.

*****

Toulon isn't your average picturesque resort. Originally a commercial and military port, in the 1970s it had little of the tourist charm of some of its neighbours. But I fell in love instantly. There was a beach, there were restaurants and clubs, and there was sunshine. Who could wish for anything more?

I was disappointed to learn that Angie and I would be sharing a room. We got on very well together but when you're living out of a suitcase and working with so many people, it's lovely to have a sanctuary, a private space to rest from the world. At least our room overlooked the main square which made me feel like I was in the heart of the town.

As soon as I'd unpacked we walked to Le Colonis, the bar where we would be performing later. The manager was friendly and the venue pleasant enough. I paid special attention to the podiums. They looked wide enough to dance on but I would only find out later.

Next I went shopping. I'd arrived with £40 in traveller's cheques which I thought would last me well but an hour later I had spent half of it on a single essential purchase: designer sunglasses! I'd never had a pair before and, I reasoned, if now wasn't the time to invest in a pair, when was? Feeling extravagant, but ever so at home in the sunny town, I wended my way back to the hotel at five for a light meal. Then Angie and I made our way to Le Colonis. Even as we walked I sensed the "professional" part of my brain clicking into gear. *This is why you're here. You're not on holiday. You're here to work.*

We were contracted to perform for fifteen minutes per hour, from nine o'clock till one. Cash wages would be paid weekly and Jo took ten per cent. Considering dinner was included in the hotel price, I had a decent amount to live on. But first I had to earn it.

Stepping into my jambières for the first time was an odd sensation. I was used to either wearing clothes or not wearing them – but these odd bits of trousers would take a while to get used to – but not as long as another part of my costume. Pulling on my g-string was an interesting experience, more like flossing teeth than getting dressed. It felt like an intrusive nappy between my cheeks and I was so self-conscious getting ready I thought I must be walking like John Wayne. But somehow I made it into the main room and onto a podium. Then the DJ played Supertramp's Breakfast In America and I was away.

I was dancing.

It didn't matter that I was topless. It didn't matter that the flared jambières only highlighted the exposed cheeks of my bottom or that I was performing on a tiny platform above most customers' heads. All that mattered was that I was feeling the music and responding in the way that only my body knew how. All the years of training, of pain and humiliation and relentless practice, were worth it. In those fifteen minutes I banished a lot of personal demons and made a lot of friends.

As I climbed down from the podium, glistening with sweat but on fire with adrenaline, Angie came rushing up.

'Fantastic, Tessa, bloody amazing.'

Jo was right behind her.

'You never said you could actually dance!' he laughed. 'Christ, Tessa, I'm going to have to get you some proper work!'

The next day I woke up feeling like the world was at my feet. For a few minutes I just lay still, smiling as the recollections of my debut performance came slowly back. The lights, the audience, the music, the owner, Jo, Angie, the walk home in the moonlight – everything had been perfect.

Over the next few days I slipped into an easy rhythm of exploring the area by day, walking for miles along the beach, or wandering down elegant, tall streets of terracotta buildings with wooden shutters, the skyline a mess of tiled roofs and aerials. There was always a strong aroma of tobacco and aniseed, especially near bars. Foreigners were not exactly encouraged, it seemed, but old ladies always broke into gentle smiles whenever I tried my French on the bus or in a shop.

Television at the hotel helped me to pick up the language. I was lucky there were so many programmes of interest. Variety shows featuring superb dancers, all ballet-trained with classic looks, seemed to dominate the airwaves like reality TV does today. It seemed I could switch on at any time of day and find a dozen lovely, topless girls, all teeth, with their hair up - in fancy chignons just like mine - high-kicking away. I hadn't been there long when I spotted a girl in the street whom I'd seen backing Claude François – one of France's most eminent performers. (He died young – electrocuted in his bath). The dancer had that French superiority, that indefinable something, but she was flattered to be recognised and warmed as we spoke. Her parting words of advice to me were, 'It's easier to dance with a group than on your own – but good luck.'

I knew it was easier to get work with a group – but to actually dance with one was another matter. By that stage I had tasted enough of solo performing, even if it was on a podium, to know that I never wanted to share the stage again.

From working in the club and seeing so many sights I soon got to know the different types of men. The young ones were mostly pleasant, clean-cut, short-haired and neatly dressed. They'd whiz up and down the promenade on their mopeds, strangely old-fashioned in many ways. The greasy, middle-aged types at the bars and clubs were different. With their white shirts open to the navel and leather wallets – the male equivalent of handbags in the Med – they all looked the same and, when they got their chance to speak to younger girls, they sounded the same as well. Angie and I sometimes compared lines we'd been spun during the course of an evening and laughed at how many were repeated over and over again.

Regardless of age, all French men would compliment and acknowledge beauty. I had a beautiful *poitrine* (chest), as I was told not just at night but by strangers if I were on the beach or buying flowers in a shop. Men were very forward in giving their opinions and they didn't appreciate coyness. A woman was expected to realise her assets and use them: to gain free entry, get the best seats at a club or have her luggage carried, and men were happy to oblige.

With my first wages in my hand I called home. Mum, of course, was too busy to answer at first but on the third or fourth attempt I found her.

'I can't stop to talk now,' she panted, 'because about a hundred people seem to have turned up for dinner – unannounced. But why don't you write me a nice long letter – and send one to Gran, too.'

I was relieved at her suggestion. Just hearing Mum's voice had made me sadder than I expected. For a moment only one thought filled my mind. *What are you doing here when your family is so far away? Haven't you always dreamed of having your family close?*

No sooner had I hung up than my feelings of homesickness had vanished. But even so, over the next weeks and months I would call home less frequently for that reason.

I threw myself into the French way of life as much as possible. The idea of having a drink outdoors in London was laughable, but pavement culture was all the rage in Toulon and there was nothing I enjoyed more than a morning coffee – their attempts at tea were risible – whilst watching the world go by. Below our hotel was a glass-fronted café with wicker chairs and a menu featuring the most delicious hot chocolate. One day I had sat at my usual table, read for a while, then ordered my bill. The waitress came back with a smile

'Your bill has already been settled – by a gentleman.'

A gentleman?

Suddenly I was aware of polite coughing behind me. When I glanced over I looked straight into the eyes of a buccaneer – or at least that's how I remember it to this day! The man had intense grey eyes, high cheekbones, wavy brown hair and a moustache. If he'd been wearing pantaloons and a sword I would not have flinched.

'Merci,' I managed to utter as my benefactor rose.

He nodded. 'You are a thing of beauty, mademoiselle,' and he bowed and left.

A thing of beauty? A swashbuckling pirate called me a thing of beauty, bought me a drink and didn't even stop to ask my name? I was falling in love with France every minute.

It wasn't long before I had fallen in love with more than the country.

As I was walking to my hotel a few days later I saw a familiar face in the café below. Gingerly I stepped in. I needn't have worried. The look on my buccaneer's face told me he not only remembered me but might have been waiting there for days to catch a glimpse of me.

I pulled up a chair and we spoke. His name was Thierry, he was of Polish descent, his family lived in Brittany and he was training to be a doctor at the military hospital. He looked and behaved much older than his twenty-four years, I could tell that already.

I saw him again the next day, this time for an arranged date. Days became logistical exercises in fitting assignations into our conflicting schedules. After ten consecutive days of lunches, breakfasts and afternoon meals I asked my boss for a night off. The next night Thierry and I had our first night together. He picked me up in his red MG and took me into the hills to a rustic, simple restaurant with food that tasted like nectar. The sky was pink and the countryside turned bronze. Then, driving higher, to a view of the glittering lights of the coast against midnight blue and a kiss that swept up my soul, I was his.

The next few weeks were intense. I had fallen in love, swift, total, liberating, tormenting and blind. Thierry showed me the real France and I began to develop a confidence conversing in the language. I began, in fact, to feel French and it suited me. I loved the women's fashion and grooming and the time people allowed for themselves to enjoy family, friends and food; all the good things.

That suited Thierry, I quickly learned. On one of our afternoon dates he took me shopping. I'd never had a man take an interest that way before. They normally only paid attention once I was wearing an outfit – not while it was on a mannequin. But Thierry wasn't impressed by my clothes: I'd borrowed a few sun dresses from an aunt and, while I liked them, they weren't the height of Parisian couture.

When we went into a smart-looking shop I saw a black dress and went to try it on.

'What are you doing?' Thierry asked.

'I'm seeing if they have it in my size.'

'Waste of time,' he snapped. 'It won't suit you. You need to be wearing this.' He gestured to another dress.

'I'm not sure, Thierry. Do you think so?'

'I don't think. I know. I'll wait for you outside.'

Thierry's fondness for having things just so worked both ways. We would travel for miles in the summer to experience the perfect sunset or taste the perfect cocktail. Nothing was too much trouble. We'd drive along the coast, with the roof rolled back, to pretty coves and little restaurants run entirely by one chef. By candlelight he educated me, as he put it, in food. Meats with rich sauces, greens eaten separately, good wine and strong, black coffee.

I took it as a compliment when he introduced me to his colleagues and friends but soon regretted entering his world. When you go out with one of them, you go out with all. Dates for two became dates for eight. I treasured our time alone but doors were always open. It worked both ways, of course. We could drop in anytime and share a meal or appear at a phone call's notice at a friend's flat and sleep on their floor rather than go home. It was always on those occasions that Thierry wanted to make love – as if revelling in my awkwardness as his friends slept the other side of the door.

Somehow I managed to keep my hours at work although on more than one occasion I got to the club by the skin of my teeth, Thierry's MG screeching up outside at a minute to nine. But I would not risk my dancing for anything. I'd already given up so much to get this far.

After a long season at Le Colonis, Jo placed me on a new contract along the coast at Hyères. I had a good feeling about the place as soon as I saw the town's white cottages draped in bougainvillea, old men playing boules, its tiny railway station and a casino set in colourful gardens. There was also a nudist bay where I swam, like a mermaid, hair flowing, and a general pace of life which suited me, slow and peaceful. Best of all, though, I had my own room above a sleepy tabac/bar run by a lovely elderly couple, him - pipe and slippers, her - apron and slippers. It was a heavenly little place.

Work was good as well. My new venue was a disco called Retro 2000, and it played lively, upbeat chart songs to a packed audience of French holidaymakers while I danced the night away. I'd never seen such an appreciative crowd. As soon as I stepped off my podium I was inundated with offers of drinks, food, you name it. On my first night there I was asked to pose for photographs with young couples but the next night I had a different request.

'Miss Skola, would you mind signing this?'

A handsome young local was holding a pen and a matchbox from the venue. It took a second for the penny to drop.

'Sign what?'

'Your autograph.'

'Why would you want my autograph? I'm not a star.'

'You were a star tonight, Miss Skola – and I think you will be for a long time.'

I couldn't believe what I was hearing but as I scribbled my signature I thought, *I could get used to this!* I thought the evening couldn't get any better. Then I saw another face – but this one did not want my autograph.

'Tessa, are you ready to go?' Thierry's voice was masterful and cold. The men around me stood instinctively aside.

'Of course I'm ready, darling. I was just waiting for you.'

He offered his arm and gratefully I fell onto it. He was so powerful and charismatic, even to be escorted out of the building in such an old-fashioned romantic way was a joy. But I could tell Thierry wasn't enjoying the moment as much as I was.

'Never forget,' he said, his voice steely and distant, 'you are mine.'

I burst into instant tears. Quickly, Thierry's tone softened as we reached his car, and he added three more words.

'I love you.'

Love! The thing I'd been dreaming of all those weeks ago as I'd trundled across the grey vista of northern France. And now I'd found it.

I was the happiest woman in Europe. Nothing could spoil it for me now.

CHAPTER SIX

DON'T CHANGE

It's amazing how environment can affect mood. On the Côte d'Azur I felt at home. I loved the language, the people and the lifestyle. I felt more French than English and, thanks to Thierry's grooming, I looked it as well. My hair went blonde in the sunshine and I even grew to love wearing g-strings on the beach. The locals had no inhibitions where sunbathing was concerned and despite my early self-consciousness – odd considering how I made my living – I grew at home wandering around topless.

And, of course, being with Thierry made the sun shine even brighter.

I knew my contract at Hyères was drawing to an end and waited for Jo's call. Excitedly I pored over a map of the Mediterranean coastline while Thierry recommended his favourite places.

'Marseilles, St Tropez, Cannes – all of them out of this world.'

'What about Nice? Or Antibes? Or St Raphael?' The names evoked faint memories of film scenes or magazine reports of celebrity lifestyles.

'Tessa, this is Côte d'Azur. There is nowhere bad here.'

'But will you always come to see me?'

'My darling, I will travel to the ends of the earth to be with you.'

We kissed, blissfully in love. A week later, however, Thierry's words would be sorely tested. Jo had a new contract for me but it wasn't in the South of France. It was in De Panne, in West Flanders. My heart sank. My lover had said he would travel to the ends of the earth – but would he come to Belgium?

I was sobbing like a mad woman as I boarded the train to Paris. Thierry watched stoically from the platform then broke into a little run alongside the carriage as we pulled out of the station.

'I love you,' he mouthed.

'I love you too,' I cried back. I didn't care who heard.

From Paris I transferred once again to Lille where Jo met me, his uneven smile ever present. He did his best to cheer me up but I must have been hard work and he soon gave up. I can't blame him. It was his job to find me decent contracts and my job to fulfil them. I'd never told him I only wanted to work in the South of France. I just hoped.

Jo dropped me off at a small hotel in De Panne and once again I forced a smile as I explored my private room. It was compact, as usual, but it was mine. My little kingdom, my little bit of Belgium. *I just wish I had Thierry here to share it with me.*

I explored the town at the first opportunity. As Belgium's most western town, it borders France and even though it's on the coast, sitting on the North Sea, any similarities with Toulon ended there. The coastline was grey and flat and the temperature closer to that of London than Marseilles. Even worse, the people seemed to reflect their environment. Everyone looked grey and worn-down. In fact the whole town had a melancholy air.

Entertainment-wise, food seemed to be of the "chips with everything" variety. I hoped my venue would be better but the Kings Disco was limited by its surroundings. The same cloudy atmosphere that pervaded the town also affected the club. I danced as well as I could and the crowds seemed to delight in my ornate crab positions and high-kicking enthusiasm, but their smiles stopped short of their eyes.

Maybe this is exactly how De Panne is or maybe there was another explanation. Maybe I was letting my personal depression at being removed from my love colour my mood. I honestly can't say but I do know that I didn't cope with the separation very well. After several months of decadent companionship I slipped quickly and too easily into my pattern of binge drinking immediately after work. The club didn't shut till four in the morning – and I was always the last one out, if I was still standing.

What is the point of going home? There's no one there. At least at Kings I'm surrounded by men who love me.

Of course, when I was drinking I allowed some of those men to love me a little too much. It was because of Thierry that I craved male company but I still should have been stronger. The other girls in the club said nothing: they didn't need to. Life on the road can never be normal. Life for a performer, in fact, is such an alien existence that friends and family left behind could never understand. At least that's what we all convinced ourselves to justify our behaviour. Married men chased married women and sometimes new relationships were formed. But then one of them would leave as easily as they'd appeared and the memory would disappear with them. That was then: what mattered, always, was now.

Not everyone was out for sex, though. Kings was a very friendly establishment, not at all intimidating for female visitors. They put on a classy dance event, not a simulated sex show. Lots of my audience comprised couples of all ages but one night I noticed a pair taking particular pleasure in my performance. When I dismounted my podium they were waiting to congratulate me.

'Can we buy you a drink?'

'That would be lovely but I can't while I'm working.'

'Okay, we'll wait till you get off. Perhaps you'd join us for supper?'

Over the next few weeks I saw them dozens of times and we became as firm friends as you can when everyone knows that time is short and contracts have to end. Pascal and Natalie were lovely people and invited me to stay at their house in Dunkerque on my day off. She was thirty-five and unable to have children so she treated me like a daughter. They cooked me snails dripping in garlic and crunchy frogs' legs, both of which I found quite delicious. I enjoyed their company but the journeys to and from their house was depressing. Dunkerque was so bleak I could almost feel the horror entrenched in the land; just walking through the dark, grey town made me feel tired and hollow. De Panne, though, wasn't much better.

The girls at Kings took every opportunity to mock my relationship with the couple.

'What do they want from you?'

'Nothing – we're just good friends.'

They all laughed. When Natalie gave me one of her necklaces as a keepsake the scrutiny increased.

'She'll expect something back for that,' my manager sneered.

'When will you understand? It's all perfectly innocent!' but I could tell my words were making no impression.

'No such thing as innocent in this world.'

I sighed and prayed that I would never become as cynical as they were. Other girls had a defensive layer, a mask they could put on in public. They looked like they knew the rules to the game.

I didn't even know what the game was called.

After eight uninspiring weeks in De Panne, eight weeks away from Thierry, Jo rang with a new commission.

'Is it in the south?' I asked eagerly.

'Well, it's south of where you are now. It's Knokke.'

Damn. But at least I knew the club was good – and I'd see Angie again because she was already there.

With two nights of De Panne to endure I fell even more heavily onto the crutch of alcohol. I danced with anyone who could keep up with me at Kings until finally the manager ordered everyone home. I still managed to hang around for another twenty minutes talking to the DJ but eventually, at about four-thirty, I staggered into the fresh early morning air.

Birdsong and the echoes of my own footsteps were the only sounds. Suddenly I was aware of a low humming noise. I thought nothing of it at first but the sound stayed with me. As I turned to cross the road I could see a grey car in the distance, just sitting with the headlights on full so I couldn't make out any passengers. A few minutes later I crossed another road. The car was still behind me: still stationary.

This time I caught a glimpse of the driver. He was bespectacled and balding. Next to him sat a dumpy woman. They were staring straight ahead, like shop dummies. Suddenly they turned in unison towards me and stared. No one moved for what seemed like ages. Then, forcing myself to break their gaze, I turned away, my stomach churning with confusion. But now I could make out clearly the humming sound from before. It was the car's engine, purring as it crawled along the shadowy Belgian streets. I chanced a look in a shop window and thought I'd explode. It was still there, exactly the same distance from me, but undoubtedly following.

Following me? My brain was sober for the first time that night. *Why would anyone follow me?*

I needed to be sure. I turned sharply down an alley and tucked into a doorway. The car swung round, stopped briefly, but then moved on. As it passed in terrifying slow motion, I caught their faces again, looking intently down the alley. Now I was sure.

But who were they? Did I know them?

Was my vivid imagination playing tricks? No, I sensed something truly dreadful and macabre.

Sweat rolled down my body. I fought a powerful urge to vomit. I needed to stay calm but it was impossible. My heart was pounding out of my dress. I was desperate for oxygen but almost too terrified to breathe.

Then I did something stupid. I should have stayed where I was, safe, until the alley's doors and windows came alive with morning activity. But I didn't. I peeped carefully back up the road I'd walked down then doubled back.

Suddenly there was a screech of tyres and excessive revving as the grey car swung violently round the corner. They'd been waiting. Watching and waiting. Taking the corner so fast made the car swing momentarily out of control. Out of sight for a second, instinctively I dived into another alley and threw myself like a rugby player behind a stack of stinking rubbish bins.

There was another roar of rubber biting the road as the car slid to a halt twenty yards from where I was lying. I didn't dare move but I knew I might have to.

I'll be cornered if they get out. If I hear a door open I'll have to run.

Eventually my pursuers drove on but I'd made that mistake before. I was not moving this time until the street was alive with other people. So I lay there, almost enjoying the smell of the rancid food sacks and putrefying waste in my relief. Then, only as a continuous stream of cars began to pass did I pull myself up and scan the vicinity anxiously. All clear. Even so, it was a very nervous walk back to my hotel. I thought I would be too scared to sleep but I went straight off.

I couldn't wait for my last night to come. As I prepared to go on the manager asked me what was wrong. I told him about the car and he promised to send me home in a cab later – whether I wanted to leave or not. Then he asked, 'Did you recognise them?'

'No, it was just a man and a woman. I've never seen them before.'

'Ah,' he said slowly. 'Are you sure it wasn't a certain man and woman from Dunkerque? Maybe they don't want you to leave?'

I was horrified at the idea and told him to apologise. But the more angry I became the more insidious his idea was.

'Think about it, Tessa. Are you really sure?'

Yes, I was sure. Perfectly sure. Or so I thought. But by the end of the night I realised I wasn't sure of anything anymore and I couldn't wait to get out.

*****

It was a pleasure to return to Knokke Casino and comforting to see Angie again, but mainly I remembered how beautifully the club lit its girls and I wanted to be part of an establishment that made an effort to get all the small things right. As I settled into a sweet single room at a nearby B&B I remembered the last words from Thierry. He had promised to visit soon but as the days and weeks had passed it hadn't happened. I'd written to him almost every day and received a postcard or two back. But that was all right, I decided. He was a very busy man.

The audiences at the Casino were very good as well. My crab earned applause every night while my handstands on the small podium just caused a loud intake of breath around the room. But it was the splits that always drew the most rapturous response. Audiences have no idea how easy they are for a trained ballerina. It was as easy for me to drop to the ground in side splits as for anyone else to sit down in a comfy chair. And yet every single performance that simple move brought the house down.

The Casino manager, forever "Burl Ives" in my memory, was as friendly as I remembered as well. When he caught me crying in the dressing room one night he couldn't have been more supportive. I can't remember what was wrong. A combination of loneliness being away from Mum, missing Thierry and recurring memories of that night being stalked by the car, I suppose. Without knowing what that couple had planned I had begun to invent ever more terrifying scenarios. I know it was stupid, but as a lone woman in a strange town it was unavoidable.

Burl couldn't have been more sympathetic. He took me out for coffee and told me why I had to be strong.

'I see a lot of girls come into this business and they get chewed up by it, quicker than you'd imagine. The ones that don't, they survive by changing. They get hard, they get cynical and they start taking. They lose respect for themselves, they sleep with men for money. They forget why they wanted to dance in the first place.'

I nodded. He was painting a terrible future for me.

'But you, you're different,' he smiled. 'I saw you six months ago and thought, *Well, she won't last.* But look at you. Bringing people to their feet with appreciation every night and doing it with a smile. Don't change, Tessa, whatever you do. Don't change.'

It was the perfect pick-me-up. Of course, I wondered if he had an ulterior motive but he didn't. He was just being kind: what a gentleman.

As if on cue I got another lift that day. Jo rang to say he'd fixed up a contract in Marseilles. I was elated. More work in the south, more sunshine – and more time with my beloved Thierry. I couldn't wait. And the best news was a week's gap between contracts so I could actually enjoy some time with my boyfriend before immersing myself in work. Perfect.

Counting down the days at the Casino kept me happy. Everyone knew what I was looking forward to and they were happy for me. Everyone, that is, apart from Patricia.

I'd seen her sort before in the clubs. She was a barmaid who, for whatever reason, viewed dancers with distaste. I think to her eyes we were all prostitutes. Perhaps her boyfriend had left her for a showgirl, I don't know. All I'm sure of is she hated me for no reason that I could think of. Smiles wouldn't be returned, she would be slow to serve me and any comments she did make were bitchy.

I tried to engage her in a discussion once but being charming didn't work either. Foolishly I ended up assuring her that I was different from the other girls she'd seen. I was a dancer, that's all. I didn't denigrate women. I didn't sell my body for sex.

I thought I was getting somewhere at last because she smiled. But then she said, 'You can't fool me.'

And I knew I was back where I'd started.

A few nights later I saw her talking to a regular customer, a blond banker called Pierre. He often came in and seemed to be an old friend of Patricia. I decided to make another effort to charm her. She can't be that rude in front of a friend, can she?

I figured correctly. Patricia was all smiles and jokes for the next half an hour. In fact she went so far as to tell me that Pierre would happily drop me off at my B&B on his way home.

I demurred. 'It's all right, I'm sharing a cab with Julia.'

Then I remembered that Julia, who roomed at the same B&B, had already told me she was seeing friends after work. She wouldn't be travelling with me.

'Don't worry,' Pierre said. 'It's really no trouble. Any friend of Patricia's is a friend of mine.'

The journey wasn't unpleasant but Pierre was a banker and, away from Patricia's teasing, it showed. When he stopped the car outside an apartment block, however, I was surprised.

'I just need to get something for Patricia,' he explained. 'Maybe you could pass it to her in the morning?'

'Fine.'

'I'll only be a minute but do you want to come up, we can have a quick coffee?'

Naturally inquisitive I decided to poke my nose around Pierre's flat. You can tell so much about a person from the way they live. I wondered what he was really like.

I soon found out.

Pierre unlocked the door and stepped in. From the hallway I could see a bed in the middle of the main room — we would call it a studio flat - lots of dawn light streaming through tall windows. I entered and Pierre slammed the door. As I jumped at the bang he shoved me hard in the back. I fell clumsily onto the bed and a second later he landed on top of me.

It hurt as he clamped a hand tightly around my mouth and groped to pull my dress up. But nothing hurt like the searing pain of being raped up my backside: such an appalling act that revolted and terrified me to the core.

I struggled, of course I did. But he was strong. The weight of his body crushed all the strength out of me and it was impossible to move. The hand smothering my mouth was so big it pushed against my nose as well. For a second I couldn't breathe at all and I groaned in absolute fear. He adjusted his weight and pushed harder but at least my nostrils were clear. For now.

I'll never forget those dead eyes as he turned me over. They stared ahead, lost in concentration while his hands did the work unguided. And then he found what he was looking for. I shut my eyes and winced. I was being invaded as a woman this time.

The only thing that stopped me being sick was knowing that my mouth was still trapped. Whatever I coughed up would stay with me. I could choke on my own vomit. Would he even stop then?

It didn't hurt my vagina. Dancing always left me with a certain level of moistness. But I felt my rear had been torn in half. Every short stroke he made was also like a blade inside my heart. I'd not given him a single word of encouragement. I'd barely spoken while Patricia was there and I was sober. He couldn't have got the wrong impression - not from me.

The rape was brutal. Suddenly he closed his eyes and shuddered. The grip on my face tightened. But then he shifted his weight back onto his knees and off me. He was finished.

In a strange way, that's when I became more scared. *What happens now?*

Surely he was worried I'd call the police. So why would he let me leave? I began to panic and pulled down my dress nervously. Cautiously I sat up and reached for my bag. All the while he watched me with a mix of contempt and smugness. As I slowly stood up he moved.

I froze.

But he didn't touch me. He bent down and started sorting some papers next to the bed. He didn't turn round as I walked to the door and gave no sign of hearing it open.

I couldn't understand it. *What is he playing at?*

I closed the door carefully then flew down the stairs. I don't know how I didn't fall over. I was taking two at a time in sheer panic. But he didn't come after me. It was as though he didn't think I was a threat to him in any way. Even after what he'd done.

When I got home I ran a hot bath but didn't get in, not at first. I sat on the floor with my back against the door, knees pulled up to my chest, and cried. I realised I had no underwear on, but there was a lot more than that missing. Pierre had taken something from me that he had no right to. I felt empty, alone, violated and afraid.

I knew I had to tell someone. I had to go to the police or tell Burl Ives or call my mother. I needed to confide in someone for my own sake, for other women's sakes. That's what I needed to do. That's what I would do.

But every time I thought of it I shrank even more. Just remembering those eyes, that suffocating hand, that sensation of him snapping away my thong elastic, brought a wave of nausea.

I can't go through with it. Not yet.

He needed to be punished but doing it would punish me more.

Eight hours later I was due back at work. I've read many times over the years that victims of rape feel somehow "dirty" or responsible. They're convinced that others are looking at them with disgust. In 1979 I thought it was just me who felt like that. I caught a taxi to the Casino and couldn't bear to look at the driver's eyes in the rear view mirror. *He's looking at me,* I thought. *He knows.*

I paused when I reached the imposing marble entrance. I contemplated going straight back to bed but couldn't. Dancing, I realised, was the only constant in my life. It's what I had when everything else had gone. It gave me life and it gave my life structure. So I went inside.

My stomach turned when I approached the bar. A man in a camel jacket and soft shoes was there, talking to Patricia.

Oh God, it's him. I've got to get out!

About to run, I spied the man's face in a mirror behind the bar. It wasn't Pierre. Still hyperventilating I made my way backstage.

Just as I'd hoped, the night passed normally. As usual I became lost in my movements, inspired by the cheers and applause of the audience into trying new and more theatrical techniques. By the end of the night, with adrenaline replacing some of my horror, I went out to the bar area to wait for Julia as usual.

I hadn't been there a minute when I was aware of someone standing behind me. I spun round and saw Patricia, arms folded provocatively.

'Got home all right then?' she spat accusingly.

'What do you mean?'

'You know Pierre's married with a baby on the way, don't you? You should be ashamed of yourself.'

I was completely mortified. My eyes glazed but I kept a fixed smile as she scrutinised my face. I felt the whole room had stopped moving. I didn't flinch.

'He dropped me off safely, thank you,' I managed but it sounded false even to my ears. She thought I'd seduced Pierre, probably for money. She'd thought that would happen even when she'd recommended he take me. It's as if she wanted to hate me. I don't know why but she clearly had issues of her own. That was her problem: but now she had made it mine.

I made a decision that night. I wouldn't go straight to Marseilles before the next contract. There was someone I needed to see more than Thierry – and that was Mum. I booked a flight and started to pack. The next morning there was a message at reception. Burl Ives wanted me to call in at the Casino on my way to the airport. What on earth did he want? Had Patricia told him something?

I nearly didn't go but fondness for the old man and the impressive way he ran his excellent club persuaded me. I'm glad I did. Burl just wanted to say goodbye properly.

'You're an exquisite dancer, Tessa. It's been an honour to have you in Knokke.'

I blushed. But he wasn't finished. He reached into his pocket and handed me an envelope containing £300 in Belgian francs.

I was open-mouthed. 'What's this for? You've paid me in full.'

'Good people need to be encouraged,' he said warmly. 'It's not easy in this world, it's certainly not easy in this lifestyle. So we do what we can for each other, okay. One day you'll do the same.'

I burst into tears. After the torrents of fear and pain recently this generosity was more than I could cope with. I hugged him and promised to pay him back.

'I don't want your money,' he sighed. 'Just promise me this. Don't change: never, ever change.'

CHAPTER SEVEN

JE TE CASSE LA GUEULE

The older I get, the more I hear people in the entertainment and sports industries say, 'Never go back.' As I approached my nineteenth birthday I'd probably never even heard the phrase, let alone considered the meaning of such advice. But flying into London, catching the tube and heading for Kensington, my heart didn't lift the way I expected. Why not? I needed to be with Mum. I was looking forward to that more than I could say. But what else was there for me here?

Number 10 was heaving with strangers, as usual, when I arrived but the first person I saw was John Schlesinger.

'The wanderer returns! I know someone who'll want to see you. Doreen. Doreen!'

I'd forgotten what a ball of energy he was. By the time I'd got my breath back he'd already been to the kitchen and the dining room looking for Mum.

'She's in here somewhere,' he laughed. 'Must be upstairs. Go find her. She'll be thrilled.'

As I climbed the stairs I saw a familiar face carrying a basket of laundry out of one of the guest rooms.

'Hello, Mummy.'

'Tessa!'

There were towels and linen all over the carpet as she ran down to meet me. I don't know who cried more, but I know I didn't want to end our hug. In fact I didn't want to leave Mum's side, even though I could see she was rushed off her feet. A few minutes later I was scooping up laundry behind her, stripping beds and shelling peas, perched on the kitchen table, while she busied herself at full speed with preparations for a large banquet that night.

'Business as usual then, Mum?'

'Nothing's changed, darling. If anything I'm getting slower.'

It was lovely to see her, and all my friends from the house who kept popping their heads round the kitchen door when they heard I was back. But we didn't really get a chance to talk that day and by evening Mum really was in demand. By the time she came to bed I was sound asleep.

The next day Mum was just as busy so I went shopping for new stage clothes. New jambière sets were top of my list so I headed to Colin Wilde, a well-known costumier behind Carnaby Street. He was a larger than life character, well-built to match, sprouting a mass of ginger hair and whiskers, dressed in velvet flares and multi-coloured waistcoats. His shop was an ad hoc meeting place for all sorts of artistes. During my fitting I met the UK disco dancing champion who had come in to collect his order. We spoke for ages about the impact of *Saturday Night Fever* on the club scene.

'It's incredible,' he said. 'You can't move for white suits and Lycra.'

I loved the fact that people were out there, normal people, just dancing and showing off in clubs all over the country, thanks to that film. If other men and women could get a fraction of the pleasure that dancing had given me, then I was delighted.

I spent my birthday sorting through books and trinkets in my room at Number 10. I wanted to streamline my luggage but on the other hand, having the right amount of personal mementoes in my hotel rooms really made a difference. Mum popped her head round the door a few times to check on me but she was rushed off her feet as usual. I didn't mind. I didn't feel like partying. I would just have loved to have a good chat with her.

I toyed absentmindedly with an old photo of us with Grampy and Gran. *What would we have chatted about?* I wondered. *Would I have told Mum about Pierre?*

I knew the answer was 'no'. If I was going to stay around where she could keep an eye on me, then maybe it would have been different. But I couldn't spring that sort of news on her then fly off again. As desperate as I was to talk to someone, I couldn't do that to her.

The next day I was in tears saying goodbye but as soon as I stepped out onto Victoria Road my mood improved. London hadn't felt like home, not this time. I was heading back to Toulon. I was heading back to my new life – and to Thierry.

Jo had arranged to meet me at Marseilles before driving me south. After an hour of waiting with no sign of my agent, however, I began to worry. Had I got the wrong day? Or even the wrong airport? Call booths worked differently all over the world, and in France I needed the operator to place a long distance call to Jo's number – on reverse charges. I heard it ring and ring. This was in the days before answering machines were common and the mobile phone hadn't even been dreamed of. Again and again over the next four hours I went through the same tortuous procedure with the same results. On the brink of panic I managed to hold myself together and hailed a cab. Thanks to Burl Ives' gift I could afford the forty-mile ride. An hour later I checked into Toulon's station hotel, a good few francs lighter, but filled with excitement.

I'm home!

I spent what was left of the afternoon arranging my room and getting myself ready for the evening. At half past eight, heart in my mouth, I opened my door. There was Thierry. The night passed in a blur of all consuming emotion.

Three days later Jo arrived, full of apologies – and not just for the hiccough at the airport.

'I'm really sorry, Tessa, but the Marseilles contract has been cancelled.'

'Why?' I felt so deflated.

'I don't know. A change of manager I think. But don't worry, I have a few offers on the table from Switzerland. I'll have you working again in no time.'

From having the time of my life working in Marseilles and being with Thierry I now had the worst of both worlds – waiting to start work in another country while not working in this one.

The Switzerland contracts were arranged but didn't start for a month. I didn't want to go back to London but I couldn't afford to stay in Toulon for that long without an income. Yet I was desperate to stay with my lover – and thank God he was desperate for me to stay as well.

'I will find a way, Tessa. Trust me, my love.'

He managed to put us both up in a friend's empty apartment at the top of an old block with stone tiled floors. For the first few weeks it was bliss, sharing our own place and enjoying its iron balcony with views across the rooftops, but we had to survive on a tight budget and Thierry was strained, assisting in the operating theatre. And after the initial euphoria of our reunion I began to feel incredibly frustrated. Not dancing and being unemployed knocked me off centre completely. Love was strong and certain with Thierry but without work I felt insecure and that affected our relationship as surely as his own professional pressures.

I never thought I would tire of Toulon and all its marvellous memories but it happened. If only I'd been able to work, I'm sure it would have maintained its place in my heart. But, like London had before, it grew unfamiliar to me. My connection was breaking with every passing day.

When the day came to leave for Geneva I wasn't as sad to leave Thierry as he appeared to be at my departure. I suspect he sensed it, too. But it wasn't him. It was that place and my role in it.

'I'll visit soon,' he promised and we parted once again.

The overnight train took nine hours. It seemed like just as I'd managed to fall asleep there was the sound of a crude whistle and dogs barking. We were at the Swiss border and there was to be a luggage search. I had nothing to hide but it was a delay I could have done without.

A stern-faced guard appeared in my carriage and asked to open my case. Without a second thought I flipped the catches. I could have kicked myself for not warning him what he was about to find. The guard held up a pair of jambières and pulled a face.

'And what, madame, are these?'

I couldn't help laughing but he wasn't amused at all. I explained that it was all part of my cabaret dancer's costume and he grunted. A moment later he came across a pouch full of spangly g-strings. I don't think he really needed to pick up every single one and by the end he was positively cross-eyed and breathing heavily. But, with a nod, I was let through.

Jo met me in Geneva at the apartment block, Le Residence. After the blip in Marseilles he'd redeemed himself here. It was exceptionally modern and clean and impressive in every way. My rooms were on the sixth floor, level with Swiss flags hanging over the boulevard below. I say rooms because as well as a bed, I had a fully-equipped kitchenette, a bathroom and even a desk and easy chair. My first own little apartment! I was thrilled.

Jo drove me around Lake Geneva with its famous fountain and exclusive hotels set in landscaped gardens, then onto a shopping area with a flower market, where he bought me roses tied with ribbon.

'To apologise for before,' he explained.

What a gentleman – a completely different person from the fellow who'd slipped uninvited into my bed on my first night.

We had breakfast in an expensive café and I spent my reimbursed fare on a little black cocktail dress with diamanté straps – and a Swiss price tag! After the disappointment of Toulon I was excited.

Then Jo explained the detail of my contract.

'It's the Moulin Rouge – the best cabaret in Switzerland,' he enthused nervously. 'This is the big time, Tessa – for both of us.'

Jo had never secured a booking there before. They normally dealt only with the bigger agents.

'This is a whole different ball game but I'm confident you won't let me down.'

It was a huge compliment – and responsibility. Jo said I was his first dancer good enough to be put forward for this famous venue. His reputation in the business could be made or broken by my performance. I was only booked to be a podium dancer – not one of the "attractions" on the main stage – but even so, I would be judged and so would Jo.

Surprisingly I was exhilarated by the pressure, not cowed by it. This was the big time: a new country, an entirely different scene with completely new rules, standards and expectations. I was desperate to put the horrors of Belgium in the past. *You can't let it ruin the rest of your life*. But it was hard.

In the afternoon we went to the cabaret. There was a grand entrance under an enormous windmill, with red carpets, gilt mirrors and chandeliers, leading down a staircase which opened into a crescent-shaped club. It was huge. Even with the normal house lights up, I was impressed by the main stage and three platforms circled by tables, where I would be performing. Finally there was a bar which, I was told, was waiter service only, and a proper glass-fronted DJ booth from where all the sound and lights were controlled.

Downstairs was just as professional. There were four large dressing rooms, showers and even a practice barre and mirrors, with a passage up to the backstage area. When we bumped into Willie, the boss, I don't know which of us was more nervous, me or Jo. He was short, grey, placid and polite and assuring. He ran through the house rules: the club opened from nine o'clock in the evening until four in the morning, I'd dance four times a night and in between performances I could change and sit in the club to watch the show.

'You may be invited for a glass of champagne at guests' tables,' he explained. I nodded, drinking in all his words. Somehow, though, I missed the true meaning – as I would discover later.

Overall I was left with a very positive impression. Glamour was the name of the game. 'You have to wear evening dress at all times when you are not performing,' Willie said. Because artistes arrived through the main entrance with the customers, he did not want the image of the club ruined by acts turning up in jeans and no make-up. 'That won't be a problem,' Jo assured him. 'Tessa is never knowingly underdressed.'

Back at Le Residence Jo said goodbye and I finally got the chance to unpack. It was a joy to have fresh linen, towels and a wardrobe with hangers! I arranged things in drawers and bought tea and milk for the kitchenette to make a proper home. But the biggest psychological difference, I realised, was putting the suitcase under the bed. As soon as it disappeared out of sight I felt settled, not like a traveller passing through. As I displayed my photos and arranged Jo's flowers in a jug I thought, 'There's no place like home.' Then, content, I slept.

When I woke up a few hours later the weight of expectation attached to the contract hit me. So far I'd been serenity itself but now the reputation of the venue and the professionalism of the set-up weighed like millstones around my neck. Even Willie's warm words now took the tone of a warning as I remembered them.

To dispel my nerves I leant out of the window to watch the world go by. I needed to smell the city, get its measure. Then I could calm down. Opposite was a basic but cosy restaurant with a sign advertising "today's special – cauliflower cheese". As usual in a new place I wasn't at all hungry. It usually took until day three or four of a contract before I settled into normal eating patterns. Until then, so desperate to please, I lived on adrenaline and air.

I watched as a taxi pulled up outside the apartments. Unusually, the driver hurried round to open the door. Out stepped a petite, olive-skinned girl with a long black plait, dressed entirely in pink. Her bags were just as striking. Cases, clothes covers and beauty boxes were all in the same leopard-print design. I had no idea who this creature was but even from this distance there was an aura about her.

According to Jo's deal, the only things I needed to pay for were my food and cabs to the club, arrangements I was perfectly happy with.

For my first trip to work, however, I decided to walk a little. It was a familiar ritual, to help me anchor, to feel I was part of the city scene. I wanted to emerge from my stroll strong, ready and professional, rather than turn up at the venue intimidated and bewildered by my surroundings. Appearances, as any performer knows, are everything.

I passed a neon café and stepped inside for a drink. It turned out to be a lesbian bar. I had a Brandy Alexander and gulped it down in silence as all eyes watched this figure in a black gown, as if dressed for the opera, carrying plastic bags and an unusually large holdall. *What must they think of me?* But no one asked. They weren't friendly at all.

Slipping back out into the city I thought, *I hope the staff at Moulin Rouge will be warmer.*

I soon found out. As I poured myself out of the cab, smiling at the doorman, he beamed approvingly and helped with my bags. *First battle won.*

Like all clubs, the Moulin Rouge came into its own at night, glowing red, plush and tempting for an expectant crowd even though it still had an hour before opening time. Soft lights lit the blonde receptionist – who gave me a pleasant nod – and display cases of champagnes on offer decorated the corridor. A cut-out image of a red windmill included photos of the DJ and various acts underneath the banner "The outstanding night-club of Geneva". Downstairs the bar was bustling with elegant waiters in black with white bowties, suave but serious, checking the tables. I saw the DJ, Paul, and introduced myself. I was pleased to find him a friendly chap because he also took the role of stage director and worked the amazing stage effects, which he demonstrated. Get on the wrong side of a club's technicians and you would always regret it. They can light you to look terrible – or play the wrong music to interfere with your choreography. The horror stories among other dancers were legion, but it had never happened to me. Yet!

On the other hand, I had never seen anything this spectacular before either. As Paul worked a couple of controls, the dance floors merged into one stage and rose to eye level. At the same time two podiums pushed up high above on either side.

'Wow,' was all I could say. But I was thinking, *I'm going to have to be at my best to fit in here.*

Paul smiled. He was used to impressing with his technology, I could tell. 'The *Star Wars* theme announces the main show at midnight,' he explained. 'You'll be first on with Dominique – she's already downstairs. When the lights dim, step onto the podium and stand still as it rises. You'll dance for about fifteen minutes.'

There were no curtains, I noticed. 'We don't use them,' Paul said smugly. He hit another button and lights transformed the view. The podiums and stage were bathed in darkness. Girls could arrive unseen, props could be introduced invisibly, then suddenly the set would come to life with projections that covered the entire walls with patterns. It really was incredible. I ran through the rest of the arrangements and we discussed the music I'd dance to.

After such a build-up I couldn't wait to get to the dressing room. I'd be sharing with Dominique, the second podium dancer. A whole room for just two of us! It was such a treat to have space, a full mirror and hanging rails, where I could leave my costumes and not worry about lugging bags around every night.

Dominique, like most performers, was incredibly friendly. She was from Martinique and had the smooth dark-honeyed skin of the islanders and an unforgettable figure: tall and slim with bosoms so enormous that to not mention them would have been rude. I'd often longed for larger breasts but Dominique said, in her sweet French, 'Be careful what you wish for. Imagine this weight pulling on your back' as she took my hands to cup her breasts. I sympathised. It was like holding two warm melons. For the second time that night I was speechless. '*Ça me fait mal,*' she sighed theatrically, but a second later was all smiles as she introduced everyone else.

A group from Thailand called themselves a ballet but not in the sense I knew. They performed traditional dances in a rainbow of silk costumes and headdresses, beautiful and exotic. There was also a male juggler, a pale, pointy-nosed Belgian who looked like a pixie. Finally, with her own dressing room, was the main attraction, who hadn't arrived yet.

Greetings over, it was time to get ready. That familiar tightening of the stomach hit me about five minutes before I left the dressing room. For once there was no curtain to hide behind but in every other way it felt identical to my first night on the famous old stage at the Windmill: same energy, same determination, same nerves.

Paul the DJ had done his work as promised. Nobody noticed as I stepped onto the flat dais. Then the music started, the dry ice poured in and I felt the podium rise. Four thousand watts of spotlight hit my smiling face as I rose through the air. Hundreds of faces watched expectantly. And all I could think was, *Don't fall off!*

A second later the podium settled, the lights altered and there was silence. Even the waiters stopped moving. There was tangible excitement in the room, like the countdown to a blast-off. Towering over my audience I knew what was coming, but when the first beats of *Can You Feel The Force* pumped out, the volume alone nearly shot me through the roof. But the audience loved it and suddenly I was on: dancing as I had never danced before.

Fifteen minutes later I was back in the dressing room, stunned by the fantastic experience. It had gone so quickly but I'd given my all. I couldn't wait to get back up there.

My second spot came and went. Still breathless, I changed into my evening dress and went upstairs to enjoy the rest of the show. There is always something to learn from other artistes, especially when it comes to making the most of the lights, sound and effects on offer.

The Thai ballet had the audience breathless with some of their acrobatics on the main stage. Halfway through their act I felt a hand on my shoulder and a voice at my ear.

'You're a fabulous dancer!' It was Paul the DJ. He'd actually left his booth mid-act to compliment me - high praise indeed.

A few minutes later I had another visitor – one of the waiters. He put a glass of champagne in front of me and said, 'With congratulations from Table Five.' Surprised, I nodded a thank you to four smiling men across the aisle. *This is too good to be true!*

I was right. Five minutes later the waiter returned, scowling.

'Why are you still here?'

'I'm sorry?'

'Why are you still here?' he repeated in abrupt French. 'Why haven't you joined them?'

I had no idea what he was talking about.

'Joined who?'

'Table Five!' His face was contorted with rage but to the guests behind he was trying desperately hard to remain light-hearted. 'You're meant to sit with them and get them to buy you a bottle. Now get going.'

Confused and upset I slunk over to the group of men. I shook hands and made polite conversation and learned they were all bankers out for a celebration. Shy and awkward, I don't think I was the best company. Once the compliments dried up we all sat in silence watching the show. I certainly didn't have the nerve to ask for another drink.

A few minutes later I felt a rough hand on my elbow. It was the waiter pulling me to my feet. 'If they don't buy a bottle, leave the table,' he hissed.

I don't remember what I said to that but he left me alone for the rest of the evening. I desperately wanted to run back downstairs to ask Dominique what was going on. But suddenly there was a fanfare, the stage was drenched in purple and from a pinpoint of ice blue, the spotlight gradually expanded, bathing a solitary figure in an ethereal glow.

I couldn't leave now. The headline attraction had entered the building.

Suddenly the music changed, the smoke cleared and I saw the most exquisite doll.

It's the girl in pink from the apartments!

There was no way I was leaving the room now. I sensed I was about to see a masterclass in performance. I wasn't disappointed. The music was a haunting instrumental score and she didn't perform any full dance movements, rather she floated gracefully across the stage, using all the space to acknowledge everyone in the balcony, smiling graciously at all times. Briefly, an opal flash caught the light, sparkling from a large diamanté fixed at the centre of her forehead. Beneath a long, stone-encrusted cloak, she revealed a glittering bikini and perfectly formed figure. Her shining skin and glossy hair swept up in a chignon played perfectly in the light. As she lifted her arms, turned and posed, we could all admire her beauty – and we did. She was breathtaking. Here was a gem of costume, colour and mood. *I can see why she is this month's attraction.*

After the show I ran down to the dressing room to tell Dominique about the rude waiter. When I reached our door, however, she was already talking to someone.

It was the doll!

Both women were wrapped in bath robes and smiled when I appeared in the doorway.

'Tessa, have you met Polly? She's our star attraction.'

I was embarrassingly tongue-tied. I tried to say how much I'd enjoyed her act but the words tumbled over each other. Polly laughed and put me at ease with her kind words about my dancing.

'I didn't know you'd seen me,' I said, surprised.

'Well I did, and you were amazing: a proper dancer. You'll go far.'

Polly was Filipino and looked about my age so I was shocked when she revealed she had a child back home. On closer inspection her body was covered in deep stretch marks as well, which was a shock. She caught my eye but wasn't offended.

'Dahling, I pay the DJ good to give me the best lights,' she purred.

'Well, it worked,' I gushed. 'I've never seen anyone more beautiful on a stage.'

Talking to Polly over the next few weeks I learned so much. There was very little she could teach me about dancing, but tricks of the trade, technical advice and performance tips were her forte. Spotlight colour gels, the most effective music for different scenarios, what enhanced or diminished your appearance – she covered it all, completely unselfishly. 'Big features come across well on stage, whereas a pretty-pretty face can be lost. Lighting makes all the difference and this is what you do...'

I didn't get the chance to speak to Dominique that night about the waiter's behaviour but the next evening I made a point of getting there early enough to get some answers.

'Tessa, you're so sweet, so innocent,' Dominique laughed. 'You honestly don't know how this works?'

I shook my head, utterly bewildered by her amusement.

'How do you think the club can afford this amazing show, all these lights and our wages?'

Eventually convinced that I really was in the dark, Dominique explained all. I was shocked at what I learned.

The reason all acts were required to wear evening dress is because we were expected to mingle with the guests afterwards and encourage them to buy as much champagne – the only drink available – as possible. Apparently it was the same in venues all over Switzerland – although I'd never heard of the practice. It was considered a coup for customers to be able to invite the exotic stars of the night over to their table – and generally the champagne flowed.

'Each glass, half bottle, or magnum, earns you a percentage of the cost,' Dominique explained. 'The waiters are perfectly reliable – you get your cut and they get theirs and the club makes an incredible profit.'

'But don't the men want anything in exchange for their champagne?'

'Ah...'

With the timing of an experienced showgirl, at that moment Dominique's flatmate, Stephanie, entered the room. After introductions she was brought up to speed on my dilemma. It materialised that Stephanie was an expert on the subject. Not being a performer, her job title was actually "hostess" – and all she did each night was encourage customers to drink. And drink. And drink.

Some of the hostesses performed rudimentary routines early in the evening to whip up interest, but most were placed at tables ready for the arrival of the first customers, to be noticed and admired. A waiter would then escort them to a table on request or present them, to encourage a gentleman to have company and start spending. The real pros made eye contact and sallied over to work their charms. 'Willie has a preference for booking French Africans and Asians,' Stephanie explained, 'as you've probably noticed.'

'I thought they were customers,' I admitted to more laughter at my country mouse naïvety.

The business of enticing drinks out of customers was known as "consummation" and the girls, all working on commission, took it very seriously. All eyes would be fixed on the stairs to see who walked down and, with a nod from the maitre d', a surge of prospective companions would greet each visitor.

If a table was getting on well, the large wooden tobacco box would be proffered by the waiter. All the girls smoked – especially at those commission rates. A suggestion from the waiter that a box of chocolates (at an extortionate price) might be a lovely gift for the lady would often follow.

'But I just couldn't drink that much, even for the commission,' I admitted. 'Especially if I was expected to dance as well.'

Stephanie smiled. 'There are ways around it. It's in the waiters' interest to get through as much as possible as well, so they will tip some into the ice bucket when the guest isn't looking or turn the bottle upside down even if it's not empty. I spend most nights accidentally spilling glass after glass under the table, or I'll offer friends a glass – anything to get through the bottle as quickly as possible. You'd be amazed how quickly some of these men can run up a bill of a thousand pounds.'

'You mean francs?'

'No, cherie, it would be a hundred thousand francs!'

'But don't the customers know what's going on?'

Stephanie shrugged. 'Most do, lots don't. Some are wise to what goes on but they like our attention, to be seen as Mr Big, wealthy and powerful – especially if they are trying to impress work clients. Some are sad and pay to talk even if it's their last savings. Young guys know it's a rip off but you'll get a few glasses out of them if they're on a stag night or out with friends.'

As Stephanie spoke I tried to remember the night before. I'd seen plenty of girls fitting the description of hostesses but most of them were incredibly "hands-on" with the customers. That's why I'd stupidly thought they were the wives and partners! But now the truth was staring me in the face. They were prostitutes – or near enough. It was embarrassing trying to raise the subject with Stephanie so I didn't. Dominique, however, filled me in as soon as her flatmate had left.

'Steph goes out with customers when it pleases her,' she said coyly. 'But really she makes her money from plying drink from the audience. Others aren't so choosy. You wonder why the tables are in such darkness! Look at some of the things going on. But the girls aren't allowed to leave with anyone until after closing time. Willie is emphatic about that. We're not a pick-up joint, but if girls want to arrange a private assignation he doesn't mind.'

I suppose in this set-up the girls were spared the intimidation of walking the streets – and men got hours to give their intended "dates" a good interview before any later transaction. But even so, I was still open-mouthed to think that this behaviour was going on right under my nose in such an up-market establishment.

Dominique was still laughing at me. 'It's the same in every cabaret club, and most of them aren't this discreet. Be careful what you agree to when you leave here!'

Once I got over the initial shock of how the club funded its elaborate shows I realised that I didn't actually mind. Plenty of people would disagree with my choice of dancing topless or nude. I'm not one to judge how others live their lives; as long as they're happy and not forced to do anything they don't want to. However, I began to notice suspicious- looking men hovering around the hostesses and I got the feeling that each girl had a pimp looking out for her. From the rumours, most of them were afraid of their bosses. Now I had a different view of their lives.

The part of the scenario that worst affected me, though, was the assumption from the customers and, I was sure, the waiters too, that I was no different from a hostess. Night after night I was subjected to unwanted invitations to join this table or that. If I was lucky I could get away with a flute of bubbly and a few kind words. Other men saw their purchase of a bottle of house champagne as their purchase of me as well. Hands roamed over my flinching body until I had enough and stormed away.

On night four Willie caught me sitting alone waiting for the Doll to appear. 'You're not drinking,' he observed.

Now I'm for it.

I was wrong.

'I was telling Jo that I think you're a great performer,' he said as Polly made her grand entrance. 'You could do that, you know, and better. I think you're main attraction material – you need to get off these podiums as soon as possible.'

Was he serious? Did he really think I could take the main stage like the amazing Filipino? I decided to ask Jo. If he thought he could get me work like that then I'd think about it. But was I even ready? Probably not, I realised. *But that has to be my target.*

Before he left me Willie brought up the subject of consummation. 'You're a beautiful performer, I don't mind,' he said. 'But the maitre d' and the waiters aren't too happy.'

'It's just not something I can easily do.'

'And fair enough,' he said. 'But I don't want you to fall out with anyone so next week a friend of mine will be dropping by. If a man called Roland buys you a drink, be sure to go over. Trust me – he will look after you properly.'

Look after me how? It sounded ominous but Willie was so happy with my work that he extended my stay by a fortnight. It was music to my ears – especially as I heard that Thierry was coming to stay for five days. He had never actually seen me perform before and if he was going to, I wanted it to be here at Moulin Rouge.

No sooner had Thierry arrived, however, than he was making arrangements to leave two days later.

'You told me you were staying the week.'

'I'm sorry, my love. I have to get back to work. But I'm here now. Shall we make the most of it?'

I couldn't help feeling dejected but I threw myself into showing him the Geneva I had grown to love, with its trams, outdoor cafés and fountains. Then at night he saw my show and showered me with compliments. But too soon he was leaving again, in tears, with no plan of when we'd see each other next. To make matters worse, Le Residence was alive with the sound of hostesses faking noisy orgasms for wealthy clients that night. I stuffed cotton wool into my ears, pulled a pillow over my head and howled tears of foul temper.

I really had to talk myself into getting to work the next night. My heart wasn't in it. It seemed as though Thierry had packed it in his case the previous morning. But I'm glad I turned up. After my second spot I received the familiar courtesy drink from an admirer. When I went to join him, cringing with every step, he said, 'You must be Tessa. My name is Roland.'

The manager's friend was a life-saver. He was a director for Honda Motorbikes and liked to watch the shows and have someone to talk to. That was the extent of his demands. After the octopus-like intrusion of the other visitors he was a breath of fresh air. A gentle, unassuming man, chubby with a beard and glasses, he came to the club several nights a week and paid for three bottles, whether we drank them or not, just so I wouldn't have to sit with anyone else – and the waiters would leave us both alone. On the third night, after a magnificent evening, he invited me out for dinner. The next afternoon, I flew on a hundred-mile-an-hour bike ride to Lausanne. The journey left me breathless with fear and delight. Roland treated me to some super restaurants; steak diane, fondue - Swiss cooking was amazing. On my night off he took me to La Reserve for dinner overlooking the lake. We sat outside, lights in the trees reflecting on the water and then to Maxims to enjoy a rival cabaret night for once.

What an eye-opener!

I had been warned that Maxims was probably even more lavish than Moulin Rouge but I hadn't anticipated by how much. The acts were truly the best in their field – dancers, acrobats, singers. Rather cheekily, in fact, I said to Roland, 'Shall we invite the attraction over for a glass of champagne?'

He of course agreed. I thought it would be fun to experience the other side of the arrangement but I regretted it instantly. I complimented the dancer's acrobatics but she didn't even pay me the courtesy of listening. She was haughty and rude and couldn't wait for the champagne to disappear. I think she thought she wouldn't get anywhere with Roland if I stayed there – but plenty of men at Moulin

Rouge bought hostesses to spend the night with their girlfriends. Bashful and bruised by the experience, Roland asked her to leave.

The hostesses were the most distinctive part of the club. Each one looked like a *Vogue* model, all dripping in Cartier watches and furs and their trademark Vitterand luggage. Roland caught me staring. 'Geneva has the best hookers in the world,' he whispered. 'Did you see the cars outside? They all belong to these girls.'

There had been a procession of Mercedes and BMWs in front of the club. If they really did belong to the prostitutes, I couldn't imagine how much they charged for their company.

I began to see that Moulin Rouge was actually a friendly place compared to the Maxims money-making machine. In fact, I was actually quite popular with our hostesses because they realised I wasn't interested in competing for male company – their meal tickets. Occasionally, the artistes, a few hostesses and even the waiters would even go to a late night Arabian café, if we had the energy.

I instinctively sat with Dominique and Stephanie – Polly rarely came out – but gradually I realised that, away from work, and out of sight of the maitre d's all-seeing eye, the waiters were actually quite pleasant. One by one they quickly lost the harshness of their professional persona which was a side-effect of working on commission-only contracts. They earned a fraction of what the hostesses did, and that's why they were so pushy with the champagne.

The hostesses, on the other hand, were mostly closed books. Apart from Stephanie, no one saw any of them during the day and only the visiting girls ever socialised. Those from Geneva had their own lives. Perhaps their loved ones didn't even know how they earned their living. I heard several rumours about girls saying they were nurses on night shift. Imagine if their partners – or parents – ever wandered into the club one night?

All in all, my spell in Geneva had been a pleasurable one. Thierry's visit had been too brief but the city was beautiful and although I found the Swiss generally distant and unemotional, the work had been out of this world. As I counted down the last days of my contract, I hoped Jo would find me work there again soon. So far it only had happy memories.

Then something happened to smash that thought to dust.

Passing a group of waiters at the bar as I arrived one night, a tall, blond chap who was one of our café crowd called me over. As I approached, he stepped a few yards away from the others. Smiling, I said as usual in French, 'Hello.'

'Don't hello me, *bitch*.'

'*Pardon?*'

He flew into a torrent of angry abuse. I couldn't follow all of it but like most newcomers to a language, swear words were an early addition to my vocabulary – and he was using all of them.

Crushed, I fled crying to my dressing room.

I was two days away from the end of my contract. I didn't need this. As I looked at my face, puffy and red in the mirror, I knew I was going to struggle to go on that night.

Suddenly there was a knock at the door. It was Stephanie. Embarrassed, I tried to hide my face but she came over and hugged me. Over her shoulder I was horrified to see the waiter standing behind her in the doorway.

'Get him out!' I blurted, and he started to leave, but Stephanie was quick to calm the situation.

A few minutes later I was sitting again, in control of my emotions, listening as Stephanie translated the waiter's words. His name was Michel and he had been told tonight that the maitre d' had information that could get him sacked. For some unexplained reason, my name had been mentioned, that's why he'd attacked me – but then he'd quickly realised his error.

Utterly bewildered, I was so relieved not to have a fight on my hands that I accepted Michel's explanation without question. In fact, when he invited me to the café for dinner that night as an apology I heard myself accepting.

At four in the morning he picked me up at the entrance as though I were one of the wealthy guests finding their limos. He was very slim and in the neon light I noticed his pale skin was absolutely flawless, almost translucent, with a head of golden curls. Combined with his delicate nose, perfectly formed pink lips and grey eyes, he looked like an angel.

'If you don't mind, Tessa,' he said softly in surprisingly good English, 'I'm going to cook you spaghetti at my home, if you will let me. Please, it is not far.'

I felt a little pang of disappointment not to be going to the café but Michel was trying to make up for earlier so I didn't want to hurt his feelings. When I said "yes", his full, comforting smile completely changed his rather serious face. When I picture him now he has the look of Sebastian from the television series *Brideshead Revisited*. Handsome, clean-cut and blond, he was not at all my type (I've always preferred solid, rugged, dark-haired men). But I could see his charm.

By the time we reached Michel's flat I'd completely forgotten the misunderstanding at work. He went out of his way to be polite, carrying my bag up the stairs, hanging my jacket for me and then making sure I was comfortable on the sofa before preparing to cook in the open plan kitchen. While I took in the neat, uncluttered surroundings, Michel put on some music. A second later he gathered me in his arms and twirled me around the lounge with a release of laughter. He'd come to life and I was actually enjoying his company.

A shrill whistle from the kitchen halted our fun.

'Ah, the kettle,' he said. 'You English like your tea, no?'

I followed him to the kitchen area and offered to help. 'Just relax,' he said, shooing me back to the sofa before returning to chop onions, chatting all the time. I marvelled as the large, gleaming knife diced its way expertly along the wooden board. Then he paused, as if remembering something. He came striding over to me and pulled me to my feet.

'Let's dance!'

He was smiling but the playfulness had gone. He held me painfully tight, with a new strength, and pressed his cheek hard to mine. When he tried to kiss me I turned my head away.

'Michel, I'd rather not. My boyfriend wouldn't approve.'

He dropped me instantly. 'Ah, your Thierry.' Without looking back he returned to his chopping. Relieved, but shaken, I went to sit down again but in a flash Michel was walking back towards me. Wordlessly he lifted me off the floor and hurled me forwards. I landed on his bed, face down.

'Michel! What are you doing?'

As I eased myself up, he slapped me hard across the face and I fell in a daze. Instinctively I put my hand to my cheek but I didn't feel any pain.

I just felt sheer terror.

The angel from the car had disappeared. Standing over me was a demon: and he was holding the large chopping knife.

'You bitch,' he snarled coldly. 'You come to my home, dance with me and expect me to let you go? Lie down!'

'Michel, *please.*' I could not take my eyes off the shining silver blade. The time for words had gone.

Oh God, I'm going to die.

Michel stared at me and spoke calmly in French. 'You will do as I say. Or I'll break your face – Je te casse la gueule. You're going to please me if it kills you.'

With one hand he tore off my shoes and threw them against the wall. He pulled my dress down tight then ran the knife top to bottom, like he was gutting fish. The material ripped in half, exposing my bare flesh. I stared immobile with fear as the point of the knife hovered above my belly. Then his gaze lowered to my g-string and with one flash of the blade it sliced through the thin elastic.

He's going to stab me. This is it. This is it.

I was crying but no tears or sound came out. I was frozen. It was like watching someone else's body being violated.

But it was mine.

I screwed my eyes tight, waiting for the end, for the knife on my skin.

'Look at me, bitch,' he hissed.

Still with one hand clamped around the knife's thick shaft he pulled down his own clothes. Suddenly he was closer, climbing on top of me, his right hand clutching the knife an inch from my head as he pressed me down. He thrust himself in and I didn't dare struggle. I didn't dare speak. All I could think of as Michel got more energetic was the knife twisting in his hand, moving with his urgent rhythm, brushing against my hair, then my ear.

I lay rigid, trying to detach myself from my body but I could feel him all the way inside me. It was too much. Everything was too much. The smell of onions from the knife was overpowering. His grunts in my ear - sickening. I wanted to scream but the glint of the knife hypnotised my tongue.

Then it was over. He stopped. His breathing changed. He was catching his breath and staring at me. It was like he was seeing me for the first time. I knew in the next few seconds he would decide whether I would live or die.

Time seemed to stop as he held his weight over me. He was thinking - but what? I saw focus come into Michel's grey, feral eyes. He had decided.

He pulled himself up, adjusted his trousers and walked back to the kitchen. In disbelief I heard him return to chopping vegetables. In silence, I eased myself up watching his back. He still had the knife.

I have to get out.

I didn't have shoes or panties and my dress flapped open like a silk cardigan. But I was alive – for now. I tip-toed to the door, grabbed my jacket and ran out, barefoot. With each stair I waited for the sensation of the knife in my back. But it didn't come. He wasn't pursuing me. I was free to go.

The cool air soothed my burning thighs and clammy skin. A yellow beacon of rescue slid into view as a taxi stopped almost immediately and twenty minutes later I was showering in my little bathroom. I scrubbed and scrubbed but no matter how hard I tried, how raw my skin became, I could not get rid of the smell of onions. And those words, *'Je te casse la gueule'*, wouldn't go away.

But I was alive. Thank God I was alive.

CHAPTER EIGHT

YOU ARE MY LIFE

Jo looked very pleased with himself as he drove us across the French border to St Julien en Genevois. It had been a successful contract in Geneva. The next one, he was sure, would be "even better".

'We're on our way, Tessa.'

I couldn't smile. I could barely speak. It was as much as I could do to stare out of the car window at the speeding trees and buildings without crying.

How had it all ended so badly?

Willie had been a great employer in so many ways but everything you hear about Swiss accounting was proved when he came to settle my earnings. I earned £25 a night but £12 was deducted for medical insurance, £25 for my work visa, £100 club commission, £125 towards the apartment – and £50 for police. I have no idea what this fee entailed. I certainly didn't see anyone in uniform. When all the T's were crossed I ended up with just £400 and a box of kitchen utensils from my flat.

And then there was Michel. He was the real reason for my malaise. I contemplated telling Jo about him but chickened out. What could he have done? But I should have told someone, I know that now. I needed a friendly ear – and others needed to be warned against him. Yet again, though, I bottled it all up, just as I had in Knokke with Pierre. In my overwrought imagination I could just picture my mother's stern admonishments. "Best foot forward, stiff upper lip, life goes on." I needed to put it all behind me.

'Soonest forgotten, quickest mended,' I repeated to myself over and over.

Time would heal me, I decided. I didn't need help from anyone, or anything, else. Well, perhaps one thing. Dancing. As usual, what else did I have to look forward to? It's not like I'd been showered with attention from Thierry.

The Macumba was a modern, white building shaped like a UFO with a massive car park. The interior was even more spectacular. It had the biggest disco I'd ever seen, with a foyer and boutique selling souvenirs featuring the Macumba logo – a silhouette of a dancing girl.

There was a bar-and-grill and crêperie counter like an American diner and a central DJ platform built as a burger in a bun. I could see how the Macumba chain had managed to expand to California. Everything was constructed in space-age design. Spongy sofas surrounded the two dance podiums and at the front were a huge stage and cinema screen. Backstage was just as impressive. The dressing rooms were the best I would ever use, with floor to ceiling mauve carpet, TV, shower, mini bar, sofas and dresser with spotlights. There was even a connecting "celebrity area" with a kitchen and office facilities. The night I arrived Fats Domino and his band were already in their rooms ready for a night's performance. The following week we were due to host Gloria Gaynor. It really was an incredibly popular venue.

I couldn't wait to get started. The club opened at nine and I danced five times on half-hour shifts opposite a French girl who performed mime sequences, silhouetted behind the cinema screen, like the logo. It was very effective. All around us a spectacular laser show dazzled the audience as streams of ultraviolet lines shot through me from the DJ's booth. It looked like a UFO landing but, goodness, those lights were hot. By the end of the evening I was exhausted but exhilarated, and absolutely drenched in sweat. I'd been through two towels before I even stepped inside the shower. What a night.

I always explore a new town at the first opportunity, but I slept through at my little apartment from four in the morning almost until it was time to go to work the next day. When I arrived back at the club I was quickly thrown into the relentless schedule – and I loved it. The French singer Michelle Tor was performing that night and so the disco was even more packed than usual. I nearly missed my cue for my second dance because it took me ten minutes to push through the crowds to my podium! But it was worth it. Dancing above a sea of three thousand faces is utterly breathtaking. And hearing shouts of 'Minion!', 'Formidable!', 'Belle!' and 'Bravo!' just made it better – if that was possible.

Sitting at the bar after the end of my shift I struck up conversation with one of the barmaids who couldn't have been more complimentary. 'Everyone else who dances on the podium moves in a certain way – but you move like a proper ballet dancer.'

I told her about my training.

'I knew it! No one else has ever managed to do the splits up there.'

The girl's name was Ava and she was from Martinique. She lived alone with her young daughter and had a Swiss boyfriend. The night ended with her inviting me to spend the next day with her. It's always nicer enjoying time with real people, rather than showgirls who are passing through, so I said "yes". We had a lovely lunch then Ava said she had some errands to run.

'You're welcome to come if you won't be bored.'

Bored? I am always happy seeing the world by car. While Ava chatted about her life, her amazing daughter and "wonderful" partner, I let my face bask in the sun as I enjoyed the scenery.

After barely a week at Macumba my luck got even better. When I got home to my flat on the Friday there was a note for me. "I'm in the bar." Tentatively I peeped into the small lounge and got the shock of my life. Sitting there with a coffee and a newspaper was Thierry.

'What are you doing here?'

'Aren't you happy to see me?'

'Of course I am. But you said you couldn't come!'

'It seems I was mistaken.'

What a fabulous few days. Thierry's new plan was to teach me to cook. 'And now you have a kitchen there is no excuse not to.'

I laughed. 'Why do I need to cook?'

'You'll never be a good wife if you can't cook,' he replied, although, as usual with Thierry, I wasn't entirely sure what he was saying. But with his help I made crêpes, apple tart and even mayonnaise! We had a divine few days, talking, walking and rearranging the flat – to his specification, of course. I wasn't able to get time off work at such short notice so Thierry accompanied me to the club. I think he was impressed by what he saw – my act included. On our last night together he disappeared for an hour in between my shows. When we returned to the apartment it was covered with roses.

'It seems you have an admirer,' he said, cool as ice until I threw him laughing onto the petal-strewn bed.

It was an amazing end to a magical weekend. I couldn't wait for him to visit again the following Friday. I felt as if I had a home life outside the bubble of club land, where the lows could almost annihilate me and yet I could bounce back with some love, laughter and kindness.

Catching up with Ava the next day it seemed I hadn't been the only one to have had my boyfriend staying. Hers had come over from Switzerland for the weekend as well.

'You'll meet him next time,' she promised. 'I'm having a party, do bring Thierry as well if you can.'

I spent the rest of the week in a blissful loop. Work, sleep and dreaming about Thierry were punctuated by regular trips with Ava in her car. I didn't mind where we went or what for. It was just so perfect being shown the sights by someone who had lived there for more than the duration of a contract.

One day, though, the bliss was shattered. As we headed down a straight, clear road, talking and laughing as usual, I screamed. Ava had already spotted the tractor pulling out slowly in front of us – but by the time she hit the brakes we were skidding dangerously out of control.

We hit the tractor head-on at thirty miles an hour but the next few seconds seemed to take place in slow motion.

I still remember the sensation of somehow seeing my body from above lift out of my seat – no one used a seatbelt in those days – and fly towards the windscreen. It really was as though it wasn't happening to me. When I put up my arms instinctively to shield my face, they weren't my arms. When my head snapped violently against the glass, the pain wasn't mine. And when I crumpled back into my seat like a doll thrown into its box, I closed my eyes and passed out, completely calm, completely at peace, completely accepting of my fate.

Completely ready to die.

The next thing I remember is waking up. I was back in my body and staring at Ava. She was giving me mouth-to-mouth. I'd been unconscious and she had saved me.

The tractor driver was unhurt, as was his vehicle. But Ava's car was a wreck. The bonnet looked like a concertina and there were bits of bumper and plastic lights all over the road.

Miraculously, I managed to dance that night but I spent the entire next day covered in ice packs as the bruises seemed to take twenty-four hours to appear. Other than that, though, I was fine.

Physically, at least.

Mentally, however, it was a different story. I couldn't stop thinking about my mortality. *I'm so lucky to be alive.* I had come close to death and somehow survived. Why was that? How had I escaped serious injury when so many don't make it?

Another day of obsessing about my brush with fate went by and then I made a startling discovery. I wasn't thinking about how fortunate I'd been to escape the car crash.

I was thinking about the rape: about Michel... *and about that knife at my throat.*

When Thierry arrived that afternoon I fell into his arms. Sobbing, I told him about the accident.

'Are you all right? Let me see your head.' I felt his fingers run softly over my scalp. 'Oh, you poor thing! You have a bump the size of an egg. You need to see a doctor.'

'You're the only doctor I need to see.'

But a funny thing happened after that. The more Thierry comforted me, the more upset I became. Eventually he asked the question I'd been dreading.

'Tessa, there is something you are not telling me. Your tears are no longer about the car crash.' He pulled me to him and kissed my forehead. 'Come on, tell me what's wrong.'

So I told him about the rape. I told him about Michel, how he'd threatened me, flattened me and violated me, all the while clutching that gleaming, deadly knife. Thierry listened in silence but his arms held me tighter. I don't know if he was hugging me or trying not to lose control. At the end of my story I felt like a weight had been lifted off my shoulders: like a condemned man released. The anguish had come from the deepest place, but what had been buried was now on show.

How would Thierry react?

He was horrified. When he spoke finally the questions came in a torrent. Why hadn't I told him? Who was this man? Why hadn't I told him? Did I have an address for this attacker? Have you seen a doctor? *Why hadn't I told him?*

'I don't know. I couldn't find the words. I thought you might blame me somehow.'

'Blame you? Oh no, no. I could never blame you. You must always believe that.'

An hour later he took me to see a doctor, not only now for the bump on my head but any possible internal injuries and a blood test.

He said all the right things to calm and reassure me but when I caught a glimpse of his reflection in windows I could see he was angry.

Later that night I was relieved to discover Thierry wasn't put off me physically. He comforted me the best he could but as we lay there together, moments from sleep, he promised, 'If I ever meet this man, I will kill him.'

With Thierry's support, I felt I could cope with anything. More than ever, when he left I felt abandoned and alone. It was for only another week but it seemed like forever. Each show seemed harder to do without him in the audience and my flat seemed unwelcoming. But five days later he was back and in good form.

'I am determined that we shall enjoy ourselves this weekend,' he declared.

That Saturday we went to Ava's for dinner. Preparing for it had made me strangely emotional – showing off Thierry to Ava's friends for the first time and also knowing that my contract was at an end were both having an effect. Everything about my stay in St Julien had been perfect. Even the accident had brought about the unplanned confession to Thierry. And, yes, I really did feel better having told someone.

We stopped off to buy flowers and wine on the way to Ava's house. When we arrived she was in her front room introducing guests to one another. As the group dispersed to fill their glasses she saw us.

'Tessa! So pleased you could come. And this must be Thierry! We never got a chance to talk at the club.'

'A tragedy we must rectify,' Thierry purred. There was no situation where his old-fashioned charm didn't work.

'Well, I've met yours, Tess, now you must meet mine.' Ava scanned the room then called over to a group in the corner.

'Darling! Darling! There are some people I'd like you to meet.'

A blond, curly-haired man with his back to us turned slowly round. As he did I felt my world come crashing down.

Ava's boyfriend was Michel the waiter from Moulin Rouge.

My rapist.

Thank God for Thierry. I've never seen someone so able to ingratiate themselves with strangers as him. Shaking hands, kissing cheeks, laughing and joking, all done with his natural charisma. All done without any input from me whatsoever, which is just as well because I could only stare at my feet.

I don't know if Michel was looking at me or not. I couldn't bring myself to check. It took all my strength to mumble, 'May I use your toilet please?'

Without waiting for directions I walked away, arm extended for balance, feeling my way along the wall.

What was going on? How had this happened? Was it really him? The coincidence was incredible. But it was no mistake. Rage, guilt, nausea and disbelief fell upon me, pressing down with an unbearable weight. I was vaguely aware of walking down a short corridor pushing doors open: bedroom, bedroom, kitchen.

If I don't get to the toilet soon I will faint.

I flung open the next door and staggered into the bathroom. Luckily, the toilet lid was up because before I could even kneel down I threw up noisily and painfully into the bowl. My throat ripped with each convulsion and tears streamed down my face, dripping into the torrent.

Gathering myself, I turned and locked the door. Now it was time for thinking. I caught a glimpse of myself in the mirror: time for thinking *and repairs.*

Could I get out of the flat without anyone noticing me? Of course not. Should I confront Michel? The very thought made me retch again. *But I can't sit there and eat like nothing has happened!*

In the end, though, I couldn't think of anything else to do. I didn't want to embarrass Ava.

With the old dancer's blend of cold water, perfume and composure I stepped out. Everyone else was seated for dinner and I felt all eyes on me as I made my way to sit next to Thierry. Fortunately Michel was the other end. But that was still close enough. I must have been terrible company. With an aching throat, bulging with suppressed tears, I tried to smile and react to the conversation but I was miles away in a silent world. Every mouthful of the meal was tasteless, a chore to swallow.

The longer the meal went on, the louder Michel's voice became. Any initial glint of discomfort had vanished. He was laughing, charming and attentive. Occasionally I sensed him glance towards me with bold looks of defiance. I held my breath each time. If he actually spoke to me I wouldn't be able to hold my anger in.

Thierry was suspicious. 'What's wrong?' he whispered. 'Are you unwell?'

'I'm fine,' I lied. Not wanting to make a scene in a stranger's house, Thierry didn't push it. But a few minutes later he saw Michel try to bring me into the conversation – and noticed how I tensed, then went lifeless.

'Excuse me, Ava, I just need a word with Tessa.' Thierry stood up and gestured me to do the same. He led me to the hallway and spoke calmly but with fury in his eyes.

'Tessa, will you tell me what is going on? You obviously know this man. Have you had an affair?'

'No!' I cried. 'No, no, no.'

I gasped for breath.

'It was him,' I choked. 'Michel is the man who raped me.'

One look in my eyes told Thierry I wasn't lying. His own eyes softened and he held me. 'Leave it to me,' he whispered, kissing my head. 'Come back, and let's finish dinner.'

Thierry helped me to my seat but instead of sitting next to me walked over to Michel.

'Could I have a word, please?'

I couldn't help but watch. Michel's smile remained but it was forced. What must have been going through his head?

Ava said nothing but she definitely wasn't smiling. Something about Thierry was troubling her. When the two men left the room the conversation continued. Alone, I gulped down my wine. When they returned I tried to read their faces. Michel was still smiling in that angelic way that had confused me. Thierry on the other hand was black with rage. He returned to the table just long enough to throw me my bag and hiss in my ear, 'We're going.'

Then with apologies to a confused Ava he led me from the room. I couldn't walk properly. A combination of fear and sickness felled me. Almost carrying me to the car, Thierry slammed the door, and delivered the cruellest surprise of all.

'He told me you led him on and you enjoyed it.'

What?

I screamed as the horror slowly dawned that Thierry believed him. *Him* – my rapist.

'He raped me!' I sobbed. 'He raped me. He raped me.'

I repeated the same words over and over. I had nothing left to say. In silence Thierry sped to my apartment, threw his things into a case and left without another word.

I pictured Michel, the monster, playing happy families with Ava and her little daughter and was sick again.

The bottom had fallen out of my world.

Crying, I lost track of time. Suddenly there was a knock. The club car was there to pick me up.

'I'm not coming!' I called out.

'Sorry? What did you say?'

I took a deep breath. 'I said I'll be down in five minutes.'

I tied my hair up and made a fist of applying some make-up. At the dressing-room my puffy face was still red and seemingly impervious to make-up. Worst of all my legs had turned to jelly. I was sick to the stomach and every other part of my body. *There's no way I can dance tonight.*

But a contract is a contract. 'If you don't perform the manager will make you pay,' the DJ warned. 'Do your best. I'll give you a much shorter set. Just do something, anything.'

I agreed. Then his girlfriend arrived with a cup of tea and wrapped her arms around me. For the first time in hours I managed a smile. You have to remember the good people.

Somehow I got through my evening. My arms were leaden and my stiletto heels seemed made of concrete. I don't know how close to the actual beat I got as I performed but I did my best. I managed a smile throughout – the hardest thing by far.

Six hours later, lifeless in my dressing room chair, I heard a cough from the corridor. Being held into the open doorway was a large bouquet of flowers, a bottle of champagne – and a picture of Thierry!

It was inscribed, 'You are my life. I love you.'

My lover walked into the room and I crumbled.

'I'm so sorry, my darling. Will you forgive me?'

'Of course, of course. Please don't leave me.'

'I'll never leave you again.'

I was speechless and suddenly so very tired. I'd performed one hundred and fifty shows that month. My body had had enough. As we squeezed each other he whispered, 'I've arranged a holiday. You deserve it. We're going to be together for a while.'

After farewell drinks and an exchange of addresses with the staff, I wrote a note to Ava who hadn't turned up for work. I referred to our friendship but not the supper incident. How could I explain anything else unless we met face to face? The pang of disbelief and sadness was eased after a short sleep. Thierry then loaded the car and we set off for Perpignan, a long but pleasant drive through countryside, towards the Pyrenees. We were going to stay at his uncle's lodge in Canet Plage. I wasn't looking forward to seeing any relatives just yet – but the chance to spend some time alone with Thierry and to recuperate drove me on. We needed time to heal together.

Canet Plage was like another planet. Miles of deserted beach punctuated with odd sculptures and futuristic buildings, all brightly coloured. I couldn't wait to find our little piece of it. During the journey I noticed I'd developed a skin rash and a dull abdominal pain that was worsening with every mile. I think it was just a bug brought on by exhaustion. I knew I was desperate to sleep. Unfortunately Thierry had other ideas.

'We can unpack later. We're meeting my uncle for dinner tonight.'

'Oh, no, darling. I'm so tired. And the pain in my stomach just won't go.'

Thierry's desire for control would not be challenged – not even by illness. As a trainee doctor he had an answer for everything.

'You'll be fine once you've had one of these.' He was holding a suppository – a common form of medicine in France. Ten minutes later, after much arguing and tears, he inserted it.

Head spinning, I watched this man who looked like my lover retreat into his doctorly mien, as though I were just another one of his patients to be processed as quickly as possible. *Who are you?* I wondered. *The Thierry I love would never be so inconsiderate.*

'What's wrong, darling?' I asked, but he dismissed the question with a wave of his hand.

'The only thing wrong is the idea that I won't be able to show off my phenomenal girlfriend to my uncle if she doesn't cheer up!'

He smiled, but I knew he didn't mean it. Something had changed. I knew it was the rape. I was the victim but he was making it his problem. When I needed him most, I sensed Thierry slip further away.

The meal with Thierry's uncle and his girlfriend was perfectly pleasant. Thierry did most of the talking and I spoke when spoken to. All I could think about was my bed, though, and eventually I was allowed to find it. When I woke up I felt even worse but there was no respite from Thierry's relentless schedule.

'Uncle and Sofia are joining us for lunch. Help me cook.'

Again I was a shadow of my normal self, nursing my ailing body through light conversations and barely touching my food. But I was used to smiling through a performance. I knew I could keep it up just long enough.

I'd like to think that Thierry was oblivious to my discomfort. If he wasn't, then his next words were unforgivable.

'Tessa, I've been telling Uncle about your sensational costumes. Why don't you put one on for him to see?'

One of my dance costumes? Are you serious?

I stared hard into Thierry's face. Was it pride or spite behind his eyes? 'I don't think that's appropriate for lunch, darling.'

'Nonsense. There is never a wrong time for a Frenchman to see a beautiful dancer.'

His uncle joined in and so with all eyes boring into my back I walked slowly upstairs.

What is he playing at?

Dancing is an approved and even respected profession in France. I certainly had never been ashamed of my career. Even so, walking down the stairs wearing little more than a g-string and jambières, I had never felt more uneasy or embarrassed. Thierry must have been able to see it on my face. But still he made me proceed. Was he enjoying my humiliation?

His uncle and Sofia were charm personified. They showered me with compliments, both on my figure and the sparkling outfit. But I knew it was in bad taste. Putting on a costume without shoes and make-up, outside of a club, away from the transforming spotlights, never feels right. I don't think I ever forgave Thierry for that afternoon.

He still refused to admit that anything was wrong and, in fact, over the next week seemed to mellow and return to something like his normal self. Finally alone, we were able to relax and enjoy each other again. One day we drove across into Spain, to Grenoa, wandering amongst its tall, ochre buildings huddled beside the river. Thierry spoke fluent Spanish and led us confidently down cobbled streets and back alleys, where we bought well-made leather shoes for a third of the usual price. Then he returned me all the way back to Annecy, with a supply of suppositories, a tender goodbye and the promise to see each other again in two weeks.

It was a romantic farewell – in a weird way even the medication was a thoughtful touch – but the cloud hanging over us, the episode with Michel, had not gone away. I wondered if it ever would.

Age nine

Hello Paris

Macumba

Tidy traveller

Slave to the rhythm

Ice Queen

CHAPTER NINE

THIS IS WHERE IT ENDS

Sometimes it's easy to forget why we do things. As I sat in the foyer of my hotel, suitcases around my ankles waiting for Jo to pick me up, I didn't have a friend within a hundred miles. But whose choice was that? I could have gone to the station, caught a train to Calais or the airport and been back at Number 10 Victoria Road by nightfall. I could have my mother's arms wrapped around me at bedtime. I could even find my way down to Cornwall and enjoy one of Gran's welcoming saffron cream teas.

I had options. There were alternatives to the miserable life I found myself suddenly living.

But none of them appealed.

What is wrong with me? Why don't I just run away?

But then the blast of a car horn made me look up. Jo was pulling up outside the hotel, ready to ferry me to the next engagement. Ready to escort me to a venue where men and women would pay to see me dance. Where I'd be a paid entertainer every night and made to feel like a somebody, for every moment I was performing.

That's why I don't run away.

I could sit in lobbies feeling sorry for myself all day and night but I had choices. I could have followed Thierry home. I could have contacted Jo and walked away. I could have drawn a line under my career for the sake of my relationship. But I didn't do that. I didn't throw in the towel to follow my lover back to his career in the military hospital.

I was looking for love: but not at that price.

Jo drove me to a non-descript hotel closer to the Swiss border and as usual helped me settle in.

'I just need to finalise a couple of things this afternoon then I'll take you to your new contract tomorrow,' he explained. 'Enjoy yourself today.'

Enjoy myself? The budget hotel appeared to be, as far as I could tell, in the middle of nowhere. If you're not in the right mood then even rural France can be an intimidatingly vast, empty place. But the solitude would help me think.

My call from Jo never came that day or the next. It's horrible not knowing what you're doing. You're not working but you can't relax in case you're summoned quickly. It's a hellish sort of limbo. Finally Jo phoned. There were problems, once again, with the contract. It would take another few days to settle.

I think I stepped outside the hotel once. I spent the days writing long letters to Thierry, pouring my heart out on every page. In the evenings I rang him but he never answered – or replied to messages. And that is when, my heart aching almost to the point of physical pain, I would order wine from the restaurant and start drinking until it was morning and I could start the day anew.

After five days Jo returned. I could tell from his face that he didn't have a contract for me. In fact, he had something better, but at a cost.

'I've taken you as far as I can go,' he said. 'You're the best dancer I've ever seen and you need a bigger agent to make the most of your talents.'

He had lined me up with a renowned Swiss agent and they were expecting my call. I couldn't thank him enough. It really was a step up the career ladder. But it was sad saying goodbye to Jo – forever.

As I watched his car pull away I thought, *Another man walking out of my life.*

Taking Jo's place was Leo Verles, the most respected agent in Switzerland. His office was in Lausanne, but I didn't have to go there to pick up my next assignment. In fact I would never meet Verles – and I only ever spoke to him once. His secretary, however, was friendly and very efficient. 'Get yourself to Lommiswil and your contract will be waiting.'

My heart sank at the thought of returning to Switzerland. Bad memories outweighed the good but work-wise I had never been disappointed. The town was halfway between Basel and Bern and it looked like a postcard as my taxi pulled in, pastureland set beneath snow-covered mountains. I knew from experience that first impressions can be misleading and I would soon be proved right. There was only one shop and no bus route.

Who on earth comes here for dancing girls?

I had a room in a guesthouse which was attached to the place where I would be working. Both were owned by the sour-faced Caverzacio family who ignored me from the moment I arrived on their doorstep. Fortunately it was their son who ran the Cavallino Bar where I would be working and he was much nicer. The bar was his pride and joy and so anyone connected with it was a friend. My contract with him was until Christmas – and for once I really did have a contract, not just a verbal agreement.

'Verles always works like this,' he explained as he peeled off the yellow copy for me, holding back the pink version for the agent and the green for himself. 'He also asked me to make sure you saw this.' He handed over a document entitled "Rules" which laid out, in laborious detail, every aspect of the contract, from arrival and departure to discipline and behaviour. Rehearsals at four o'clock in the afternoon were obligatory on the first day. Verles took 8% commission. I paid £20 a week towards my room from my wage of £25 a day. I was also entitled to a daily meal at the café. The club calculated its own deductions for police and tax, as I'd already discovered.

My own description on the contract was as "topless go-go girl" which made me smile. *If Miss Brooking could see me now!* But I knew there was more to it than nudity. Work started at half-past seven and I had to do seven shows, each lasting the length of one record. Once again I couldn't wait to get started.

The bar was more like a private club, frequented by wealthy, bored friends with Ferraris identical to the owner's. There was a lot of money in this area, obviously. My first night passed enjoyably. Yes, the venue had none of the glamour of the cabaret scene, but I was the attraction and I wasn't required to coax customers into drinking to plump up my salary. It was just a very nice, straightforward gig.

I was fortunate that I could dance at almost any venue unlike groups and speciality acts that needed space and all the stage effects, but without consummation it meant I wouldn't always get contracts at the top clubs.

With Christmas approaching I began to make plans. Mum said she'd love to have me there so I said yes. No sooner than I had put the phone down to Number 10 it rang again. It was Thierry.

'Come and be with me at Christmas,' he insisted.

'I can't. I've agreed to go home.'

'Well,' he sniffed, 'I shall just have to come with you then.'

In one short sentence he lifted my heart for the first time in weeks.

'That would be lovely,' I said quietly. 'I can't wait to tell Mum.'

It had been six months since I'd set foot in London and Mum was quick to point out the time hadn't been kind to me. 'You look run down,' she scolded. 'Come on, you need to rest.'

For once I did as I was told as she led me to my old bedroom. I slept so soundly, in fact, that I missed a call from Thierry. When Mum told me the message I cried.

'I'm afraid he's not coming to London,' she said quietly. 'But he did tell me something else.'

'What?' I struggled to keep the petulance from my voice.

'He said he wants you to come to Brittany for New Year – because he is going to propose to you!'

I was ecstatic. Mum, for once, wasn't rushed off her feet so we opened a bottle of champagne and talked the night away. Funnily enough, practical questions like where would we live or what I would do for work, never came up!

'I've never seen you so happy in love,' Mum cooed. 'I can't wait to meet him.'

'You'll love him,' I smiled. 'Everyone does.'

A few days later I flew to Brest to meet Thierry's parents and stayed at the chalet they'd given Thierry, set in an orchard below their house. There was a blazing log fire and Christmas decorations, a perfect romantic retreat. It was an odd feeling knowing what he planned to do – but not when he intended to do it. On New Year's Eve we ate at a lovely restaurant festooned with chandeliers and flowers. The lights were dimmed just before midnight, which is when Thierry whispered something in my ear. As the twelve o'clock chimes rang out, everyone in the restaurant stood up and kissed each other in the candlelight for New Year.

But Thierry and I were kissing for a different reason. We were engaged.

We're going to get married!

Still high on happiness we were forced to part the next day. Thierry drove back to Toulon while I had another season in Lommiswil to honour. But this time I went armed with plenty of books and writing paper to correspond with my fiancé. Fiancé – the word made me smile just thinking it.

Who would have thought that little tomboy Tessa Skola would be marrying her dashing French pirate?

Thinking about the wedding sent my mind wandering and for the first time in months I found myself thinking about my father. Who would give me away? Suddenly I felt guilty for not thinking of Mum's feelings when we'd discussed it back in London. How could she think of my wedding without remembering her own – and the man she left behind?

I couldn't help drawing comparisons between her life and my own. Look how far away I was living from Thierry. That would need to change, wouldn't it?

Once again, returning to a place I had previously enjoyed had unsatisfactory results and after a slow season I couldn't wait to move onto my next contract, in Basel.

After months in a sleepy village it was exciting to be back in a city – especially one with shops. Armed with all my wages from Lommiswil (there had been nothing there to spend money on) I embarked on a shopping spree and bought outfits from designer boutiques and had my hair styled. I felt such freedom, out of the gloom, and spent with gay abandon. It was a kind of madness, combined with a sense of release and relief. It culminated on a Saturday night when I went to the Hilton disco, drank too much and bought everyone in the club a drink.

Back in my guesthouse I cried myself to sleep, suddenly lost without Thierry. His absence cast the same cloud over me as the absence of my own father. But at least with Thierry I knew what I was missing.

The only way I could not be crushed by the loss was to ignore it.

Work this time was at the Happy Night disco, a dilapidated building along the road from the main train station. My photo was added to the advertising board outside and I had to do five shows a night. Home was an uncomfortable flat on the first floor of the same block, directly above the main entrance, and overlooking the railway track. I shared with a girl called Audrey – born in Sierra Leone, brought up by Barnardo's and living in Hackney. She was the first Brit I'd met abroad since Angie in Toulon; big-eyed, slim, with a wicked laugh, and fun to be around.

With Audrey I broke one of my rules and we often had a tot of whiskey before going to work. That didn't stop me drinking plenty more afterwards. Fuelled by the adrenaline of work and the buzz of having a good friend for a few weeks, I let myself go. We both had our reasons, it turned out. Audrey confided in me about being raised in an orphanage then said, 'So what are you running away from?'

Me? 'I'm not running away from anything.' I was sure of that.

'I'm not so sure. There are things on your mind. Maybe you're looking for something then, but you don't know where to find it.'

I told her about Thierry. How I didn't know where I stood with him from one day to the next. How he had the power to lift or drop me and seemed to revel in wielding that power.

The night ended as usual with more drinks than I could handle. The next day, as though his ears had been burning, I heard from my fiancé. He was coming to visit that weekend.

The next two days flew by in a blur. Friday night I went to work just before midnight as usual, expecting to see him stroll into the club as agreed at any point. But he never arrived.

A phone call the next day apologised for the change of plan. I was crushed. But it wasn't the first time and, I cried to Audrey, I knew it wouldn't be the last. 'In my darker moods I swear he messes me around on purpose just because he can.'

Basel is a pretty city with its picturesque squares and bridges crossing the Rhine. You have to be careful not to get run over by the trams, coming in all directions and, like so many beautiful places, it hurts to be there alone. The views and the restaurants and the galleries need to be shared.

Each night I watched lovers at the club holding hands, and more, and my body longed to feel the touch of a man. It was only a matter of time before the inevitable happened. Inspired by alcohol, of course, I was flattered by the attention of a smart businessman – dark, rugged and handsome, just the type I always find irresistible. He was visiting from Zurich and staying at the Hilton and he invited me back for a drink after work.

Why not?

We continued drinking in his room then lay down and kissed. God, it felt good to be held. Thierry was nowhere in my thoughts. All I could think of was how my body was alive at this stranger's touch. I needed to be loved that night.

As I took off my dress, the man reached for the phone and spoke in German. I could only imagine what delicacy he was ordering from room service. Oysters? More champagne?

When the knock at the door came I was in the bathroom freshening up. I emerged, naked, to be confronted with the sight of my date – and three of his business colleagues. All of them were as nude as me.

Panicking, I darted back into the bathroom.

My date banged on the door. 'What's wrong? Come out!'

'Give me my clothes! I don't want this.'

'Don't be silly. We'll pay – *the normal rate!*'

I wrapped a towel around me and opened the door. The men had pulled some clothes on. They all had faces like thunder.

'I'm sorry,' I mumbled, scrabbling for my things. 'I'm not a prostitute.'

'Are you sure?' one of the men said.

I fled the room still wrapped in the towel and pulled my clothes on in the lift. What on earth had just happened to me? How could I have made such a mistake? I was suddenly sober, panicking and, I realised, completely without money. I never needed it at work because I lived above the club, my purse left in my room. I walked back to Happy Night cold, tired, feeling dirty and cheap, in floods of tears: that's when things got worse. The front door was locked and I hadn't brought my key. It was four in the morning and no amount of yelling up to Audrey could penetrate her own drunken sleep.

Eventually I gave up. A small hotel further up the road let me in, taking my jewellery for a deposit on one of their smallest rooms. It was obvious what the night porter thought I needed the room for but I didn't care. I woke the next morning in a dismal and empty mood. The previous night had been a close escape and I hated those men for thinking they could use me. But worst of all I despised myself. I had been weak and I had nearly paid for it dearly.

For the next few nights I performed on autopilot. In between shows I stayed in my room and read or stared out the window. I never knew going through the motions could be so easy. But it was all I could manage. Those men had triggered memories of Geneva that I wanted to stay buried. I wouldn't recover from this episode until I could put Michel's evil out of my mind again.

But that, it turned out, was going to be harder than I hoped.

Nearly a week after my fright at the Hilton I was still avoiding company. A British-style pub near the station offered a suitably miserable escape from the burning sun and smiling faces outside. As I sat there with a drink and an English newspaper I heard a familiar voice.

'They said I'd find you here.'

I looked up, unable to believe my eyes. It was Ava. My good friend Ava.

My face broke instinctively into a grin but, as she stepped away from the glare of the entrance I could see Ava wasn't smiling. In fact, her face was dark with intent. In four or five short strides she reached my table and without a word slapped me hard round the face. I flinched and fell against the wall.

The barman heard the noise and called over.

'We're fine,' Ava snapped and ordered a drink. Then she pulled up a chair next to me and glared into my eyes. It was like she was trying to read something from my mind. I hadn't said a word. The sting of her hand was still raw but I didn't want to give her the satisfaction of seeing me cry. But, God, I wanted to.

She spoke quietly. 'Why did you do it? Those lies about Michel. Why did you say them?'

Hatred was burning up her face and finally I had to let the tears out. I went to speak but she held up her hand.

'Forget it. I don't want to hear any more of your poison.'

Ten seconds later she'd stormed out of the pub, her drink untouched. I don't know where she went or why she'd come without getting to the truth. I only knew one thing. I had had enough.

I want to die.

I remember actually picturing the trams in the main square. I imagined stepping out just as one pulled into the plaza. I visualised the impact of that fast, heavy carriage against my body. In my mind I didn't feel any pain. And that is when I knew what I had to do.

I staggered out of the pub and stared blinking into the daylight. I was nineteen years old and I had come to the end of my tether. I'd come to the end of my life. *This is where it ends.*

I turned to walk to the main square. In truth I could be run over by a tram in any number of places but at the time it seemed logical to go to the place where the trams were most frequent.

I'm really going to do this.

To get to the square I had to pass Happy Night. I walked straight past without stopping, focusing on the pavement. But then an urge swept over me. I turned to give the building one last look of farewell, and as I did I caught a glimpse of my photograph fixed proudly to the promotional board: "Tessa Skola – Dancer".

I repeated its words, 'Tessa Skola – Dancer. Tessa Skola – Dancer.'

I found myself walking towards the poster as I spoke. I got within a yard and reached out an arm. I felt my hand touch the plastic board.

Tessa Skola. Dancer.

It was like a car being jump-started. That's who I was. I was Tessa Skola and I was a dancer. I was respected and admired in every venue at which I appeared. I was bloody good at my job. In fact I was a bloody good person. The idea of taking my own life had vanished. What had I done wrong?

That night I performed one of the best shows I'd ever managed. I had a new lease of life – quite literally – and I was determined to make it count. Life wasn't perfect, I realised that. I just had to make the best of it that I could. Not for the first time, I wished a certain someone were there to help me achieve it.

With the timing of an actor, Thierry turned up unannounced the next day. Completely out of the blue, he just appeared at the door to my room. If my life were a film script critics would say it was too far-fetched. But it happened. One day I wanted to commit suicide because I felt alone. Twenty-four hours later my fiancé was standing in my room promising to fix everything.

It was an odd reunion. Thierry's grey eyes were crackling fiercely and he insisted we had fun during his stay. Every moment he was there I thought I would burst with pent-up emotion, but before I could even say anything he'd disappeared again as suddenly as he'd arrived. Despite being so much in love with him, I found myself wishing he'd never come. He'd churned up my feelings of love and pain and for what? One afternoon, one night and one morning's company.

A few months earlier I would have been badly affected by his usual vanishing act but now I was stronger. *If Thierry wants to have his mysterious distance then so can I.*

An hour after he left I booked a holiday to Barbados.

With my stint in Basel over I moved onto Burgdorf, Biel and then the well–known Mocambo Club in Berne. This was my favourite city with its famous bears, steep roofs, tightly-packed, and tall church spire set prettily against the surrounding mountains. It was in Berne that I instigated the next steps of my recovery. I whizzed through, shopped, saw the sights and had a taste of the high-life with excessive money and excessive drinking.

I also had sex and didn't feel guilty. In fact I did it to help me forget Thierry. *I can either let his silence torture me or get on with my life.* I met two brothers and made love to them both, on their balcony overlooking the river, for all to see. I also encountered a pilot, who took me up in his glider, an Olympic slalom skier and a bank manager who opened an account for me with Credit Suisse. It felt good to have a Swiss bank account!

My newfound confidence extended into my holiday. I met a Canadian architect working on the new airport in Barbados and he drove me around the island. We walked along the white sand past Churchill's house, meandered through plantations and dined outside with calypso bands playing in the sweet night air. I ate flying fish and coconuts and sipped rum at brightly painted wayside shacks. And yes, we made love without a thought for my fiancé. I healed my wounds a little and began to think about my future. Was Thierry going to be in it? It was up to him. I knew I couldn't let him make me a victim. Enough men had already done that.

There was something else on my mind too: my career. I'd had two good years as a podium dancer or a sideshow to the main event. But the time was approaching for a decision to be made. *Am I going to stay a go-go dancer or step up to be the main attraction?* At that exact moment I knew I still wasn't ready. But if I wanted it – really wanted it – I had to start working hard now.

By coincidence I met a couple in Barbados who ran the Madewis Agency in Switzerland. They'd actually heard of me!

'We can find you all the work you need,' they promised. 'Whenever Verles has a gap, let us know.'

I did not trust the other elite Swiss agents I had seen and heard of – more like high class pimps disguised by expert charm and flashy suits.

I returned to work in Basel for Madewis, on the other side of the river which was full of gay clubs and beer cellars, home to a huge transvestite community. I performed for them at the Hotel Soleil where I also stayed, and the show place was a twenty-four hour basement bar, frequented by drag queens – a home from home! Mountains of flesh in kaftans and five inch lashes, flirty and feisty, they seemed drawn towards acting like mothers to me, giving me little gifts and watching the shows proudly.

The highlight of my act here was dancing to Sister Sledge's *We Are Family*. That song got everyone going. I was paid £20 a night plus tips.

When I phoned England I wasn't homesick as usual, but when both Mum and Gran said I must sort out my relationship with Thierry, I agreed. A few weeks' earlier, that sort of honest talk would have been enough to break me. But something had changed. *In me*. Was it confidence or experience? Or had my love for Thierry gone once and for all?

I had been grateful that he forgave me. But I should have been the one being asked for forgiveness. When I needed him most he turned on me. And he'd been turning his back on me on and off ever since.

After a number of my messages went unheeded, I finally called Thierry's family. They told me he hadn't been in touch for months. I'd have to find him myself.

I finally moved onto Zurich. Whatever hopes I had of that city didn't live up to expectations. A contract at the famous Le Terrase club eluded me and I danced on billiard tables in bars in bad areas with disgusting accommodation in a call girl guest house. Men rang the bells all day, the stairs smelled of cum and I had to disinfect my room after finding tampons and condoms left under the bed. I was relieved to hop across the German border for my next Verles contract. *If I never see Switzerland again I won't be unhappy*, I thought. It was a new country and it was even further away from Thierry. I hoped it would be a new start.

CHAPTER TEN

THERE'S NO PLACE LIKE HOME

They say appearances can be deceptive. Everything about my new contract screamed respectability but the truth couldn't have been further away – and I loved it.

The Black Bottom cabaret occupied a large house, set on a parapet, in the small village of Grenzach. I arrived, as instructed, in the afternoon and rang the bell. A sweet middle-aged lady in a tweed suit and flat shoes opened the door. Behind her stood a timid looking chap in spectacles and a country squire's suit.

Have I got the right address? 'I was looking for the Black Bottom,' I said nervously.

'And you've found it!' the woman replied in good English. 'You must be Tessa. We are the owners. I'm Frau Weiss and this is my husband, Herr Weiss. Come in, come in.'

The owners? This couple looked like they'd both just stepped out of church, not the region's most famous nightclub. Their teenage daughters, I soon discovered, had the same conservative, butter-wouldn't-t-melt look. *What have I stumbled into here?*

I couldn't imagine a more ordinary family but their club made them thoroughly extraordinary.

There was a lot more to the Black Bottom than its smart appearance and perfect design, with a good-sized stage extending into the room and black sofas and stools giving audiences a perfect view. From the pretty bar girls who served topless while they chatted away, to the dancers who, this being Germany, were expected to strip completely naked, the club ran on sexual energy.

On my first night I went out into the main room to enjoy the rest of the show and get a feel of my latest home. I'd been there a few minutes, enjoying the loud music, before I noticed a large cinema screen in front of the stage curtain. Something was being projected onto it.

It was a porn movie!

Bearing in mind all the things I had seen in my twenty years, I was surprisingly shocked to see this completely hardcore film beamed beneath a soundtrack of the latest 1980 records as though it was a video on MTV. The most startling aspect was just how nobody seemed to be taking any notice. There were plenty of husbands and wives here and everyone just treated it like background entertainment. The screen was lowered between acts and over the next few weeks I saw things to satisfy any curiosity – not that the incredibly prim and proper audience seemed to take much interest. Once I glimpsed a scene involving animals which made me look away in disgust – but no one else batted an eyelid.

The films were only the tip of the iceberg. Three or four striptease girls doubled as hostesses and everything was so discreet I'd been there almost a week before I noticed guys being led through a curtain behind the bar. The next evening, before opening time, I asked one of the waitresses what was behind the drapes.

'Come and see for yourself.'

Intrigued I followed her through into a smart corridor that had a wall on one side and a row of doors on the other. I opened the first door and couldn't help gasping. Just when I thought the club couldn't surprise me anymore, here I was amazed at finding a little booth, called a "separate", just big enough to house a bench seat, a side table and a box of tissues.

'No prizes for guessing what goes on in here!' the waitress laughed.

'How often do they get used?'

'Are you serious? Pay attention tonight. I hope you can count!'

That night I kept an eye on the bar and sure enough one by one each hostess disappeared behind the curtain with a customer – and a bottle of champagne – within half an hour of the club opening. The waitress wasn't joking. By the end of the night I'd lost count of the comings and goings but as usual nobody else took a bit of notice. There was so much else going on in the club to keep everyone entertained. I was surprised at how little I minded. In other clubs I would have felt sullied by association. But everyone at the Black Bottom was so charming and likeable that it was hard to take offence at anything.

The acts themselves catered for all tastes. A French magician and his girlfriend assistant amazed me with their spectacular tricks. I watched a little silver ball levitate every night for a fortnight and never once worked out how he did it – and he would never tell me either. Another couple, a husband and wife from Vienna, performed a balancing/acrobatic act. The highlight involved her posing as a space queen on a revolving rocket, in a silver bodysuit that cleverly came to pieces. She was thirty-one, with a model figure and Hollywood features and we quickly became friends.

The main attraction was stupendous. I'd heard about The Paper Dolls from one of the bar girls but even so, watching four nuns standing in a row, holding candles and miming to angelic voices, made me tingle with expectation. Suddenly the music burst into *Don't Tell Mother* from *Cabaret*, and habits were ripped off, veils flung asunder and spotlights hit four leggy figures in dazzling corsets and suspenders, with black manes tousling down. They weren't nuns – *they weren't even women!* But somehow their flawless take-offs of Donna Summer, Diana Ross and Liza Minnelli worked so brilliantly.

The Dolls' guys were from Indonesia and Argentina and we bonded instantly. It's funny to be given tips and make-up lessons from men but they all transformed themselves into such beautiful women that I had to take notice. They also taught me a lot about costumes – what works, what doesn't – and made me start to take more interest in choreography. My dancing steps were still improvised then, but, inspired by The Paper Dolls, I began working out some Latin moves for the Fat Back Band's *Spanish Hustle*. One of my ideas was to strike a pose to start my show. I was rehearsing it one day when there was a burst of giggles from the doorway. The guys were all there, screaming with delight and hips to the left, arms outstretched, right hands across their faces.

'We're doing the Tessa pose!'

I was genuinely sad when the contract ended at the end of July. Michael, the manager, took all the artistes out for dinner and I was showered with champagne and given a gold good-luck charm. As I looked at it, through tears, I thought, *I'll need this*. Verles was sending me back to Switzerland and I wasn't looking forward to it.

But first I had a free week. Fired up by the generous spirits of my German experience I came to a decision. I called Mum and said, 'For the sake of my sanity I'm going to sort everything out with Thierry once and for all.'

Even on the Express train to Lyon I had plenty of time to rehearse what I was going to say to the elusive man whose ring was still on my finger. I was on a mission and I felt strong, not emotional. I wanted answers that only he could give. And if I didn't like what I heard? Well…

As I stepped out of the familiar little station in Hyères I was suddenly nervous. I'd left messages at his hospital telling him I was coming. As soon as I'd checked into my room at the Bar Tabac I called him again. *This is his last chance,* I promised myself. *He's got one day.*

Once I'd done all I could, I decided to relax. The scorching heat, the sea, the palms – it was my idea of paradise and how, I realised, I'd missed it all. The afternoon came and went and the evening followed. By noon the following day I was mentally packing my bags. *He's not coming, is he?* But five minutes later there was a knock on my door.

'Mademoiselle, there was a telephone call for you.'

It was him.

'Is he still there?'

'No, but he gave a message. "I'll be round in an hour."'

Totally Thierry! No excuses, no chit-chat, no hint of regret. Just him, seizing control.

My room had a window overlooking the back street and sixty minutes later I was sitting, waiting, as I always seemed to do for this man. I heard the roar of a sports engine and saw a familiar MG pull up and Thierry stride out – with a Doberman at his side. If I'd seen cameras filming a period drama I wouldn't have been surprised because he looked like a country squire from a Lawrence novel. And he'd changed. He'd lost weight, his hair was longer. But anyone can change their appearance. Had he changed for the better in any other way?

In the end it didn't matter. After all the tough-talking I'd rehearsed, as soon as the door opened I was totally under his spell. Again. The dog bounded in and I was instantly light-headed. Thierry seemed to move in slow motion and I was captivated. He was measured, deliberate in his words and actions and the effect was hypnotic. When we kissed and fell into bed it was more loving and passionate than it had ever been.

We drove to the hills to eat and it was as if we'd never been apart – from his point of view at least. He told me about how busy he was in the army hospital, he listened to my concerns about our relationship, but did he give any reasons for his silence? None. Even after ten hours with him I still didn't know what he'd been doing or thinking. But the whole day, the evening – and the night – were all so perfect. *Am I looking for problems that aren't there?*

The spell was broken the next morning. As I watched the familiar sight of Thierry dressing distractedly, already mentally at his next destination, I felt that onerous pang of sadness and disappointment.

'Are you sure you can't stay? I have another four days off.'

'I'm sorry. But I'll make it up to you. I'll come to Chur for your birthday.'

'You won't remember.'

'How can you say that? We're engaged to be married. I wouldn't miss my fiancée's birthday for anything. You know you mean the world to me.'

For that moment I think he truly believed it.

*****

By the time I arrived in the alpine city of Chur, Switzerland, I had been travelling for nearly twenty-four hours. Whereas its neighbour, St Moritz, was fashionable and glitzy, this village in the mountains seemed uninteresting and drab. The journey through the lakes and cypress forests had promised much but, as I dragged my case into the Vulkano Bar, my heart sank. There was a small bar with a dance floor in one corner, backed by a wallpapered alpine scene with one red light shining down. Rows of pine tables and benches served as a restaurant and seating area. My exhaustion didn't help, but first impressions were awful. *I've come all this way – for this?*

The owners were a strange, young couple; him dark, stocky and silent, her tall and grouchy with a face deeply pitted with acne scars. She showed me up another steep flight to a maze of small bedrooms and bathrooms above the club. Partition boards had been put up to split the rooms in imaginative and ridiculous ways. She opened a door and I realised I was staring at a shower cubicle.

She gestured blankly. 'Through here.'

Through there?

Sure enough, she stepped into the enamel shower tray then pushed a door the other side of the hose and walked out into a small walk-in wardrobe. When I saw the single bed and narrow cabinet I realised it was my room.

As unclean as the bed looked, I just wanted to collapse onto it and recharge my batteries for the next day's start. But the sullen woman had different ideas.

'You start tonight. Get your costumes. Follow me.'

'But I don't start till tomorrow,' I said weakly.

She shrugged indifferently. 'You start tonight or you don't start at all, I don't mind.'

An hour later I was sitting at the bar trying to get the measure of the clientele. It was obviously the cheap, local place to eat and sit in all day. Farmers in knitted jumpers and boots, self-conscious young men too shy to even look at the girls, and old men staring into their beers were the only customers. And it was my job to make them buy me drinks. *I can't believe I'm doing consummation again. I'm terrible at it.*

At least the other girls were nice. There were two Thais, one Italian and, to my surprise and relief, an attractive, well-spoken Caribbean girl called Delia who lived in Knightsbridge. She wore the most exquisite cocktail dresses – Estee Lauder everything – and looked completely out of place. When I learned that she was the mistress of someone well-known in London I was even more confused.

'Why on earth would you work here then?' I asked.

'I wanted some adventure.'

As usual my only respite from the unpleasant atmosphere in the bar was when I was dancing. Suddenly all faces turned to the stage and the owner and his wife sat nodding their heads in approval. As soon as I stepped down Delia ran up with congratulations. But how I got through until one in the morning I don't know. I had never known tiredness like it. Afterwards I walked back to my room. I had to wait for a man to finish in the shower before I could pass, wet-footed, through to my door but eventually I fell into bed and slept for twelve hours solid. I awoke, parched, and, with no kitchen facilities, drank water from the shower using a hairspray cap.

It was only my second day and I couldn't have been more miserable with my set-up. But at least I had Thierry's visit to look forward to. We would share my twenty-first birthday together. I couldn't wait. It was the only thing that got me through the week.

And then, the day before my birthday, he rang to say he couldn't come.

I don't remember the excuse. Maybe he didn't even give one. I'd dropped the phone from my ear and it was swinging on its metal cord. *He's done it again. He's let me down. Again.*

Our changing room at the club was actually an under-stairs cupboard with one bulb. That's where Delia found me, huddled in the corner, mumbling, nose and mouth running. Somehow she pulled me through, and even bought me a cake the next day. But I couldn't wait to leave that place and when the day came we were both up at dawn and after fond farewells I started my journey around the country. After several elegant clubs as top billing my final destination was in Schinznach-Bad. I had accepted a contract for a hotel with a cabaret show, as a last minute favour for Madewis. But wherever they sent me were the lower end, small scale venues and, unfortunately, this was one of the worst.

I knew it was a mistake as soon as I arrived. The station was in the middle of nowhere and after five miles in a taxi I realised the rest of the village was no better. Pulling up outside the Hotel Rossli my hopes of an upturn in fortunes were dashed. This was no hotel. No tourist would have been desperate enough to be drawn there to make enquiries.

It had the look of a brothel about it even to my newcomer's eye: and that was where I was staying.

As I arrived, a slim, brown-haired, pretty woman beckoned me toward her office at the end of the hall.

'Sit,' she ordered, and sat looking at me across her desk. I burned with discomfort. She was about forty with cold, brown eyes and a permanent sneer, as if laughing privately to herself. Eventually she spoke.

'I am Madame Arn. I run this hotel, restaurant and club.' She paused and looked at some notes on her desk. 'And I've heard about you.'

The way she said it, in such a superior manner, made it sound as though I had a criminal record. But after the initial shock I realised what she meant. Talk of my attempts at consummation had preceded me. I bit my lip and looked forward to four long, hard weeks in her establishment. I began drafting a letter to Verles in my head even as I trudged to my room. *I need to get out of Switzerland. Please – get me work anywhere but Switzerland, as you promised.*

I soon learned that the hotel only employed acts to disguise its real purpose as a brothel. Even so, Arn had hired an eclectic group but they were all friendly, including Count Cristos, an Italian magician with an older German wife who acted as his assistant. Their room smelled like a zoo with all the creatures from their show: two snakes, rabbits, two dogs and a flock of doves. There was also a hostess/striptease from Brazil, who was a sex change with an astounding figure and the best breast job I'd ever seen.

On my first night I danced with as much passion as I could muster and won many approving glances from customers and staff. But not from Arn. As soon as I stepped down from the stage she snapped, 'Stop looking so pleased with yourself – find a man and get him drinking.'

I couldn't do it. If someone approached me and offered a drink then I would never say "no". But forcing myself on customers was not in my nature or my make-up. When I looked at the hostesses it only made me more desperate to ignore the owner's bullying. They were mainly around forty, all sharing a look of sadness. Many of them had once had plans and ambitions but had got lost along the way, trapped on the circuit, cheated, alone and empty. The luckier ones ended up with a large bank account and a little pet dog – but hardened by their lifestyle and unable to forge a meaningful relationship.

On the second night Arn warned me it would be my last if I didn't sell five bottles of champagne. I looked nonplussed and walked onto the stage. It was midnight and I danced to Christopher Cross's *Sailing*. There wasn't a sound in the house as I moved slowly and dreamily, lost in a faraway place, with chiffon veils added to my blue bikini and no jambières for a change. When I stepped down from the stage I was deluged by admirers and Arn was congratulated as well for finding me. I can only imagine how annoyed that must have made her. Every part of her gnarled mind wanted to fire me because I didn't sell enough alcohol – but it looked like she had a cabaret hit on her hands, so she couldn't do much about it.

The real hostesses drank gallons of champagne, bottle after bottle each night, then whisked customers upstairs. Some of the regulars were sinister men, who looked as if they despised the world and everyone in it. A wealthy dwarf in a wheelchair was a frequent visitor. To my horror, his chauffeur approached me, but only with an invitation to join them the following afternoon for tea. I said "yes", just to get out, and despite initial nerves had an enjoyable day. That night I arrived happy to work. Arn soon punctured that.

'Skola, it's entirely up to you what you do in the afternoons. If you want to fuck a cripple, that's your business. But this is mine – sell me those five bottles.'

I enjoyed trips into town with the Brazilian sex-change. I could always recognise hostesses from other clubs, wearing dark sunglasses, like vampires, uncomfortable in the ordinary world.

The magician and his wife never seemed to go anywhere because their animals couldn't be left for long. They gave everything for their show – even their health. At the start of the act, Cristos would get a pile of razor blades, a reel of cotton and a glass of water and swallow a blade and piece of thread, one at a time. He made it look painful. At the end, when you'd forgotten this, he would cough and splutter, hit his chest and, looking alarmed, begin to pull out the cotton between his lips, revealing ten razor blades hanging from the long thread, like a washing line. He often cut his mouth with the pre-threaded blades there all evening so I told him to drop the trick.

'Drop the trick? Audiences love it. I do it for them, not for me.'

I knew what he meant.

I never once got a decent night's sleep at Rossli. Every night I would be woken by men knocking on my door. I'd hear footsteps creak by, pause, then try me again. The regulars soon cottoned on that I wasn't that sort of girl, but one of them must have complained. One night there was a knock, then a familiar voice.

'It's Arn. Open this fucking door.'

She was standing there with a man and a bottle of champagne.

'This gentleman is a very good friend of the club. I've promised that you'll show him a good time.'

I watched in shock as the man put a thick roll of notes on the side. He hadn't even looked at me. What on earth was he expecting me to do? Arn looked like she would rip my arms off if I didn't move but I was frozen. Could I do this? I wondered. *He's dark, not too bad.* But could I do it just for the money to keep this horrible woman off my back?

I looked at his impatient eyes and said, 'Sorry. You've made a mistake.'

Then I turned my back on the pair of them. He exploded with rage, which Arn had to deal with in case her other customers were concerned. I didn't turn around until they'd gone back downstairs.

By the fourth and final week I was ready to go. But where?

With days to spare I received a letter from Verles. An agent called Gavaraggio had a contract for me. In Florence! I'd never read sweeter words. Arn never said goodbye but my wages, though well under half the amount, were doled out by the barman.

To celebrate I caught the train to Zurich and checked into a luxury hotel on Bahnhofstrasse, an exclusive shopping area, where I bought a set of Loewe luggage in camel-coloured suede and a pair of pink silk pyjamas and kitten-heel slippers. I ate a four-course meal and ordered champagne (which I could still enjoy and not associate with the clubs).

I deserved this. I felt I'd been let out of hell.

The next evening, a porter showed me to my first-class sleeper carriage on the train to Italy and as I changed into my luxurious nightwear, I was happy to be leaving Switzerland.

*****

I arrived in Florence in the early morning. As I stepped off the train, I could sense the buzz of a city stirring to life. I had one week before my contract started and continued my holiday spree, booking into the Hotel Savoy. My black and white suite overlooked one of the large squares where all of Italian life seemed to play out like an opera beneath me.

A few hours later, the concierge opened the heavy glass door and I was drowned in the midday bustle, drama and aroma myself. I'd only taken a few steps when I paused, my senses assailed by the commotion and emotion in the street. The square was alive with language, history and smells that spoke directly to the soul. The Mediterranean spirit and lifestyle was untidy, unruly and totally liveable – everything the other countries lacked. *And I loved it.*

The maze of streets suddenly opened up to majestic piazzas. I was side-tracked through alleys into courtyards, overlooked by balconies adorned with plants and washing. Bazaars lined the walkways and elegant rows of exquisite shops stood beside crumbling old churches with tiny doorways. Cafés in the piazzas were swamped with people under awnings, chairs and tables spread out, as mopeds and little square cars zoomed around. The decay and beauty, the passion for style and speed, the joy of family and friends, even the gloom and tradition of the Catholic religion, couldn't stifle the zest for living.

The view from the park of the River Arno and Ponte Vecchio bridge at sundown was magnificent, as if the city were ablaze. The red tiled roofs turned to smouldering rose in the last rays as I sat and stared, brimming with emotions and appreciation. Over the next weeks I would discover and take immense pleasure in art, artefacts and architecture and this is where it started. I remember the exact moment.

I felt like a millionaire dealing with the hundreds and thousands of lire spilling out of my purse and I shopped like one too. I bought silk scarves for Gran, silk dresses from Bellini's for myself and the softest leather bag for Mum. The shade of plum was just her style, I thought. And it was from Florence!

On my third evening I was walking back to my hotel when I paused by a supermarket window. I glanced to my right and, sure enough, saw a young man with a mop of hair, sideburns and beard look quickly away. *He's following me.* I panicked and darted into the shop. When I emerged ten minutes later he was still there. But the expression on his face didn't seem threatening at all. I scanned the packed streets. There were no police in sight.

There was only one thing for it. 'What the hell do you think you're doing?'

From his shocked reaction I knew immediately my shadow hadn't any evil intentions. He was an intense-looking student with dark brown eyes and a sort of mediaeval look, like a painting in the Uffizi. He was horrified at my conclusion about him.

'You are so beautiful, I just wanted to sketch you,' he explained in broken English.

Well, what could I say to that?

Gianni was a delight, yet serious and intelligent. He immediately took me to a café and introduced me to a creative clan of writers and photographers all pursuing the same artistic dreams. But I also saw a side to him which, I later realised, characterised Italian men. We dined at the best restaurant in the city later that week, as a treat for him and company for me, and afterwards he escorted me not to my hotel but to his flat – for sex.

'I'm sorry, Gianni, but I don't want to sleep with you – not yet.'

'But you allowed me to buy you dinner. What game are you playing?'

In actual fact, I had paid for dinner. But, as I soon learned, a response from a woman in any way was seen by young men as an invitation. We parted that night and I never saw him again.

For all their flowing compliments and romance, it took time to find a meaningful relationship with an Italian.

The next day I finally met Gavaraggio. He was a towering, heavily-built man, pale and brown-haired, in contrast to the short, dark, typical Italian. His office was a shambles but he found my contract and escorted me personally to my new employer. He chatted freely but had a warning.

'They like consummation here.'

I cringed – he'd obviously heard my reputation as a poor saleswoman as well.

'But they adore good acts. Hopefully you'll be fine.'

Hopefully? Flashbacks of Madame Arn flooded my mind as we stopped outside the Liberty nightclub. It was decorated with Tiffany glass and had quotes on the board outside. "Elite in name, elite in place" said one. "The marvellous furnishings, the shows, the disco and management by Valerio and Livio, make Liberty the princely nightclub of the city" said another. Five minutes later I was sitting opposite Valerio and Livio and composing my own reviews. They were stony-faced, sallow and humourless, and never met my gaze. Direct contact from anyone seemed an affront. I think if they could have spoken only to Gavaraggio they would have done.

This would sum up future work in Italy – sumptuous nightclubs but some of the most cold, cruel bosses I would ever encounter.

Tiffany's show offered a female magician and a solo dance attraction and I'd perform my dance spot four times, throughout the night.

When I returned to the club at eight o'clock I was shocked by the number of girls milling around, forty in all – with twenty-six from Poland. The dressing room was full of gowns and I learned there was some racket going on with hordes of European hostesses passing through, borrowing the dresses for a week, then being replaced by a new crowd.

They were pretty girls but it was one of the slim Italian hostesses who stood out. A Kim Novak look-alike, she had dyed her hair white and in the ultraviolet club lights it glowed an eerie shade of green. The effect was startling. Customers were mesmerised, like moths to a flame, and she was busy all evening.

I was pleased to have my own dressing-table but the performance space left a lot to be desired. There was no elevated stage. I'd initially been so nervous of dancing on podiums but I'd grown to love the authority they gave. I was literally on a pedestal for ten or more minutes – but not at Liberty's.

I made my way through to the dancing area and waited nervously for the DJ to hit the "play" button. First night in any club is always fraught with butterflies in the stomach: that never changes. But this seemed matter-of-fact, with no curtains or black out. Anyway, I dived into my improvised moves. Now I was in my element. After a week off, I was back doing what I did best.

But something was different. Normally I tune out and let my body take over. But something definitely wasn't right. I let my mind wander.

They're not looking at me. They can't even see me.

Between me and the seated audience, were a bunch of revellers doing their own disco moves, as I was pushed into the corner. I was on the same level as the customers and, despite being flamboyantly dressed and topless, I may as well have been invisible.

What on earth am I doing? The only people who could see me don't even know I'm here.

I continued dancing but it was hard. Every lunge, flick and toss of my head seemed strained, artificial and ultimately pointless. I couldn't wait for the music to stop.

Is this the best I can do?

I was miserable as I sat in a side-booth near the bar afterwards. I didn't care about the consummation and none of the waiters bothered me as I was tucked out of the way. I watched enviously as the stage was cleared for the main acts. The magician's show was amateur and at the end, she took off her cloak, to stand topless. It didn't work. But at least everyone could see her. I felt a glow pass over me as my spirits rose. A plan was forming in my mind. When the main attraction took the stage it crystallised.

Mayling, from Korea, was a glossy, raven-haired beauty with perfect skin and teeth. She wore a white chiffon dress, edged with ostrich feathers, that caught the breeze and she danced like Ginger Rogers to a Frank Sinatra song, polished and elegant. With such style, looks and personality, edited music and gorgeous costumes, she had the complete package. In fact, I thought, she was too good for this disco. She should be headlining on a proper cabaret stage. *And,* I finally admitted to myself, *so should I.*

As I ran through the motions, ignored again, during my next spot I was convinced it was time. *I need to upgrade to main attraction.* I was getting stale. I craved the discipline of a choreographed routine and, more importantly, the respect of higher billing. Jambières and improvisation had taken me as far as I could go.

Mayling turned out to be as incredible a friend as she was a performer, but beneath the stage confidence was a fragile girl, a naïve dancer propelled into an unsavoury world in search of her dream. She was more like me than I cared to admit. If I'd seen on my own face the stresses I saw on hers when we were alone, wrought by touring the world as a solo attraction, then perhaps I would have stopped. But I had a drive, just like her, to perform. I craved an audience and the opportunity. Everything else would have to work itself out.

Mayling was halfway through a one-year contract and miserable. She was born to perform but she hadn't the confidence to be proud of it outside the club, for in Italy, "dancer", unlike in France, meant "prostitute" to most people. She was only working in Italy because her fiancé lived in Fiesole. His family, she said, would be horrified by her profession. In fact, even her landlord had no idea.

When I moved into a room in the same pensione she warned, 'Tell him you're a teacher – anything but a dancer.'

I paid a week in advance as demanded by the greasy-haired, mean-looking man in creased mustard trousers with a paunch. An hour later, as I laid out my costumes on the bed, my door swung open. Standing there, open-mouthed, was my landlord. Staring at the g-strings he yelled, 'No whores! Out! Out! This is a respectable place. No night girls!'

He gave me a minute to throw my things together then literally frogmarched me out of the building.

I was furious. 'What about my rent?'

'No rent for whores!' he shouted and slammed the door. He must have been spying on me to know what my work involved.

Humiliated but relieved, I settled into a delightful pensione that had advertised a room, near the Savoy. Full of aspidistras and lace doilies, it was run by the charming Mr Mario, who played opera on his old turntable and loved to cook spaghetti for all his guests. A gigantic dish would be placed in the middle of his table, dripping with herbs and tomatoes, accompanied by chunks of bread and Chianti.

'Help yourself'.

Much chatter and laughter would ensue and at the end we would return to our rooms spattered with sauce but sleepy and content. What a stark contrast between the two ways of existing, the different ways of being treated.

I once again shuddered at Mayling's life. How had she surrounded herself with people who made her despise her own life? I determined never to let that happen to me. But it was easier said than done. There were dangers when I least expected them.

Two nights later, sitting in the dressing room, I heard footsteps in the corridor and saw Mayling burst in, out of breath and trying to drag me up.

'What's wrong?' I asked.

'Hide,' she panted. 'In there.'

She pushed me towards the large laundry baskets at the side of the room. Unnerved by my friend's terrified expression I did as I was told. I folded myself into the wicker crate and saw her do the same. Two other girls threw themselves out the window.

What the hell is going on?

A minute later I heard more footsteps. These were heavy and hurried. The door burst open and loud, angry Italian voices filled the room. Peering through the slits in my pine prison I could make out expensive shoes, trousers and a tie. And there was something else beneath the jacket of one of them. Carefully I shifted my weight and strained to see through a lower gap.

It's a gun!

After that I closed my eyes and held my breath. Above angry voices I heard make-up boxes hit the floor and chairs kicked over. But then the sound of footsteps retreated from the room. Only when the door slammed did I let out a huge sigh of relief, but I stayed immobile, petrified.

Suddenly the lid was being lifted from my crate. Mayling's beautiful but terrified face was looking down. She was alone, but for how long?

'Who were they?' I asked, still not moving.

'Mafia,' she said quietly. 'Looking for payment.'

'In here?'

'They're happy to take girls instead of lire. But we never see them again.'

I shouldn't have been so astonished. Liberty was a strange club. It was usually half empty but apart from the young couples who would come for a snack and a dance there was another scene, groups of mysterious men, in dark suits, wearing lots of gold. I'd seen them bent over tables in hushed conversation. And now I knew who they were.

I made sure to keep my distance that evening but I had another problem. Livio and Valerio hated my attitude to consummation. I was performing the best I could but it meant nothing to them if I didn't equal the payment in bubbly. But that night Livio had a proposition.

'There's a television company coming here tomorrow. They want to expose the club as a brothel. We want you to talk to them.'

Defend this club? Why would I do that?

'If you don't want to, I think you should leave.'

They still owed me two week's wages and I got the distinct impression I'd be leaving without it. So I agreed.

The female interviewer, who spoke good English, arrived with the preconception that all dancers were prostitutes. Considering the attitudes of most of the Italian men I'd met so far, I wasn't surprised. Yet when she started attacking me I wouldn't be bullied.

'I'm a topless dancer, not a courtesan,' I said gently. 'If you have a beautiful body there's no shame in showing it off.'

'But aren't you just being exploited for men's titillation?'

'Would you say the Venus de Milo is titillation? No one objects to female nudity in art. Watch our shows. Dancing is just sculpture in motion. No one is being sexual, no one is simulating anything unpleasant. We train hard and we work hard to be as beautiful as we possibly can.'

All the arguments from Mrs Henderson's Windmill flowed out. By the end of the interview Liberty had a new convert and she stayed until the end. I didn't see the broadcast but Livio actually congratulated me and I managed to see out the rest of my contract without another word about consummation.

But Mayling's plight was beyond my control.

She staggered into the dressing room one night, sobbing uncontrollably, her eyelashes peeling off, revealing small eyes that wiped away the mature, sophisticated lady, to look more like a twelve-year-old Asian child.

"Help me", she drawled. "They put something in my drink. They want me to go with that awful man and I can't".

The awful man wore a white suit and sat with the bosses, arranging some deal. The DJ quickly manoeuvred Kim Novak to replace Mayling. The bosses were furious but they saw that Mayling was out of control. The DJ exchanged strong words with them. He was an essential go–between and they knew it. I helped walk Mayling home. I didn't care anymore, only for Mayling.

As I walked back to the club, distressed but determined to finish my last show, I passed a notorious street corner where ravishing transvestites waited for business. One of the 'women' smiled, softly, in recognition of a fellow artiste or perhaps catching my thoughts. I managed to smile back, a moment of kinship in this mad world of the night.

It was sad saying goodbye to Mayling and Mr Mario but I was anxious to get away. Mayling had opened my eyes to my own future. I made myself the solemn vow that I would never go-go dance again.

From now on it's main attraction or nothing.

I just needed somewhere to train and create the next, arduous step-up in my career. Where was the best place to do that? I wondered.

A second later all was clear and I smiled. If I'd had a pair of ruby slippers I would have clicked them together because the answer was staring me in the face.

There's no place like home.

CHAPTER ELEVEN

THIS IS GOODBYE

It wasn't my plan to be a striptease artiste. I stepped into the role to be able to dance as a solo act and remain employed. In any case, I never considered myself to be a straightforward "striptease" because I didn't "tease". If anything, I called myself a nude dancer. Other people, however, had a problem with this. 'Who are you fooling?' one old family friend asked me and I'm sure others thought it. But once people saw my show they took a different view. I got used to hearing two comments in particular: 'I didn't realise you were so good' was one. The other was: 'I didn't even notice you were naked.' I took the latter as a compliment!

As proud as I was of the work I'd done so far, the initial responses to my profession were generally looks of baffled wonderment, distaste or embarrassment. Worldly folk thought it intriguing and brave; friends' fathers thought it saucy and their wives felt sorry for me – although one, memorably, confided later, 'I would love to have done what you're doing!'

I flew back from Florence as nervous as any smuggler. It was only at the departure gate that I realised I had too much lire to carry out of the country legally. It was too late to wire it home – or spend it – so I did the next best thing. I stuffed the wads of notes into my bra and walked through, heart beating wildly.

It was great to be back at Number 10 with Mum and all my old friends, but I had a month until Christmas and I intended to use that time wisely. I contacted Verles and said, 'I'm stepping up to main attraction. Will you be able to find me work?'

'More than ever!' his secretary declared. 'As a go-go dancer you are restricted but as an attraction show we have contracts world wide".

That was great to hear and a real boost. But now I had to justify her faith. I needed to develop an act and for that I really had to knuckle down.

During my ballet school days The Dance Centre in Covent Garden was the only studio in WC2, with its warren of rooms and a café for dancers to meet in. By the end of 1980 it had been modernised and had lost a lot of its cosiness. Certainly the people using the facilities seemed less friendly. The cheapest studio was the smallest, on the top floor, but as I wended my way through the queues of girls waiting in corridors to audition or attend classes, I could sense the icy competitiveness that the building seemed to create now. Even the changing rooms had an air of intense silence. There was nothing of the camaraderie of true dressing rooms. Maybe when these young girls tasted success they would mellow.

Young girls! I wasn't even twenty-one myself but I felt like an old dame of cabaret. I'd seen so much in my few short professional years.

Armed with a tape player, notes and water, I settled into the studio and stared at myself in the mirror. All the tools of my profession were right there in front of me. Now I just needed to make them work.

Pushing my body, I experimented with creating beautiful shapes and remembering TV, film and stage shows. I found it easier than I'd thought to choreograph. Musicals were a great inspiration. *The Pirate* with Gene Kelly, my hero and dancing genius. "Talent makes you insecure" was one of his well-realized quotes. Juliet Prowse in *Can Can*, dance numbers from *Seven Brides For Seven Brothers* and *Singing In The Rain* all gave me ideas for my new routines. I aspired to become Cyd Charisse in *Silk Stockings* and, ultimately, Ann Reinking in the 1979 movie, *All That Jazz*. And this was my opportunity.

Every day I trudged into the studio, pushing wordlessly past the curious queues downstairs. I didn't feel one of them at all. I'd seen auditions at their worst – one of my friends from the Windmill had won a part in the musical *Piccadilly*, just because she fitted the costume they'd already made! Producers always know what they're looking for and the odds of you fitting that bill are slim to none. But if you can survive the audition process you can survive in the business. Like me.

I must have cut a solitary figure, rehearsing alone every day, calling out to myself, marking time, counting intros, all the while staring into the mirror. I learned to let the music lead the choreography. I didn't count the beats, just listened to the sounds – a twist in the chords, the highs and lows – and responded. As soon as I had a dozen steps in place I'd jot them down, rewind the tape and repeat until perfect. It was a lonely few hours and of course there were moments of despair. *Am I really up to this? Who'd pay to see me when I can't even remember my own dance?* Endless run-throughs, stale through repetition, were occasionally lit up by the introduction of a new, unusual move and in those moments my confidence would return and I felt as if in the company of an invisible audience.

Sometimes there *was* a real audience. Mum popped by whenever she could, partly to chat, partly to report back to Gran. But occasionally I would look up and see familiar faces from downstairs peering in, which filled me with immeasurable pride. If I could entertain those hard-faced hoofers I stood a chance in cabarets around the world!

The choices for dancers in Britain fell into West End theatre, summer seasons, pantomimes and TV – but only if you were part of a group or production. The one thing I was most certain of was that I wanted to work alone: and to get contracts as a soloist I would have to return abroad.

I knew I could earn a living as a main attraction if I could just get the right ingredients in the act. I needed power, technique, emotion and colour. I wanted to leave my audience with goose bumps.

But most importantly I needed to be different and skilled. I wanted to be booked without the threat of consummation, on the strength of my show alone.

Everything was coming together. I decided on three acts, three colours – black, red, blue – and three pieces of music – funky, Latin and instrumental in the form of Isaac Hayes' *Tequila, Chi Mai* (the TV theme for *The Life Of Lloyd George*) plus other musical inserts and an intro and exit from *Saturday Night Fever*. Now I just needed my costumes, and for these I turned to an advert in *The Stage* for Florence Foley, who worked out of her converted greenhouse in the suburbs.

She listened expertly to my parameters. I needed to be able to become topless quickly, if necessary, but without appearing to undress like a stripper, and the timeless fashions of *Star Trek* were my unlikely inspiration. With Florence's ingenious ideas, we came up with striking designs which enabled me to dance fully-costumed or topless. For the disco number I wore a silver leotard with trousers split to the knees. They unzipped all the way down one side enabling me simply to let them drop and step out. The leotard was high cut, shaped like an hourglass and from behind it looked as if I was naked, with a flesh-coloured elastic g-string and shoulder straps. No tea dye in sight! This peeled off in a second to reveal just the g-string for topless work. The Latin costume was a clash of red-, pink- and orange-layered satin frills on a waistband that was open at the front with a bolero jacket and a rose for the hair. For the ballet number, a pale blue Grecian toga with diamanté, that unzipped one side to reveal a bikini underneath plus a small silver headdress. I paid just £70 for all three costumes.

I cut up a tough plastic bag, to sew strips in the g-strings, so that sweat and any discharge could be wiped clean. Often nerves and exertion could cause a leak and it wasn't healthy to always insert a tampon. Costumes were aired but rarely washed except by specialist cleaners. A standard joke was that you could smell an artiste arriving before you saw them!

I ordered my shoes once again from Freed, the shop where I'd originally bought my kit for Brooking's. Standard cabaret shoes were silver with two-and-a-half inch heels, open toes and a diamanté T-strap. I had them rubber-soled and trimmed the tips down myself, so I could grip the floor with my toes. They needed to be elegant but tough, as leaping into front or side splits, the inner heels would take the force and the slide.

Turning up at The Dance Centre laden with my costume bags caused more of a stir. Changing into the diamanté numbers raised a few eyebrows as no other groups would rehearse in full costume until they were at their entertainment venue, under the lights.

Rehearsing in full stage garb was completely different from rehearsing in a leotard and more restrictive. I quickly found myself adjusting the timing. I had to slow the pace down, make it easier for myself. *Come on*, I encouraged myself. *You can't fill every beat with movement. Sometimes standing still can be very dramatic.*

I discussed with Mum the idea of giving my new act a stage name and she laughed. 'You've already got one! If Tessa Skola isn't a catchy name then I don't know what is. Just be grateful you're not called Doreen like me.'

She had a point. "Tessa Skola" has a ring to it and I knew I'd never find anyone else with the same name! I'd already seen it on posters in Switzerland and, yes, it did look like a proper star's billing.

With Christmas approaching, I hurried to get the last details done. Sarah at Island Records in Chiswick edited all my music onto a reel-to-reel, splicing the different pieces together. Henna-haired and pierced, she was enthusiastic and patient and when we needed a voiceover for the intro she called in the technician from next door who recorded it in one take: 'Ladies and Gentleman, please welcome a dancer of stage, screen and television, Miss Tessa Skola'. It had to be long enough to allow me to take position and dramatic enough to give an exhilarating build-up for the audience. As I heard him say the words for the first time I felt goose bumps up my arms. I couldn't wait to hear it played over a club's PA system for real.

Next I had black-and-white nude shots taken, to show my physique to full effect, but without exposing anything, and colour shots of the Latin number. I then typed a new CV. The list of venues I'd appeared at looked impressive – although each one had its own horror story. Finally I was ready for work.

Verles still hadn't sent a contract through so I looked for other agents. James and Jackie Russell worked from their home in Earls Court. They seemed an ordinary, relaxed couple, but Jackie turned out to be a petite, dark, striptease artist while her husband was a towering Canadian and professional compère. After a look at my pictures and CV Jackie smiled. 'I think I can guarantee that worldwide venues will be queuing up to have you".

After handing over my passport details and other information I asked to use the bathroom.

'Just upstairs,' James said.

Still on top of the world, I skipped up the stairs and ran into the bathroom. As I turned to close the door I saw something move out of the corner of my eye.

Two huge snakes were sliding around in the bath!

I screamed and fled. Jackie was racing up the stairs but I couldn't help noticing she was laughing.

'I'm sorry, love, they're from my act. James should have told you to use the hall loo.'

After I'd caught my breath, I laughed as well. I knew as I left that I was in good hands with these two.

Just before Christmas I heard from Verles. I raced squealing with excitement through Number 10.

'Mum! Mum! Guess where my next contract is?'

'Not Switzerland again, is it?'

'No, of course not. I'm going to the Seychelles!'

Verles had promised me the world and he was living up to his word.

I couldn't have been happier as Mum and I caught the train to Cornwall on Christmas Eve. I was bursting to tell Gran about my big break and when I did she was as supportive as I'd imagined.

'You've worked hard enough, Tess. You deserve this. Think of that lovely weather while we're freezing over here!'

It wasn't just the weather that excited me. The chance to prove myself on the international stage as an attraction was thrilling and intimidating in equal measure. I could think of little else. It took a comment from Gran, in fact, to bring me back down to earth.

'I see you're still wearing your engagement ring.' she said. 'You haven't sold it yet?'

'Oh, Gran, I don't know what to do,' I admitted. 'I don't hear from Thierry for weeks, I don't see him for months and then when he does appear I'm the happiest woman on the planet. But I can't live like this, can I?'

'I wouldn't have thought so, darling. But I do know that if he couldn't keep up with you in Switzerland he'll have a hard time finding you in the Seychelles!'

It was true. My passion for travel and the need to dance were the two most important factors in all my decisions. That's why I kept going in the face of so many hardships. I'd been honest with myself all along, hadn't I? If Thierry meant enough to me I would have already given up everything to be with him. Wouldn't I?

It wasn't that I didn't want to think about it – but my forthcoming trip filled my mind. Christmas calls from The Paper Dolls and friends from the Windmill further convinced me that my future happiness lay on stage. By the time Mum and I caught the train back to London after New Year I thought I was going to burst with excitement.

1981 is going to be my year, I thought. *With or without Thierry.*

*****

The itinerary for the Seychelles was complicated but that, in a way, just heightened the excitement. I needed travel injections at the British Airways clinic then a ticket to Paris Charles De Gaulle where I would transfer to Orly for the nine o'clock flight to Reunion Island. I was so happy I think I could have flown there without a plane, but when I joined the queue at Orly my hopes came crashing down.

'I'm afraid your suitcases are overweight,' a check-in steward said. 'There's an excess to pay of one hundred pounds.'

A hundred pounds? The contents probably weren't worth that. I didn't have more than a twenty pound note to my name and wouldn't until I'd got my first pay cheque.

'I haven't got the money. Can I leave some things here?'

'If that's what you want to do. There's a bin over there.'

I started going through my cases. Books and toiletries were the heaviest things so, with reluctance, I threw them out and dragged my luggage back to be weighed.

'I'm sorry, it's still over. You have five minutes before this desk is closed.'

Five minutes?

'Please, you have to help me. I need this flight.'

'I'm sorry, madame, there are no exceptions.'

I stared again at my belongings. I'd chucked everything apart from costumes, a few clothes, shoes and photographs. There was no way I could part with any of those. I felt the tears welling up and even though I was dressed in my finest travel outfit, I didn't fight them. What was the point? I felt like my world was ending.

Well, there goes my career, I thought as the gate officially closed. *What a joke that was.*

It was about twenty minutes before I'd recovered enough to face anyone again. When I did, I realised my situation was about to get worse.

'If I can't go to Reunion Island then I have to get home,' I said. 'How much is a ticket to London?'

'Sixty pounds.'

'Sixty? I only paid thirty to come here.'

'You probably booked in advance. If you want a flight today, that is the price.'

I slumped down against the counter. Not only couldn't I afford to go to my contract in the Seychelles but I couldn't even get home. I was stuck at Orly airport.

My faith in human nature had taken some knocks during a few recent contracts but even amongst the worst moments, I always met someone who made it all worthwhile. And that, believe it or not, happened to me again that day. Out of nowhere, it seemed, a man with a windswept face and a ponytail knelt down next to me and said words I'll never forget.

'How much do you need for your ticket back home?'

I couldn't believe what he was hearing.

I'm afraid I was suspicious. 'Why would you give me money?' I'd met enough men in Europe with ulterior motives.

For a second he looked shocked. But then his face broke into a smile and he said, 'I'm from Reunion myself and am just helping a fellow traveller get home.'

He gave me fifty pounds which, with my twenty, was enough for the ticket and onward journey. I couldn't think how to thank him so I just threw my arms around him and hugged him for all I was worth. I took his address and promised to reimburse him as soon as I could. Then with a renewed enthusiasm I ran for my bus to Charles De Gaulle. When I staggered into Number 10 I think Mum thought she was seeing a ghost. And I must have looked like one. I'd been up for thirty-six hours.

'I'll explain it to you later,' I promised and fell, fully-clothed, onto my bed. The last thing I remember are the tears. I'd blown it. I'd blown my big chance. And it was all my own fault.

Making the call to Verles the next day was one of the hardest things to do. Mum stood next to me to make sure I went through with it.

'There's no point. They won't hire me again.'

'Come on, don't be silly. Just explain.'

So I did – and Mum was right. They were annoyed but understood.

'These things happen, Tessa. We'll have something for you again in a few weeks.'

It had been instilled in me that a contract had to be honoured. If it was tough, one just had to see it through and get on with it – as a true professional. No ifs or buts. Though in all the years of travel, I never missed a flight again or lost a piece of luggage.

Relieved to have got away with letting Verles down, I spent the rest of the day streamlining my luggage and even investing in a new soft, lightweight case. I wouldn't be caught out like that again. I had to borrow the money from Mum – so I desperately needed work. Fortunately the Russells had a project.

'Have you ever been to Finland?' Jackie asked.

'No, but I'd like to.'

'Well, a couple of things you need to know. The good news is there's no consummation.'

'Thank God for that. And what's the bad news?'

'You might not think it's bad news, but they want full nudity. At the last minute, just take your bikini off and pose.'

*****

I never thought I'd meet more unlikely-looking cabaret industry workers than Mr and Mrs Weiss at Germany's Black Bottom. But the woman who introduced herself to me in Turku as my Finnish agent was more Mrs Doubtfire than Miss Whiplash. Wrapped up tight in her fur coat, hat and boots, she was like a doting aunt but incredibly efficient and very supportive. After she'd settled me into the hotel where I would be staying and performing, she said, 'Well, good luck, dear. Make full use of all the rehearsal time. I look forward to seeing your show when you get to Helsinki.'

My show! The words were music to my ears. After so many performances as a support artiste – or, at worst, background entertainment – I was thrilled to be the main attraction at last. I wasn't just filling in space. I had been booked for what I could do. I felt the pressure rise in my stomach but I didn't mind. I'd dreamed of this moment and when the time came I was sure I could deliver.

The Rantasipi Hotel, part of a countrywide chain, was a warm, log cabin-style complex. It was also, without doubt, the best accommodation I'd ever had. If this is how solo attractions lived then I could definitely get used to it. I had a smart guest bedroom and full use of the restaurant, sauna and pool. When I thought back to my weeks of having to check if anyone was using the shower before I could step into my bedroom, I wanted to laugh.

The disco club in the hotel had tiered seating, excellent lighting but a slippery floor. Two out of three, but I knew I'd have to be careful.

After a run-through with the DJ I retired back to my room to prepare. When I returned to do it all for real two hours later I thought I'd walked into a silent movie. If Doris had been unexpected, the veneer of respectability that covered the audience was shocking. Middle-aged couples, pensioners and even children packed the auditorium. Was I really going to dance nude for this crowd?

The lights dimmed and my *Saturday Night Fever* introduction rang out. By the time the voiceover announced my name I was on stage and in position to start – to absolute silence. As I whirled, kicked and leapt my way through *Tequila* I counted down to the moment of revelation. Then it was time. Facing stage back, I slipped my hand under the hooks and eyes sewn into my g-string and yanked. Then I turned round, smile beaming, in a presentation pose to finish – completely naked.

You could have heard a pin drop.

Oh God, I've gone too far!

A sea of pale, blond faces stared up at me, all smiling but utterly controlled. I think if one person had clapped they all would have. The whole room seemed to suffer from chronic shyness.

But they weren't the ones who were naked!

I held the pose for about five seconds but it felt like five minutes. Then as my exit music played I grabbed my costumes and exited as fast but as gracefully as I could on the slippery floor.

I was in shock in the dressing room afterwards when the DJ came in.

'What happened there?' I asked him. 'Did I offend them?'

He laughed. 'It will take more than a beautiful woman to offend this audience.'

'But they didn't clap. Did I go too far?'

'You'll find Finnish people are very reserved. They loved you. If they hadn't, then you would definitely have heard about it.'

So – my first performance as a solo main attraction on the international circuit had been a success. Apparently! I wrote to Mum and Gran that night to let them know.

Turku, in the south-west of Finland, was a small, pretty town. But everything, in my experience, looks pretty covered in snow. The place had a civilised air if a little dull. Government-run liquor stores called Alcos seemed well frequented by the locals. There was a fish market and a few cafés, an art gallery and a church on a hill.

I made the most of my hotel's sauna, birch twig massages and cold plunge pool and the entire stay ran like clockwork. But it was lonely when no one wanted to talk and inevitably I used much of my time alone to fret about what I could do better in my show. By the time each performance came round I'd all but destroyed my confidence.

If the nightly experience at the hotel was strange, the set-up that greeted me at the Foija restaurant, where I was booked to perform at the weekend, was surreal. A square performance area was surrounded by dozens of neat tables fully prepared for afternoon tea. But what did I expect? I was due to perform, in bright daylight, at four o'clock in the afternoon.

Nervously I approached the manager. 'I don't have to take everything off here, do I?'

He clapped his hands. 'Oh yes! My customers will be very disappointed if you don't.'

For my rarefied afternoon audience I selected the more colourful and skilled Latin piece. As daylight streamed in through the windows I got changed to the accompanying hum of conversations getting louder - and the chink of china cups and plates as sandwiches and tea were served.

I'd performed in brothels and hidden in laundry baskets to escape Mafia henchmen. But somehow this scenario seemed the most unbelievable of them all.

My intro piece started and I ran on quickly to take my lunge with a downward glance, just in time. The trumpets rang out and as I threw my head up on the first beat I saw ladies – little, old ladies in neat suits and hats – smiling intently at me and sipping their tea. Aghast, I started dancing with gusto, in surprise and shock, trying to bluff that I was about to undress. *They loved it.* I moved like a graceful ballerina during the slow music, and their heads followed every movement. Then the crescendo of flicking heels and head, finishing with the g-string off, a triple spin into flying jump splits – and a full minute of rapturous applause!

What an unexpected honour. I had a lump in my throat as I put on my skirt and picked up my pieces to leave the stage. Passing through the tables, one of the smallest and most stooped of the ladies came up, kissed me on the cheek and gave me a bunch of roses. I was overwhelmed. What an extraordinary afternoon, appearing nude in front of forty Mrs Wilberforces from *The Ladykillers*.

Next I flew to Oulo for another hugely successful week, this time at the Hotel Vaakuna. I was almost in tears as I stood outside, mesmerised by my own name and picture on the entertainment billboard. Even the whiff of rotten eggs wafting over from the nearby sulphur factory couldn't spoil the mood. In fact, the realisation that here I was on the professional circuit with top acts, being treated as one myself, gave me the biggest lift of my life. I couldn't see anything ruining it for me.

And then Mum's letter arrived.

It was lovely to hear from her, of course, but it was the envelope she'd enclosed that I was most anxious to read. The handwriting on the front was recognisably Thierry's. What on earth did he want after all this time?

I tried to read each word but I was impatient to get to the point. The lines tumbled out. 'I've been sent to West Africa with the army' ... 'I haven't been fair to you' ... 'I'm sorry' ... 'I love you' ... 'Are you still there for me?'

I was floored: physically knocked back. *What does he mean 'Are you still there for me'? I've always been here. Where has he been?*

Suddenly my large room felt very claustrophobic. I needed to get out. I found a café, ordered a large coffee and thought about a reply. Drawing a pen and paper from my bag, I started writing.

My Finnish adventure continued the following week with a fortnight in Helsinki to play at the Seurahone Hotel, the oldest and most historical in the city. After the shock of hearing from my fiancé I wasn't prepared for another face from the past. But as I got chatting to the DJ setting up my show in the hotel's basement Rose Room, he said, 'You worked at the Windmill? My wife used to work there as well.'

'Really? I wonder if I've heard of her. What's her name?'

'It's Gillian.'

'Gillian? I've heard of her all right. I know her!'

A quick phone call later and my old Soho friend joined us. She was just as demure off stage as she was shapely and beautiful on it, and I was so pleased to see her unharmed by the industry.

'I can't wait to see your show, Tess. You're perfect for this country.'

I really think I was. I didn't have a single bad night. Every evening was exciting, there were full audiences in classy settings and I was being treated like a star! When Doris, the agent, said that she was delighted and had sent a glowing report to the Russells, I felt so proud I could cry.

From Helsinki I went north to Pori, a small town in a seeming perpetual state of hibernation. My venue was a restaurant with enormous floor space where audiences would dance to "oompah" music between acts. Incongruous as it seemed, once again I was a hit. Relaxing in my more modest B&B afterwards, I realised I hadn't had a single drink since I'd arrived in the country. Even the reappearance of Thierry hadn't driven me to the bottle as it had so often done in the past. I smiled. *Even if I'd performed drunk my audiences wouldn't have minded.* Finns were renowned for their heavy drinking, hence the government's monopoly on owning the only alcoholic retailers. Drunks were seen but rarely heard. Sometimes, while performing, I'd notice a gentleman propped in the same position for the entire evening until someone removed him. In Helsinki I saw a police car roll up silently to a body curled up on a bench, put him in the back seat and lock him up overnight to recover. It was a common occurrence.

I was told there was a Finnish saying about the good things in life; 'Sauna, sex and Salbiac' (like Victory V pastilles) that summed up the mentality, but it missed out the alcohol!

My last booking was at another Rantasipi, this time in a woodland setting. The snow was two feet deep and the trees burdened with fresh falls, but as the automatic hotel doors opened, the scene was chaotic, noisy and tropically hot. I had to change immediately for a show in the foyer to welcome a coachload of new arrivals. Quite what the travel-weary newcomers thought about being greeted by a topless Latin dancer in the doorway I don't know. I was just grateful that full nudity wasn't required.

And happily, it was my first booking with another attraction on the bill, a duo, Hugo and Barbara, from Majorca. They had the most magnificent costumes and props and offered advice on making my shows bigger but after the recent luggage fiasco, I couldn't afford extra weight or freight.

What they did give me was support and encouragement, which I constantly needed; it was difficult propping myself up all the time.

I was quite sad to leave Finland but Doris promised she would have me back anytime. I arrived home to a pile of contract offers from Verles and the Russells. For the first time in my life, I had choices.

I also arrived to a phone call from Thierry. He'd received my letter and risen to my challenge of calling at that exact time.

Perhaps he really has changed?

He rang me every day at the same time, always promising that we would be together forever as soon as his army commission finished in a year-and-a-half. It seemed like such a long time. But I said 'I will wait for you.'

After the restrictions of Finland I rushed around London, seeing everything with new eyes. Why hadn't I been so happy to return before? I realised it was because I had felt like I had a point to prove abroad. But now my career was at a new level I could take my time at home and stop for breath at last.

Sifting through my contract offers, I came across one in Senegal, West Africa. I couldn't wait to tell Thierry.

'If I take it, do you think you'd be able to get away to see me?'

'Of course! Would you do that? Would you come all this way?'

He knew full well I would. When we spoke again he had a new plan. He'd spoken to his commander. For two hundred pounds he could buy his way out of the final year of his army contract. By the time I finished in Dakar he would be free to return with me and open a practice in Britanny. There was only one snag: he didn't have two hundred pounds, and neither did I.

My mother, of course, saved the day as usual, although I noticed she was surprisingly dubious at the time.

'Are you sure you want to do this?' she asked, yet again, as I sealed the money she'd lent me into a registered post envelope. 'Are you positive Thierry means this much to you?'

'Mum, he means everything to me.'

I finalised my travel plans with Verles and worked hard on new choreography and traipsed around the theatrical accessories stores; Ellis & Farrier for diamanté, Borovicks in Soho for feathers, Mr Gandolphi's ballet wear shop on Marylebone Road for Lycra outfits and theatrical make-up stocks from Charles Fox in Covent Garden. Everything was coming together with the wise tips from Hugo and Barbara to "up" the glamour. I was flying to Dakar, I would meet Thierry there, and somehow, at long last, we would live happily ever after.

The day before I was due to leave Thierry rang at his usual time. I could barely pick up the phone for nervous excitement.

'Thierry!' I cried. 'This time tomorrow we'll be together!'

There was silence on the end of the phone.

'Thierry? Are you there?'

'Yes, I'm here. I received the money this morning and I've bought my freedom from the army.'

'That's brilliant!' But I could tell there was something on his mind. I wasn't prepared for what it was.

'This is goodbye, Tessa,' he said coldly. 'Forever.'

CHAPTER TWELVE

HELLO PARIS

I always like to make an entrance but the walk towards the large, tinted doors at Dakar airport filled me with dread. It was a hot, dry afternoon – as far from the weather in Helsinki as possible. But temperature was not the only reason for my malaise. Once I'd pushed my luggage through that door I would be in Africa - on my own.

The heat and disorder swamped me as I pushed through crowds of Senegalese of all heights and shades of black, in widely-assorted garb. I seemed to be the only person who noticed the chickens running around the straw-covered floor. I was the only one the nagging scouts were trying to manhandle suitcases from for a hefty tip. And, I realised as I scanned forlornly for any sign of my contact, Madame Esther, I was the only white female in the area. I'd stood out enough in Finland for not being blonde. Now everyone seemed to be staring.

I picked the least dilapidated taxi and asked for the Le Brummel club. The driver smiled and told me the meter wasn't working. I knew how this would end - with a huge bill - but I was tired and I gambled on the fact that he would at least get me there. We drove slowly towards Dakar, picking our way through the weaving traffic throwing up dust. Old buses with boys clinging to the roof racks and standing on the mud-guards rattled by, while children ran naked and women carried everything on their heads, walking slowly with straight necks and a rhythmic sashay. It didn't seem that anybody was getting anywhere fast.

A few miles outside the city centre, along a quiet dirt road leading towards the edge of the desert, the cab slowed.

'Le Brummel,' the driver said.

Before us stood a castle of sand-coloured stone guarded by four young men sitting on turrets. They stared at me with something between curiosity and contempt, then one unlocked the small door cut into tall gates which opened onto the drive.

I was met by Madame Esther, one of the owners. She started by apologising for not picking me up. Apparently she'd sent a waiter to the airport but he hadn't been able to spot me – the most distinctive person in the whole city! Either her man was lying or she was, I realised. *I hope this isn't a sign of things to come.*

I was to live on the ground floor, behind the club – the only artiste with this privilege, I learned. My room adjoined the dressing room, so I had a key for both doors. There were no kitchen facilities but a local chef lived in a hut on the grounds and would cook lunch and dinner on a gas burner.

It was too hot to unpack properly so I went to look over the performance area. The club had a long bar and generous floor space. As I marked through the show, I heard voices. Anna, a thin boyish-looking French dancer, introduced herself and Gus, the club's DJ. She, quiet and serious, had been there for a year and lived with a French professor in Dakar. Gus, on the other hand, was Lebanese, short and grizzly with curly hair and a happy disposition. And, I soon learned, he was still only eighteen years old.

I relaxed a little but halfway through a story Gus went quiet. He nodded towards the shadows and called out, 'Hello, Madame Silla. Come and meet our star turn.' Exposed, a familiar-looking woman with a sour, pale face, lipstick bleeding over her down-turned mouth and badly-bleached hair, walked slowly forward. The smell of cheap perfume on her heavy lace dress burned my nostrils but I fought the urge to flinch. She was Esther's business partner and, I could sense from the others' deference, not to be messed with. When Esther came over a few minutes later, I realised why Silla had looked familiar. She was Bette Davis to Esther's Joan Crawford, the sisters in *Whatever Happened To Baby Jane?*.

Gus did his best to promote me. 'Tessa's been sent from Verles,' he told them. 'It will be nice to have a proper show here at last.'

I blushed but welcomed the opportunity to hear a few more details.

'You dance between ten and four,' Esther explained, 'and in between you'll be expected to do your share of consummation.'

'Oh, didn't Verles tell you? I don't do that anymore.' I tried to be friendly but firm.

Baby Jane looked me up and down and smiled. 'You'll do what we tell you.' Then she added, 'I'll need your passport for the paperwork.'

I sighed with relief when they'd gone but Gus winked and said, 'You'll be all right. There are five hostesses every night and not enough clients to go round anyway. Just concentrate on your show and you'll be okay.'

It was kind of him to get involved but as I started my first performance I couldn't shift the fear that I'd made a terrible mistake. When I heard a commotion by the door and saw a group of French military come in a minute later, my anxiety increased tenfold.

Is he there? Is Thierry with them?

Heart in mouth, I desperately tried to concentrate on my movements while straining with every opportunity I got to scan the faces of the soldiers.

As soon as my applause had died down I ran towards the bar. But Thierry wasn't there and now I had half a dozen infantrymen trying to give me a kiss. What a disaster. Close to tears I retreated to my room while the soldiers turned their attention to three hostesses.

Unable to sleep that night in the oppressive heat I listened to the scuttling of cockroaches beneath my bed and stared at the open window. I'd been so stupid trusting Thierry and where had it got me? Dakar, the most western city in Africa. In a club that was depressing and smelled of sewage that wafted up from the river below and owned by people who disliked me already.

I hoped everything would seem better after a few days but, if anything, it was worse. My room looked like an assault course with every available object - magazines, a table or bottle - thrown down over a squashed cockroach. As I began one show I noticed a hostess sitting astride a customer in a dark corner. Ten minutes later, as I finished in splits, I looked beaming out to my left and saw another girl giving a blow-job under the table, right there in the front row. After the clinical cleanliness of Finland I was back in this sordid world again. I was living too close for comfort below Silla and Esther and they increased the feeling of unpleasantness. A familiar feeling of being out of control lurked at the back of my mind. As soon as my last dance was over on the Friday, I gave into it.

'A large brandy, please,' I ordered. I hadn't drunk since I'd returned to London the previous year. But I needed it now more than ever.

Thierry loomed larger in my dreams every night and I drank more and more heavily to drown him out. I was dreading my first Sunday alone. So when Gus invited me to join him at the beach, I could have kissed him. In fact, I did kiss him and by the following weekend we were lovers.

Maybe life isn't so bad. We drove through a small village above a bay with mud and straw huts and puffer fish hanging out with the washing. There was rubbish everywhere, alongside cooking utensils and the odd wooden bed frame and straw mats on the floor. I got used to seeing bodies lying by the road, catching sleep wherever they could. We passed the main port where hundreds of people queued for work outside the gates and at midday, when they'd been passed over, would settle in groups with their stoves, as if they were in their own dining room, oblivious to the passing lorries and cars.

The Senegalese were tall, slim and noble. The Mauritanians from across the border all looked like Jesus with their white robes against olive skin and their dark beards.

The Lebanese were hard-working and enjoyed their leisure time. Their sector of Dakar had a glitzy European style.

Gus and I would enjoy coffee and croissants at a French patisserie. We would buy extra pastries to hand out to the beggars who hung around the area, wheeling towards us in makeshift prams, socks over arm stumps or crawling in a mass of rags. It took me some time to get used to the poverty and the deformities people suffered.

Gus's brother lived with his wife and baby son on the top floor of a block with good views. I stayed for dinner and had never tasted anything so utterly delicious as that Lebanese meal: hummus, vine leaves, kebabs, cold potatoes and beans in oil and salad dishes of whole vegetables that we broke off as we wished. I loved eating with my hands. When I was invited to sleep over, I felt transported to another time, woken by the five o'clock call to prayer. The chant, amplified over the city in the dawn light, evoked something exotic, mysterious and ancient.

Unfortunately I couldn't return the hospitality. In fact, as soon as the Mesdames discovered my relationship with Gus, Baby Jane banned us from seeing each other.

'You've got no right,' I said.

'We'll see about that.' Whatever Silla had in mind, I was worried. At work that night I watched her make a beeline for me.

'Earn your money,' she spat, and dragged me over to a table where a wizened chap was slumped over an empty glass. He came in every night and stank so badly the hostesses had given up trying to entice him. When he saw me standing awkwardly with tears in my eyes, he seemed to come to life. Shaking his head at Baby Jane, he proffered a stool and ordered champagne.

'I know the rules,' he whispered in French as I sat down. 'Just stay here as long as you like.' I couldn't believe what I was hearing. How funny to think the person we all thought was a loser was probably the sharpest man in the club.

I still spent every day with Gus, of course, although I went to great lengths to walk along the desert track until I was out of sight of the castle before my date would pick me up. Someone must have spotted us though. When I got back one afternoon Baby Jane was waiting.

'Key, please,' she snapped.

'What key?'

'The one to the gate.' If I gave her that I'd have no route out of the compound.

'But you can't expect me to stay here all day.'

'Can't I? Let's see what other choices you've got considering I'm the one with your passport.'

How could a woman be so spiteful to another woman? That night I told Gus what had happened. The following morning, when the guards weren't looking, I managed to climb over the wall, there was no way I was going to let that hideous woman win. Or so I thought. A couple of days later I watched a workman cementing shards of glass along the top of the perimeter wall.

I couldn't get out but that didn't stop Gus from getting in. Some nights he somehow "forgot" to leave with everyone else. On other occasions he managed to sneak in past the guards by other means. I literally don't know how he did it. But I did know that if he was ever discovered, he would be fired on the spot.

Night after night I performed to an excellent response from a half-full auditorium and in between I'd be dragged by Baby Jane from customer to customer. I began to count down the days till the end of my contract but I was barely halfway through a three-month run.

At least, though, I was being paid. After every show Esther would hand over that night's wages and I would lock the cash in my beauty case, stashed beneath my wardrobe. At the last count I had five hundred pounds.

When Baby Jane disappeared to France for a few days Gus and I found ourselves with more freedom. But returning one afternoon from a day of swimming across clear but shark-filled waters, to the Isle d'Or where there was an old prison and colonial hotel, I was horrified to see my beauty box on the bed, open – and empty.

I've been robbed. All that work for nothing. All those weeks of bullying and humiliation. I looked at the door. The lock hadn't been forced which meant it had been someone with a key. And that only left Esther. Gus tried to comfort me but I was inconsolable. He ran down to the guards who woke Esther from her afternoon nap. She wasn't sympathetic.

'I can't believe you had that much money,' she sneered. 'Not with the lifestyle you lead.'

I went to fight back but Gus stepped in.

'We'll let the police decide, shall we?' he said and went to make the call. Suddenly Esther changed.

'Let's not be too hasty. Come on, if we all search the building I'm sure it will turn up somewhere, the guards would have seen anyone entering.'

She wasn't fooling any of us – but she managed to pull the wool over the eyes of the police. They asked lots of questions but in the end said there was little that could be done.

Gus and his brother even hurtled me off in their car to wasteland, miles out of the city to meet a Marabou – a wise man – who lived in a simple hut amongst a small cluster of mud buildings. His dwelling was full of interesting figurines and jars. He took my hands and looked at me with watery-brown, knowing eyes. He asked for a list of suspects and placed a branch over the paper. Suddenly the twigs snapped the note over and opening the crease, there was a line - through Esther.

I was dropped back a mile from the club. "Thank you" – I managed a smile after our fascinating trip. It was dark by now, there were no streetlights along the sandy bank, but I could make out a faint orange glow from the lanterns along the club roof and various dots of wayside fires. I heard a distant purr of a bike, otherwise the night was peaceful and I slipped into my own thoughts.

Then, from nowhere, I heard footsteps crunching on the stony road: several pairs, getting closer. Without slowing I scanned around but could make nothing out in the surrounding black expanse. Suddenly there was a rustling and a large hand clamped around my mouth. Two men each side snared my arms and others took my legs. I was dragged down onto the cool sand and smothered by bodies.

It all happened so quickly, the breath literally punched out of my lungs. I was pressed down into the grit and I felt my nostrils fill with sand. Focusing all my strength, I managed to turn my head enough to breathe freely.

I'm going to die, I realised. And I felt my body let go – almost disappear, only my head remained aware.

There were about five men crouching round me, raping me in turn; one after the other. Fuck, in – out. I didn't resist, I didn't scream. I'd switched off, resigned. And then after a timeless nothing, a dead silence, I jolted back and realized they had disappeared into the black. I hobbled back to the club. I had to get ready for the shows and though my mouth was dry, managed a shout, up to the guards, to let me in.

I stood in the shower with all my clothes on and prepared for work on automatic pilot.

There was a power cut all over town that night but the club remained open, lit by candles. Gus could hold my hand under the bar without fear of being noticed while we waited for customers. He thought I felt ill and did his best to cheer me up but I think I was hard work. A cloud had descended which just wouldn't shift and one night I begged Gus to stay with me – even though Baby Jane had returned which meant maintaining the charade of not seeing each other.

'I don't care if they find out. I don't want to be alone tonight.'

He didn't ask any questions and we fell asleep in each other's arms.

Two hours later I woke up screaming. Gus was shaking me, trying to get through to me.

'It's all right! You're all right!'

I'd been lying in a long boat floating into a dark tunnel and was about to go into a suffocating blackness. I can't remember a more vivid nightmare.

Gus had done so well, comforting me and being strong when I needed him. But then he blew it. His healing arms ceased hugging and began stroking. He misread my need for contact as desire for him.

'What are you doing?' I said, pushing his hands away from my breasts.

'Come on, Tessa. I want you.'

'I don't feel like it. Not tonight.'

He wasn't taking "no" for an answer. 'It's my right.'

The Gus who said those words was not the man I loved. I consented, after a fashion, but it was our last time. When Baby Jane fired Gus later that week I was pleased.

I'd not spoken to Mum in a month, my money had gone and I hated every minute of every day. The following morning I scaled the wall once again and spent the day eating fruit at the beach. As I watched the waves rolling in, the only thing that stopped me walking out into them, and not coming back, was knowing I'd bounced back before.

You owe it to yourself to keep fighting. Then, two days later, I was saved.

Baby Jane called me over. She looked extremely pleased with herself. 'This is Mr Hanul. You're going to work for him now.'

An extremely elegant Lebanese man smiled.

'I saw your show, Tessa. You will be perfect for my casino.'

And that was that; I was "sold" by the Mesdames. Hanul was handed my passport and agreed to pay half my wages, so with two-thirds of my contract over Esther and Silla made a profit. But I didn't care about them.

Less than an hour later I was in Mr Hanul's limousine on my way to dinner at the casino. I was shown the disco where I would perform, with under-floor lighting, heaving with French tourists, wealthy Lebanese and airline pilots and crew – a different world. Later, I was escorted to a cool, clean ensuite bedroom, my new "home". Just being there was like having the slate wiped clean. The other side of Dakar, away from the nightmare.

'The restaurant staff will serve you breakfast when you ask,' Mr Hanul said. 'Rehearsals will be at six tomorrow evening and you'll have one show a night. Sleep well.'

It was an incredible end to my African nightmare. The other acts were supportive; one, Apollo, shared their vast agency contacts list. They were a husband and wife acrobatic balancing act, who sprayed themselves with gold paint all over except for a small circle at the base of the spine.

After four months away, I eventually returned to London. There had been times in Dakar when I didn't think I'd ever get home. I stayed in bed for almost two days. I finally got out of bed on July 29th to find the whole country celebrating my upcoming twenty-first birthday – or so it seemed. Number 10 was adorned with flags and bunting from top to bottom and JRS was opening champagne all day. As we all sat down to watch the wedding of Prince Charles and Lady Diana, my mind began to wander. Part of me wanted to stay safe in London, with Mum, forever. And why not? Life at that moment seemed so happy. But another little voice was already whispering to me, 'Remember Dakar Casino, remember Finland. Remember how good it feels.'

I went to bed still confused by my own mixed emotions. But when Mum handed me a letter the next day carrying Verles' logo, my mind was made up before I'd even opened the envelope.

'I'm going to Paris!'

*****

The Moulin Rouge is still, as then, renowned for its superb dancers (mainly British) and the famous can-can routine. The top venues were considered to be the Folies Bergères, Paradis Latin and Casino de Paris but the Lido was the ultimate for glamorous showgirls. "Showgirls" referred to trained dancers, like the Bluebell girls, who were hand-picked for their minimum height of five feet, ten inches and the long legs and elegant carriage required for parading the enormous and expensive costumes.

By coincidence, Verles had offered me a year's contract at the Crazy Horse, one of the leading clubs in Paris, an all-nude show like Raymond's. But that was not why I had gone to the French capital. I didn't want to commit to a year anywhere. Instead, armed with Apollo's list and carrying my costumes, music and CV, I knocked on every door of every agent, around thirty in all. I also introduced myself at the clubs around Pigalle as well as at the cabaret clubs advertised in the tourist brochures. It was exhausting.

On the fourth day I left my costumes behind as instructed by the agent I was meeting. As soon as I walked into their offices, I discovered why.

'Show me your breasts please,' a woman said, very matter-of-factly.

I lifted my top and tried not to squirm as this middle-aged lady walked around me, taking in every inch of my body. I'd been warned about the French obsession; only girls with not too large, perfectly-shaped, pert bosoms would be accepted for topless work, whether it was the Lido or a strip club.

They didn't want to see some dance moves or publicity.

'Congratulations,' she said at last. 'Very good breasts.'

I was accepted onto the books of four agents and offered club-to-club shows around Pigalle for £5 a spot, plus a venue similar to the Crazy Horse with a choreographed show. I said I'd let them know. I'd turned down Verles' offer because I didn't want to be tied down for twelve months. On the other hand, I was hoping for better offers than these. But it was still early days.

The last office I visited, on the Champs-Elysées, was that of Roland Bertin, one of the few male agents. He was straight-talking, capable and calm. He liked my publicity and considered what to do with me.

'I'm afraid you're too short to appear at the Lido, but there are opportunities to travel with ex-Lido dancers, as part of a show. Would you be interested in that if you could perform your own act as well?'

Bertin was friendly and persuasive. But did I want to travel in a group, even one so expertly qualified?

'It's for five months,' he continued, 'near Tokyo, on an Equity contract.'

I was sold. Japan was renowned for being obsessed with putting on the best Paris-style shows. Most acclaimed dancers had a string of Far East contracts under their belt – I'd never heard of anyone having a bad time working there with a top agent. As an added attraction, I only needed another six weeks' work on an Equity contract, added to the thirty-six I'd already completed at the Windmill, to qualify for full membership. I signed there and then – without having to show anyone my breasts.

Paid rehearsals plus accommodation commenced mid-October at studios in the Place de Clichy. I couldn't have been more elated – I was dancing in Paris after all, like one of my idols, Shirley MacLaine, who had performed at the Lido! It was an incredible introduction to how troupes were prepared at break-neck speed, learning and understudying twelve numbers in a fortnight. Fitted, kitted and packed off.

Yet, when the moment came to show the rest of the group what I could do, I shrank. They were all tall, beautiful and supremely gifted, having worked with Bertin for several years. *I'm about to be judged by the cream of the crop. Have I still got it?* The pressure could not have been greater but Bertin, Madame Luska, his choreographer, as well as Clive, the head boy and his girlfriend Diana, the troupe leader, were encouraging. But most encouraging of all was Deborah, the lead in Bertin's second ballet, using the other studio. I had never seen anyone rehearse in gym shoes and these belonged to the most outstanding dancer that I could hope to equal. Deborah had long, thick, black hair, large dark eyes, legs up to her armpits, with the deportment of a Goddess. When I finished performing one of my solo routines in full costume, she led the applause.

'Super!' Madame Luska cried. 'Just what we need.'

'You've got it girl, don't worry. Keep doing what you're doing,' smiled Deborah.

It was a momentous day for me as a person and as a dancer. This was the culmination of all the years of training and the ultimate test of where I stood as a cabaret/show dancer. I'd been acknowledged. I was good enough. I was going to Japan.

I was to be in the opening and finale of the *Hello Paris* show, which included mostly presentation steps due to the huge headdresses and feathers we would be wearing. The music was pure Hollywood; big musical scores and French songs which gave cabaret the edge that only the French could. A song entitled *Hello Paris* opened the show, while the more familiar *Hello Dolly* provided the climax – with me in the title role.

I really did feel like I'd arrived. But then, two days before we were due to depart, I woke up shivering. I'd had a bad dream, but even before I could remember what it was about I burst into tears.

I can't go through with it, I realised. *What if it's another Dakar?*

Out of nowhere I suddenly found myself in the vice-like grip of depression. Everything I'd bottled up in Senegal came flooding out in new fears, nightmares and physical pain. I couldn't understand it and I certainly couldn't fight it. There was only one thought in my head.

I have to get away. I need to go home.

I packed my suitcase and prepared to flee the hotel at the first opportunity. However unprofessional, dancers occasionally "do a bunk" from a contract for all sorts of personal reasons. I hadn't got far when Luska appeared and held my hands and looked into my eyes.

'You are a beautiful dancer with a great future ahead of you, don't do this'.

An hour later I was sitting, crying guilty tears, in Bertin's office, and feeling a failure. I couldn't believe it when he appeared so calm, so understanding – so fatherly. He really lifted my spirits, even knowing I had been trying to cheat him out of his contract.

'We need you Tessa,' he said in a quiet, considered voice. 'Clive will look after you and you can call me anytime. I'll halve the contract and you can return at the end of January. But please do Christmas and New Year – as a favour to me.'

*****

Japan was everything I expected and more. The contrast, upon landing, of the hi-tech, polite and so very small Japanese with the lumbering, antiquated Aeroflot crew that had flown us there was immediate. Even I felt tall in Tokyo!

Our local agents, Mr Ito and Mr Hamada, greeted us like royalty. They spoke perfect English and couldn't do enough for any of us. As upset as I was even to have made the journey, I recognised a slight thawing in my mood watching these two men do everything in their power for my comfort. In a small way my world order was being rebalanced and I was grateful.

We took the bullet train, slicing through the suburbs, through countryside to the National Park area of the Tone Valley. The Juraku hotel was also the biggest hotel I'd ever seen, and the best equipped. Our accommodation included shared rooms – although being the odd number, I had one to myself – plus, along the hall, a kitchen with TV and utility room. We were well supplied with basics, including boxfuls of Yakult, the staple health drink, and told to write down any other requirements which would be delivered every Monday. It really was incredibly well-organised, right down to the pale blue, embroidered silk kimonos and slippers to be worn around the hotel and backstage.

The foyer and theatre in the hotel were huge. High glass ceilings, mauve and gold furnishings and a red carpet led to the auditorium, like the gangway to the Lido. Inside, the room was decorated in all shades of pink with large, circular tables and pink chairs arranged around a high black lino stage which set off the rainbow of spotlights around the backdrop and "Hello Paris" written in fluorescent paints. My jaw literally dropped when I realised just how prepared our hosts were for our visit. I'd never seen anything like it.

At our first rehearsal we had every number photographed, then individual head shots were taken. As I stepped into the lift the next morning, I was startled to see my face staring back with my name underneath in large black print. My shows were advertised to start in two days. For the first time since my wobble in Paris, I began to get excited.

After such intricate preparation from the agents, our first night was nerve-wracking. We had a full house and an electric atmosphere backstage. I'd never rehearsed for anything so much but it was worth it. At nine o'clock, the curtain went up and we never looked back. Everything clicked into place and the whole show flew past. There were highlights, of course. I performed *Chi Mai* to complete silence followed by an eruption of thunderous applause immediately afterwards. I felt prickles up my spine and wanted to cry but there wasn't time. I was part of an ensemble now. I had other scenes to prepare for.

Typically a troupe will have ten or so numbers in a show. After an eye-popping opening, acts could include a jungle theme, then perhaps sexy cowboys or French courtesans, Latin moves or softer, fan dances. Some we loved and some we cursed.

In our *Hello Dolly* finale some girls were dressed as waiters, with black trousers and bowties, white shirts, orange waistcoats, holding trays; the number was set in a café scene. Others were dressed as saloon girls or wearing evening dresses in all designs of peach and black. I made my entrance with Clive. I was topless in a diamanté-strapped bikini which ran over my shoulders and crossed at the waist, with orange gloves and a harness of orange feathers. The diamanté headdress curved over my cheeks with a huge orange pom-pom on top. The effect of this luxuriance was mesmerising. I thought the room would explode as the cheers rang out.

This costume was light compared to the heavy, restrictive harness of the opening number, which was dripping with silver feathers and ostrich plumes, and almost caused me to topple over if I didn't retain my posture! It was an entirely new dancing technique to get used to. Also, performing in flesh-coloured fishnets hid a multitude of sins, covering bulges and bruises, and from the audience's view, gave us all flawless, shapely limbs.

While the others wound down afterwards I dashed to my room to freshen up. Then it was back down to the hotel's Bally Hi nightclub for the first of my solo engagements. The Japanese love jazz and there was a great band at the Bally Hi.

Whilst I worked till dawn, the troupe started at five o'clock some days, for early conference shows in a smaller theatre, where business men sat cross-legged at traditional tables, served by geishas. So we all had our work cut out.

The Japanese focus on hard work and we were rewarded for our professional conduct by being shown great respect and given every available back up.

When I slipped and hurt my knee at the Bally Hi, I was whisked to the medical centre on a stretcher covered with a blanket but still in my g-string, like a scene from a *Carry On* film!

The doctors used the latest technology alongside natural therapies. After being examined I was given the okay with a stock of mustard plasters to apply. As I was carried out the nurses giggled, circling round, asking for a signed photograph and the doctor beamed and bowed.

We earned £100 a week – much less than I was used to getting as a soloist, but on my first night at Bally Hi one customer tipped me £17. I thought, *If I get many of those I won't have to worry about the wages.*

As the first week turned into the second, I settled into an exhausting, yet fulfilling, pattern. Everyone who saw my show complimented me on it – including the hotel management and Clive and Diana. They all said they'd put in a good word for me with Bertin so even though I was cutting my stint short, perhaps he'd still work with me again.

Beneath the thrill of the successful show, however, the curse of Dakar wasn't far away. The fearsome loss of confidence I'd suffered in Paris had subsided but every couple of nights a dream would trigger memories I'd tried to squash. On the days following I would be quiet, thoughtful and in desperate need of company. That was when I loved being part of a troupe, enjoying the luxury of shared experience and common ground, listening to the anecdotes and complaints. We formed a camera club, aerobics club and had a mystery tour day to liven up our week. But on my stronger days I liked nothing more than exploring on my own. I found solace in the serenity and simplicity of the temples, dedicated to nature.

'Don't you get lonely on your own, Tess?' Diana asked, for she was fortunate to have her boyfriend Clive as her dancing partner and companion. My answer was "no". Not usually, anyway.

One of the regular topics of conversation, of course, was sex. It's the same in any dressing room. I discovered early on that Japanese men didn't appeal to me sexually at all and since there were few foreigners in the hotel, my options were limited. Then a Filipino band arrived for a month's stay and I got friendly with their pretty-looking guitarist called Sam. It was only when their contract finished that we realised he'd been to bed with all of us!

Japanese celebrate the New Year and don't emphasise Christmas as much – decorations were taken down on Boxing Day – so it was left to us to celebrate as best we could. We ate lunch around the large kitchen table and we all sang carols drunkenly. A week later, every temple gong reverberated, as worshippers made wishes for the New Year. I was dreading that night. Memories of Thierry's proposal a year earlier were still raw and so much had happened since. But Japan worked its magic.

The manager of the Juraku presented me with a thank you card and a silk purse, saying it had been an honour to work with me. I was deeply moved and shed a tear when I returned to my room to pack.

Later, standing on my balcony I surveyed the snow-covered scene and the outside spa baths, with steam rising, causing the whole valley to quiver like an underwater scene. The gongs echoed, and the golden flickers of a thousand candles blinked from the hillside temples. It was a dreamy, soothing, yet crisp and expectant scene, and the perfect image to take away with me as I said goodbye.

CHAPTER THIRTEEN

HE WOULD HAVE MENTIONED A SON

All good things come to an end. In 1982, worn down by the sometimes twenty-four-hour workload, Mum handed in her notice with JRS. It was a sad day for everyone but there were no hard feelings. It says something for the pressure at Number 10 that she found it more relaxing becoming housekeeper for five luxury flats rather than one house! Things weren't exactly dull at Providence Court, a cut-through between Grosvenor Square and Selfridges, especially in the top floor flat owned by the theatrical agent Laurence Evans. Mum and I had only been there five minutes when we were serving tea for the likes of Sir John Mills, Sir John Gielgud and Marti Caine.

It was a time of change for me, as well. Gung-ho with the success of Japan I had taken the advice of Anita, one of the Lido girls in the group. She had done some solo work and recommended her agent, who sent me a contract for Abidjan, the capital of Côte d'Ivoire. These days sport, especially football, has exposed the world to players like Didier Drogba, but in the early 1980s Ivoirians and their country were a mystery to Europeans.

I had only been there a few weeks when I found myself worrying that perhaps I couldn't cope with cabaret in unusual places anymore, or whether I was good enough.

The show line-up included a talented Italian singer, Aldo, who could break glasses set along the bar when he hit a certain pitch, and Catherine the Great, who performed acrobatics with a hoop set aflame. I never forgot her words as she teetered over me, tall and thin in her high heels, after she had seen my show; 'You'll never make it on your own as a dancer if you don't do magic or fire'.

Just what I needed to hear, though it did have a ring of truth, I know.

The streets weren't safe. Once out of the French and Lebanese quarters it could be risky on your own. One weekend there was even an attempted coup – all the highways were deserted, families locked in their homes. But the club still operated; of course.

The four giant doormen warned that in the shanty area, not far from the club, you could get your hands chopped off for a watch or ring, just for starters!

Taxis were costing me a fortune to get about in and, once again, my boss was a spiteful woman from Marseilles who seemed to detest the very people she made her money from. For once I was honest in a letter to Mum. 'When I'm home I can't wait to get back on the road, but then I walk into a contract like this and remember all the things I hate about it.'

I sensed the time for change in the air. But would I have the nerve to go through with it?

Then another factor came into play during my four months in Africa. *I met a man.*

Matt Hart was a forty-year-old, stocky, grey-haired divorcée from Yorkshire, who came to the club a few nights a week on business for the oil trade. One of the hostesses pointed him out to me. 'He's a loner, not interested in anything except his beer.' It wasn't the most flattering of reports but we got talking and he asked me out for dinner. The most important rule for artistes working in clubs is to never go out with a customer. But for Matt Hart, I broke that rule.

Looking back, I realise now he was yet another father figure in my life. At the time I saw a comforting, supportive older man who seemed to understand my inner struggle. He was the one who took me to Le Wafou on Sundays, an outside dinner show with tribal dances, fire-eaters, a family of acrobats and musicians playing local instruments. He was the one who insisted I ate a good meal every day and made life exciting. And, when I became ill, he was the one who nursed me.

Matt was also the first person to ask me why I continued to do something that made me so unhappy. Mum had never challenged me about that. She was so supportive of every wild plot I concocted that I don't think it occurred to her to try to pin me down.

But Matt did. He said to me one afternoon, 'What does your father think about all this topless dancing?'

I told him how we'd never met. He could see it was a hard conversation for me so took it slowly.

'Well, if I were your father I'd be concerned that you were putting yourself in danger all the time.'

'But you're not my father – or I couldn't do this.' And I kissed him.

Later that night I mused on that conversation. His words were one thing – perhaps I was making a big mistake dragging myself around the world not knowing if I was going to be treated well or not. But it was the fact he'd asked that really struck me. He was my lover now but he was showing the sort of concern I imagined a father would show his daughter. After so many years of telling myself, 'Even if I had a father he would never have been able to stop me doing anything,' I began to doubt my own conviction.

Would having Daddy around have protected me from my own decisions?

After two months together my contract was up. I had some tough decisions to make.

The night before I left I danced as usual then went with Matt onto the hotel roof to look at the stars. That's when he proposed to me.

'On one condition,' he said.

'What's that?'

'That you give up this horrible job and let me look after you.'

I didn't have to think twice.

*****

That first week back was hectic. Matt returned with me and had quite a few meetings with his bosses in Euston to try to get officially transferred back to London full time. He then travelled down to Hampshire to arrange for the house he owned there to be put on the market.

'We're going to make a fresh start together,' he promised.

Mum and Gran were delighted with my new plans. They found Matt amiable enough, although they foresaw the thirteen-year-age gap as a potential problem. 'But as long as you're happy…'

Home for Mum now was the ground floor rooms of Providence Court, comprising a sitting area with sofa bed, kitchen and bathroom. It was fine for her – but now I was home it seemed cramped. In the end I bought an inflatable mattress and slept in the downstairs storage area. I didn't mind. Home was where Mum was and we were extremely lucky to be so central. And in any case, I wouldn't be there long.

There was the wedding to prepare for and the world seemed our oyster. On our first weekend Matt took me on an extravagant shopping spree in Knightsbridge and bought an emerald engagement ring from Kutchinsky and outfits from Harrods. By the end of the day my one thousand pounds earnings from Abidjan which we had used in the interim had gone and I was several hundred overdrawn at the bank. But after spending so many years counting every penny, it was lovely to be able to splash out.

Matt was organizing his finances, and to repay me and tide me over, he opened a bank account in my name and told me not to worry about spending – he would cover it all.

While Matt flitted around the country getting his affairs in order, I started looking at flats in the Kensington area for us to buy. Matt was confident he could afford somewhere very nice when his house had sold.

Everything was going so well that I began to wonder what could possibly go wrong. When the first test of my new life arrived it wasn't what I'd expected – but that didn't make it any less formidable.

One of my contacts in France, the Galli agency, had written to me with a contract for three months work in Nice.

Nice! This wasn't Africa or Switzerland – it was the south of France, just along the coast from my beloved Toulon where my life in many ways had started. I'll admit I was anguished. I didn't dare tell Matt, but I carried that offer around with me for a week, weighing up every aspect.

After so long looking for love, I'd found it and my spring wedding at the Savoy had been booked. And yet, I didn't just want to be a housewife. I couldn't give up dancing completely. That was my life. It had been my life for as long as I could remember.

'You'll have to sacrifice something,' Mum warned. 'If you take this contract you can kiss goodbye to your wedding.'

'But dancing as a solo attraction in Nice, Mum! Do you know how often I've dreamed about that?'

'Then go for it. But only you can make your mind up.'

I remembered the circumstances under which I'd met Matt and smiled. Then, with a heavy heart I rang Galli and rejected their offer. *My future's here now, with my husband.*

As a compromise I started going to the new Danceworks studios around the corner from Providence Court in Balderton Street. *Jane*

Fonda's Workout video had just begun to take its grip on the world and aerobics was the subject of many women's conversations. With seven studios and a full timetable of classes, I was able to keep fit and stop my dance moves getting rusty.

I was soon grateful I had kept in shape. Out of the blue Matt said he had to go to Japan and St Lucia for as long as six months. I was shattered by the news. *After the sacrifices I have made.* He saw the concern in my eyes and was quick to explain.

'I'm not going if you can't come out there and join me sometimes.'

Why not? I let Matt get settled then flew out first-class with the immaculate Japan Airlines to Tokyo. As soon as he saw me the spending started; the best restaurants, the best evening's entertainment, a whole new wardrobe. He just spent and spent, always laden with gifts and gadgets whenever he walked back through the door.

I thought I would be okay enjoying the city but I soon got that familiar feeling of itchy feet. I needed to do something. Looking at the brochure of entertainment at our hotel, The New Otani, I decided to approach the manager. A few days later, thanks to Mum posting my lighter costumes over, I took to the stage at the hotel nightclub, utterly elated.

Even Matt was supportive. 'Just promise me you'll never do consummation again.'

He had my word.

After six weeks of spoilt luxury it was time for me to return to London. I arrived drowning under the mountain of electrical goods Matt had sent back with me. There had been no stopping him.

'We'll need these in our new home.'

Two days after getting back I picked up the keys to our beautiful flat in South Kensington. It wasn't huge but it was empty and all ours! I ran from room to room singing, dancing and laughing. I couldn't believe it was real.

I threw myself into designing the interiors and ordered the furniture on my account. I took photographs of each new purchase and posted them to Matt. The only blot on the entire landscape was the fact that I was doing it alone. I'd spent most my working life on my own but that was always by design. It seemed wrong designing a home for two, alone.

For my twenty-second birthday I just stayed in and cooked a simple meal for myself before calling Matt in St Lucia. We were so near and yet so far.

Two weeks later paradise was shattered. I returned from Danceworks and noticed something wrong. The front door was flapping in the breeze – and I knew I'd locked it. Escorted by a builder from a site across the road, I poked my head into the hallway.

'Anyone there?'

The builder was brave and impatient. He pushed past me and returned a few seconds later shaking his head.

'I'm sorry love. I hope you've got insurance.'

We'd been burgled. The television, video player, kitchen gadgets and lots of jewellery were all missing.

I was in tears as I relayed the situation to Matt. He said all the right things.

'Get the locks changed and stay with your mother if you're uncomfortable. Just don't worry about anything.'

I knew though, that despite the brave face he was putting on it, as we weren't insured, the losses would hit us.

But a week later, I opened the door to a delivery lorry carrying replacements of the stolen items. Matt's extravagance had risen to new levels.

Unfortunately it was all in vain. Two weeks later the bubble well and truly burst – literally. I was in bed this time, awoken by an odd swishing sound. Swinging my feet onto the heavy rug, I screamed. It was soaking. The entire flat was filled with four inches of water.

I should have run out immediately but I didn't have the strength: not on top of the burglary. I pulled my feet back into the bed and curled into a comforting ball. Where was Matt? Why was I having to cope with all this without him? When was it all going to end?

The end, as it turned out, was closer than I thought. Two days later I went to the bank to withdraw some money and I was refused.

'I'm sorry, Miss Skola, your account has been frozen,' the teller explained.

'But there's lots of money in it. My fiancé puts thousands in every month.'

'Not according to our files.'

I hurried round to Mum's, which was closer, and called Matt. It didn't matter what the time difference was. I needed him urgently.

When he didn't pick up, I left a message with his hotel. When he didn't ring back I tried again an hour later. Then again, an hour after that. He didn't ring back that day, the next or the next. In fact, it would be a fortnight before I heard from him at all.

Worried, I caught a tube to Euston and went into the Fluor offices myself. After a two-hour wait I was finally seen. Where was Matt Hart? I demanded. Is he all right?

The secretary disappeared again. When she returned it was with a tired expression.

'Mr Hart is fine, according to our records. His work is up-to-date, he is in daily contact. Anything else, I'm afraid, is confidential.'

'It's all right,' I mumbled, shell-shocked. 'I've heard enough.'

Another week went by and, as was my habit, I turned to my friend the wine bottle for support. We were getting on so famously one afternoon I almost didn't hear the phone ring.

'Hello?' Any hope of playing it cool had vanished already.

'Is that Tessa Skola?'

It was a woman's voice.

'Yes,' I said nervously, suddenly very sober indeed. 'Is this about Matt? Is there something wrong?'

'The only thing that is wrong, Miss Skola, is you. Matt Hart is my husband and the father of our nine-year-old son. If you don't get your filthy claws out of him God help what I'll do next.'

Husband? But he was divorced. I poured another glass. A son? He'd never mentioned a son. He would have mentioned a son, surely.

I knew then my dream was over. The next day I cancelled orders for furniture and watched the deposits disappear. I walked into the Savoy personally to cancel our booking of their River Suite. Most humiliating of all was selling my wedding dress.

I didn't have a clue what was going on. Finally a letter arrived. I recognised Matt's scrawled handwriting immediately. If he was trying to spare my feelings, he did a bad job. The note contained barely three clumsy lines: "I do not love you anymore. Get out of the flat. I am in debt for £77,000."

By then I didn't care. I sold the furniture and appliances to the builders across the road and haggled for a measly two hundred pounds for my engagement ring. As I left the keys on top of a pile of bills and closed the door of the flat for the last time, I didn't look back.

*****

Danceworks the next day took the full vent of my pain and anger. There were fitness classes running back to back, and I took part in all of them. In between I ran through exercises on my own in the large, light studios. It was a purely physical reaction to the mess I'd been landed in. But it seemed to work for me.

Danceworks was the home of aerobics and when Jackie Genova, one of Jane Fonda's students, came over to audition to find her British training team, my name was first on her list. It was a fast-paced set of exercises to funky music, much like a choreographed dance, and I was chosen alongside an actress, two other professional dancers, an Australian ex-ballet star working as a waitress and a disillusioned hairdresser.

Work began almost immediately, alongside the training courses. Demonstrations at The Empire, Leicester Square led to a regular slot on the breakfast channel, TV-AM. In no time at all I was taking four classes a day, instructing with a microphone in front of large groups of ladies wearing puff-sleeved, brightly striped leotards and leg warmers.

Out of the blue a minute, blonde lady approached me one afternoon.

'I've been watching you for several days,' she said. 'My husband and I would like to bring aerobics to Greece and to do that we would like to bring you as well.'

It sounded too good to be true but, still pinching myself, the following month, I found myself on a flight to Athens. As Sophie and her husband Peter picked me up, I told myself it was no different to starting a dance contract, except I'd be working during the day, not at night, and I would have my clothes on. I wondered if any other differences would present themselves.

Dark, grumpy Peter soon proved himself to be as erratic and possessive as a club boss. During the first week, I stayed as their guest and was driven to and fro to classes and hardly left alone for a second. I was longing to explore the city but the boss wanted total control, as if I had no other interests outside of working for him and being stuck in his modern house on the outskirts of Athens.

The Academy studios were spread over three floors of a stately building near Syntagma Square, in the heart of Athens, with skirted, bobble-shoed guards marching nearby in front of the grave of the

"Unknown Soldier". Miro Zolan, an ex-Royal Ballet star, was ballet master and two Americans, Bruce and Janet, taught jazz. Greek staff included a delightful gay, who ran the café, and Angela, the receptionist. We eventually became great friends but they were a little cool to begin with. Only when they realised that Peter and I weren't bosom buddies did they open up. 'Beware Greeks bearing gifts,' they warned cryptically.

Peter financed his wife's whim to be a ballerina but gave her very little power. He bossed her around, like a crow hovering over a wren, which was unpleasant to witness. Watching that relationship every day added, I realised, to my gradual malaise. Not having any freedom, the alien-looking language and the unfriendly hosts threatened to break me within a fortnight. Despite all my travel experiences, I felt so out of place particularly with a language I could not decipher at all.

But then I met a French lady, Hélène, at a café near the studios. An elegant lady of about sixty, she spoke good English and shared my love of travel, cats and poetry. She had an apartment to rent and I would be an ideal tenant. Only when I moved in did I begin to enjoy myself. But it took a good couple of months to feel comfortable in Athens with the heat, pollution and Greek way of life.

Hélène's apartment was my first ever real "home" abroad, at a proper rent too, but private and quiet. Most of Athens spilled over, everyone's life was lived outdoors, as seen in many modern apartment blocks which were surrounded entirely by balconies with half the furniture piled up outside.

Four people turned up to my first class. That soon zoomed to thirty once word got round, and at weekends Peter would squeeze in forty if he could. I had Mondays off and collected my wages every Tuesday but sometimes Peter wasn't there and I had to chase him. I met a diverse cross section of students, mainly female, and a few brave men, astonished by the tough hour-long aerobic session. I was soon invited to their homes for supper and started to glimpse Greek family life and how warm and hospitable they could be. Suddenly my social life was non-stop, talk about all or nothing.

With my days taken up I exploited every moment of nightlife. That's when Athens truly sparkled and the doors of a hundred concealed bars and clubs opened to revellers. The dull-looking family-run tavernas served the best food at old wooden tables with a paper cloth and basket of bread; and there were dozens of places to go until the small hours, thanks to the nationwide afternoon siesta between two and six o'clock.

Kolonaki, unbeknown to me, was the centre of the gay community, awash with young Apollos with marvellous physiques. At a smart gay club near the Square I met Costas, a model with large, brown eyes, and his friend Dimitris who was a huge fan of Margaret Thatcher. But that's not what linked us. We danced well together and would go on drinking binges and cause a stir on the dance floor.

'How many places can we fit in before you pass out?' Dimitris squealed one night.

'Six!' I bet.

'Then I say nine!'

When and if I did pass out they would escort me home then scoot off in a taxi to continue partying alone. I led a *Looking for Mr. Goodbar* life, waking up a shade of green to take the early bird aerobics, followed by baklava and coffee with someone's grandmother, afternoon classes and then into the night again....

After a couple of months I plucked up the courage to demand a week off. Peter gave me four days so I used them to go to Mykonos, the Mecca for partying and the Greek gay scene.

The first thing I noticed when I arrived on the island was the fuchsia hibiscus bursting over the balconies of blistering white, tub-shaped buildings. It created a spasm of colour and I found myself wandering routelessly to drink in the scenes. I hadn't been there a few hours when I sensed eyes staring at me. I noticed a boyish, dark girl with glasses at the end of the street. She had been following me. I watched as she came and settled beside me outside the church. She didn't say a word and, as we walked back down in silence, she reached for my hand.

Being gay was all out in the open on Mykonos and I felt delightfully free being part of it. Catherine was a scientist and we toured the island in her rented jeep and watched the colours of the sun set over the sea and wash the buildings with a lavender hue. Four days later that micro-episode of my life was over as quickly as it had arrived – but another adventure was just about to begin.

Karina, who looked like a Grecian goddess, and her partner Cristos, the image of Alexander the Great, were regulars at my classes. They performed at open air venues in the parks with two other dancers and invited me to their show at a bouzouki. There were bouzouki theatres all over Athens and this one was huge. Singers, male and female, of all ages, sang superbly, in pairs or trios or all together in a long line. Musicians and the bouzouki players, seated on stools, would start slowly and increase in tempo. Then, just before the guest singer, it was time for my friends' group to perform. Just watching them reignited a flame in me that I thought had been snuffed out. Afterwards I confessed my past experience as a dancer.

'Then you have to dance for us!'

'Yes, next week, in the park.'

I shook my head. 'I don't have my costumes or make-up. It would never work.'

But I realised there was a way. My mother was arriving in a couple of days' time for a holiday. She could bring my costumes and music.

I enjoyed a fantastic week with Mummy. Not only did I have company but it was so lovely to be able to treat her for once and show her all the interesting sights of Athens. And, best of all, she was going to see me dance for the first time since the Windmill.

Taking my pose for the Latin number, I tried to put the huge crowd out of my head. As my intro music began I could picture my mother out there, somewhere, heart in her mouth as I started to move. *I'm doing this for you, Mummy.* But, as I took my bow ten minutes later, I knew that wasn't strictly true. I'd enjoyed it so much and there was only one person I'd been dancing for. Myself. And now I'd done it once I couldn't wait to do it again.

My career isn't over yet!

The next day I gave my notice at the Academy. Sophie was distraught, even when I told her Peter hadn't paid me for more than six weeks. When he found out, of course, he was apoplectic.

'I'm going to sue you for six thousand pounds for loss of earnings!' he screamed.

'Do that,' I said calmly. 'And when you send the papers remember to enclose my wages.'

Parting from my friends was hard and I regretted giving up my lovely apartment. *But*, I thought, *I'd rather be in crummy digs and happy spiritually, rather than materially.*

As usual that was a wish I would come to regret but the saying, that Greek friends make the most loyal, is true; they remain friends for life.

CHAPTER FOURTEEN

AN UNDISCOVERED STAR

When I think how close I'd come to settling down with Matt and giving up my career, I recoil. Could I have done it? Could I have put the costumes and g-strings in a box for good? I think the honest answer is, if I were doing it for me, if it were my decision, then yes, I might have left that world behind and been happy.

But it hadn't been my decision. 'Give up this life. Let me look after you.'

Those were Matt's words. He wanted to love me but he wanted to control me as well. For almost a year it had worked. I was under his spell, chasing the same dreams. But when it crumbled and I found myself back at the beginning, penniless and with nothing, I discovered an inner strength.

I still had my suitcases of costumes and contacts all around the world.

After my incredible experiences in Athens I leapt at the chance to go to Cyprus, Crete and Israel where my agent billed me as "Tessa Skola – Dancer from *Fame*". I choreographed a show to the music of the popular film, performing around the disco circuit. The Bouzouki clubs featured my classical cabaret numbers, where there would be much plate-smashing in appreciation!

Cyprus had a number of small cabarets but also stunning open-air discos.

Unfortunately, it was called by artistes, "The cesspit of the Med" because wealthy Arabs used it as their gateway for sex with the numerous prostitutes working as hostesses.

In Acco, Israel, I performed at an open air club built into the walls of the old city. I literally enjoyed the fruits of the lush countryside by day – visiting moshavs, harvesting oranges, avocados and roses. I led a much more balanced life for a while and even worked on a banana plantation for a fortnight after my contract. Most exciting was standing in the town square after eleven at night, waiting to be approached by quiet men in striped T-shirts who would change shekels into dollars on the black market. Somehow they knew what I was there for and the transaction was speedily completed under the corner palm tree.

I endlessly refined my act and kept learning, especially touring with the same artistes, like Mario Marinelli from Argentina. He and his wife were professional gauchos and he had four backing dancers who were superb movers but looked identical. Mario demanded they all be thin, tall, blonde and severely classical.

There was also "Bo Peep", a petite, white-haired French girl with her six white tumbling poodles. She amazed me how she travelled and coped with the dogs and her living arrangements. How on earth did she manage?. I felt I should have no complaints at all!

The Russells then sent me to Hong Kong where I was managed by Danny Chan, the most popular agent in Asia. This is where Americans, Australians and Europeans congregated, to work in the Far East. At its peak, in the 1980s and 1990s, this was the world's meeting place for every type of act.

I lived in ChungKing Mansions in Kowloon; four huge skyscraper blocks interconnected with a warren of tiny apartments, guest houses and eateries.

Artistes phoned in for their show times every afternoon and were ferried around in a van. From deluxe nightclubs on Hong Kong Island, full of gangsters in sunglasses and black suits, to basement bars including the famous Bottoms Up club featured in the Bond movie *The Man with the Golden Gun*.

Mamasans, as they were called, were employed back stage. Dressed in tunic and slippers, they were like Chinese nannies and would serve us tea and a towel after each show.

I featured at the Sheraton hotel and then a stint at the casinos in Macau. Every venue usually employed a hugely-talented Filipino band, who were terrific vocalists and musicians. They were always so welcoming, kind and unaffected. I eventually worked, on their advice, at the Holiday Inn in Manila.

But it was Taiwan that left an indelible mark. The air was yellow. It was a mix of muddy towns and high-rise business blocks. Swarms of men and women would flock to see the international line up of shows at venues ranging from huge theatres with names like Golden Dragon, to floors set up as a boxing ring like my first destination, run by "Fingers" – a lesbian in black leather who wore a two-finger black gauntlet. The three missing digits cut off by the Triads, she explained.

We played alongside Taiwanese singers in fabulously sequinned Chung Sam dresses and local prostitutes, who performed explicit acts and closed the event around midnight.

We worked every day often with eight shows a day from eleven in the morning until nine o'clock in the evening. The performances were topless only. We seemed to live on fried eggs and moved every week to a new location and private en-suite rooms in a guesthouse. It was the toughest regime but I was in my element. Not every artiste agreed. One reason was the request they called "Flashing".

In every club there was usually a police check sometime during the day. As soon as they left, there would be a yell in the dressing room 'Flash flash' and a group of volunteers would strip naked and each put on a long sequinned cloak provided by the venue.

We would then parade on stage as if in a fashion show, opening the cloak now and then to reveal our naked bodies. The audience were like hungry little boys, all craning to get a better look but at a strict distance away and ordered to remain in their seats. It was odd at first and quite laughable but we were given twenty dollars there and then, for three minutes on stage. I didn't find it degrading.

In one dressing room, the wall was covered with comments about the gruelling experiences; "In Taiwan the law of gravity is a myth, it sucks". "Want to look like a skeleton and crap like me ? Come to Taiwan". "On my way home to receive an OBE for not letting traditions of showbiz fall to level of what these lot want".

These were wonderful new places, people and experiences for me. But the unifying thing wasn't the dancing or the travel or the money. It was doing it *for* myself and *by* myself.

From feeling I'd conquered the world, with a book of almost two hundred agents, performing about one thousand shows a year, the next twelve months took a downward spin. I can trace it back to one decision. I had offers for Rome, Rhodes and the former Yugoslavia, and interest from several new English agents including Jackie Harris, Beryl Denise, Rex Grey, Sardis and Al Heath. But I turned them all down. After all the long-haul travelling of the last months I wanted to go somewhere more familiar. And where had given me greater pleasure recently than Athens? Unfortunately, none of the agents was offering a contract there.

So I decided to go on my own.

Why not? I was the strongest I'd ever been, dancing the best and feeling more worldly-wise. With compliments and warm words still ringing in my ears from the Far East, I felt that I couldn't fail.

I contacted a top cabaret, Maxims, in Syntagma Square and set off with two new numbers. One, an Ice Queen theme set to classical music and Liza Minnelli's *Maybe This Time* - the words of that song almost a copy of my life - and *Yankee Doodle*, a Paul Jabara disco track, wearing an American top hat, bow tie and red, white and blue sequinned tails. Paul had been a regular at Number 10 all those years ago and had won an Oscar for a Donna Summer track. He had just died of an AIDS-related illness. This was my tribute.

But Athens didn't feel the same. I knew it well but the city had changed - I had changed.

The boss welcomed me and he and his staff applauded my rehearsal, stopping in mid flow, to sit and really watch. But then the bomb dropped. I'd have to sit until four o'clock in the morning for consummation.

'That wasn't part of the agreement,' I spluttered.

'It's part of my agreement,' the man said. 'Take it or leave.'

It was Baby Jane all over again. I was gutted after all the effort and organisation. Even if my dancing took their breath away, it accounted for nothing. I only enough money to last a fortnight, I had no choice.

Or did I?

Completely unexpectedly the boss took my chin in his hand and stared into my eyes. 'Perhaps you're not right for Maxims,' he said kindly. 'Let me make a phone call. We'll find you somewhere more suited to your talents.'

It was a powerful lesson. Having been told I was the best dancer the club had ever seen I was still not as valuable to them as a hostess who foisted watered-down bubbly on punters. But there was another lesson: don't judge people. Later that day I arrived in the office of one of the boss's contacts who immediately signed me on a two-month booking at a hotel near Alexandropoulis, close to the Turkish border. I was flown up with directions to take the bus to Didymoteixon.

"Be careful what you wish for" is an old axiom that seems to bite me every so often. This turned out to be one of those moments.

Alexandropoulis wasn't a beach town geared to foreign tourists and the bus depot toilet could rate as the worst in the world. A gruff guard actually took payment for this health hazard, which had excrement smeared on the walls, piles of filthy rubbish on the floor, swarms of flies and a stench that brought up bile. It wasn't the best introduction.

The ugly concrete Hotel Plotini, with nightclub attached, wasn't much better. As the bus dropped me off, it looked deserted. I found the short, balding owner after calling out in the plain, lino-covered foyer. He stomped down the stairs and was abrupt to the point of rudeness but his wife was even less charming. This made me all the more polite and gracious. After showing me to my room she led me down the back stairs to the hotel kitchens which didn't look like they'd been busy – or cleaned – for a long while.

Pointing to a gas hob she said, 'This is your ring: and use that saucepan only. Touch nothing else.' I could tell she thought I was contaminating her property just by being there. There were no utensils I could use and the gas never worked to boil water for tea so I didn't go down there again.

The room opposite mine was home to a four-girl Thai ballet and a very good soloist from the Philippines. I don't know how they squeezed into the same space as me but they managed it. They were young and funny but a total mess backstage, throwing rubbish, used sanitary towels and dirty costumes on the floor and always losing their things. Slovenly, but likeable. When I told them that I'd be going out to explore the next morning, if they wanted to join me, I got a shock. The mood in the room changed instantly and one of them pushed the door shut with a bang.

Only then did anyone speak.

'We don't go out,' she said in almost a whisper.

'We're not allowed.'

'Not allowed? Don't be ridiculous. You're in Europe now. You can go everywhere you want.'

I realised that all five girls suddenly looked terrified. I hadn't seen it coming at all. I realised they must be telling the truth, as impossible as it sounded. At the very least, they believed it to be true.

I could see the conversation was making them uncomfortable so I walked back to the door to my room. One of them followed me. 'Don't trust anyone,' she mouthed. 'They have spies.'

At nightfall it fitted the picture when search lights swept the border like eerie UFO's.

*****

I'd told myself on my last trip to Athens that *I'd prefer to be in crummy digs and happy spiritually, rather than materially.* So far I only had the crummy digs. I prayed the happiness would follow.

Fortunately the shows did go well and I wasn't pushed to drink with anyone. For one fantastic week we even toured the military camps, where an outside carpet formed our "stage", a tent became a dressing room and the stars our lighting. The weather was glorious and the soldiers were incredibly appreciative and well-disciplined, sitting in neat rows behind the line of top command.

It was a few miles' walk to the town, past farmhouses serving basic Greek dishes at the family table. I enjoyed nothing more than following a sign, knocking on a stranger's door and eating whatever was on the stove that day. For added "luxury" in my digs I even purchased a travelling kettle from the only electrical store, run by a charming middle-aged man called "Papa V", balding, with big baby brown eyes and a soft smile. He spoke good English and was a dance fanatic.

As soon as he found out my trade he asked, 'Do you know my good friends Karina and Cristos from Athens?'

Minutes later we were buddies. I had lost contact with them. Papa V said they had split up and were teaching dance in Corfu. I became a regular companion for Papa V during his business trips around the area. I would be thrilled to see a new bit of countryside and he would enjoy the company and buy me lunch. There were fields upon fields of sunflowers that looked like happy faces in bonnets and a feature of the area were storks that nested on the chimney pots of village roofs.

The only drawback was his friendship with my boss at the Plotini. 'Not a happy place for dancers,' Papa V conceded, but he wouldn't say a word against the owners.

I had only been in bed a couple of hours one night when I was disturbed by a knocking. Someone was at the door. It was the soloist, and she was obviously distraught.

'Tell me what's wrong. What's happened?'

She could barely speak through her tears.

'Mr Plotini promised I could leave, go to Athens. When I went to get my passport from him there was a man, a customer. The boss said, "Make my friend very happy or no passport."'

She didn't have to go on. She'd been shamed into going with the stranger and I knew she still didn't have her papers.

I went into the other room. The Thai girls were just as terrified and I knew immediately that not only were all their early warnings true, but they'd held back most of the sordid details.

Half groggy from sleep I tried to be calm and helpful. I suggested contacting their embassy. Did they have a customer who could help? Could they go to the police? Did they have visas? But had I ever done those things when I was in trouble?

'He can't keep you here forever.' I gestured to the five cramped camp beds, clothes hooked over nails and a table as their larder, piled with food, drink, toiletries. This was their little world, but for how much longer?

'I've got a friend,' I said finally. 'He'll help.'

The next day, still bleary-eyed, I found Papa V and told him everything. He said, 'Leave it with me.' When I returned to the hotel, Mr Plotini was waiting.

'A word,' he said, leading me into his office. Once inside his face changed to one of fury. 'You whore!' he roared. 'I know what you've been doing.' He flicked a piece of paper at me in disgust. It was a list of times and dates covering my every movement, the buses I had caught, the beaches I had sat on, the shops I had used. I couldn't believe it. 'How dare you have an affair with my best friend? I know it all. Get out of my hotel.'

Affair? Get out? I was still struggling to come to terms with being spied on. But Plotini was still ranting.

'The train to Athens leaves in an hour. Be on it!'

I felt terrible, but not for me. Poor Papa V. I had tried to help the girls and I might just have made it worse. I hugged them all and left them smiling bravely, to God knows what end.

Even though I now faced a twenty-four hour journey with no food or wages, I knew I wasn't the loser. But I was back to square one.

*****

The Copacabana was now the number one club in Athens and was booked months in advance through the best agents. But it was the obvious and only destination left for me. I waited outside the club to catch the manager and literally begged to be seen. He was so taken aback by my gall, if anything, that he allowed an impromptu audition.

The stage was magnificent, extending out into the audience. What a wonderful chance for me. A cleaner switched on the spotlight and my music as I took to the floor. Even though we were a few blocks away from Maxims, this was new territory. I didn't feel associated or connected with what had gone before. One thinks the cabaret world is small but it's not. A new day, a new boss, a different area, a different outlook – always worth a try!

'We're very full', he said. My face must have screamed disappointment. 'Okay, I'll take you for one spot a night but really I am full. Ten pounds a show is all I can pay.'

It was a ludicrous wage and he was obviously surprised I accepted. But I was desperate and it really was a fantastic scoop. A pink carpet led up to the entrance, designed as a pink scallop shell, under which stood uniformed doormen. I shared a dressing room with local hostess/striptease acts and was accepted immediately as a guest attraction show.

English dancer Susy was on a one year contract. Flame-haired and vivacious, she'd been a showgirl in Madrid for ten years and was now living full time in Athens and spoke fluent Greek.

Through until five in the morning, the Copacobana produced a sumptuous showcase. There were the best bouzouki singers and the Baross Ballet, Hungarian ex-Olympic acrobats, who performed the best can-can I would ever see. Top-billing of the evening were the Sophisticats, a singing/dancing family, so gorgeous, tanned and mesmerising, you could not tell it was father, mother and daughter. They had their own lock-up room for all their wildly expensive costumes. Every night there an unforgettable buzz and lively audiences would send champagne and congratulatory messages backstage. It was incredibly stress-free but so poorly paid I could barely exist.

One evening, a gangly, silver-haired gentleman came over to talk to me as I sat with Susy having an after show drink.

'My name is Jack Pallas,' he said holding out his hand. 'And you, my dear, are an undiscovered star.'

Pallas was a big agent, I learned, and he wasn't joking about liking me. The next day he took me to his office to sign an exclusive contract with him, as he started planning my itinerary for the following year. I couldn't believe my luck and it happened to be my birthday!

Susy's birthday was a few days later, so for our joint celebration we shared a cake she had made in the shape of a giant penis – a joke at her expense rather than mine, as a truly sassy, sex-mad Leo! I'd be sorry to leave her but, when Jack offered me a three-month contract in Lebanon, he added, 'Susy will be joining you in a month, as soon as she finishes here. It's a small club but they need top solo acts.'

The key word was "solo". The week before, the director of Baross had given me a boost by offering a year's contract in Madrid, dancing at the famous Scala revue! But I was on my solo crusade with dreams, if not plans, laid out. On the one hand it would be long term security, but the routine of repetitious group work just didn't appeal. I knew I had to give Pallas a chance now.

Jack escorted me to Beirut, the war had been and gone but there were still rumblings. I was to stay in the "safe" Christian district. But even so, as we were collected from the airport that mid-September day, I struggled to take in the sights. There was a sense of after-shock in the air. Buildings were pock-marked or lay in ruins and the streets were eerily deserted. The sense of devastation was claustrophobic.

Yet Pallas was upbeat. 'This used to be a Mecca of five-star hotels with top shows. And it will be again.'

I couldn't imagine how, but then our cab turned a corner and I saw a physical change. The city began to take form, the buildings were intact and life was carrying on.

My accommodation was a pleasant apartment block opposite the Casino Liban staff quarters. We were not allowed to fraternise with them but waved across the back lot. The Paradise Club however, failed to live up to its name. It was a heaving, rough and sweaty joint, the only cabaret in the Christian sector, and I'd have to sit out front with the other acts between shows. 'Don't worry though,' Jack insisted, 'you have not signed up for consummation.'

The club boss agreed, but as soon as my agent had left said, 'If you don't earn through the drink we'll need you to help with choreography'.

The shows went well and the customers were complimentary. But people lived hard and played hard. They all carried weapons, usually a handgun, and they over-indulged to excess. J&B whiskey disappeared by the gallon and the toilets were littered with needles on the floor and traces of cocaine on the counters.

There was a five-girl group from Austria headed by a mother and daughter – blonde and attractive but none of them dancers. The boss said they needed my help and I put together three new numbers. The last act of the evening was a coarse, dark haired belly dancer in her fifties. She had stamina if anyone did, often dancing for half an hour. All were friendly enough but my life improved dramatically when Susy arrived.

We spent our days on the deserted beach in front of our apartment, not daring to stray too far. The coast curved to the promontory where the Casino stood, once famous for its showgirls, now just open for a few gambling tables. At least the weather was warm and we enjoyed the Lebanese meze at a small café opposite.

At night we often heard bombs exploding and sharp machine gun fire. 'It's far away,' the landlady said, but it was still too close for comfort. We were in the "green zone", which was designated safe. But the airport was just outside the zone. For days at a time it would be shut down for security reasons.

Sometimes we daren't go out to even buy food and the club wouldn't open. After a few days' confinement I got the surprise of my life when a limousine pulled up beside Susy and me as we walked out.

There, smiling up from the saloon, were two faces from Dakar, Lebanese friends of Gus the DJ's brother, whom I had met several times! We were driven to a pretty restaurant in the hills and seemed to have the place to ourselves.

Guy and Pierre made sure we ate several courses with plenty of wine, and chocolates to finish. Guy talked about Africa. He was flying back the next day. Susy and I were ravenous, quite petrified still after being indoors for days, yet nervously happy, feeling relief at such unexpected kindness and, full stomachs!

All the while, the driver and another well–built man waited, just out of view. They didn't speak, not even when they saw us to our apartment, laden with fruit, biscuits and gifts of Lebanese embroidery. Saying farewell, Pierre whispered, 'Don't be startled, you will be safe, I promise. Guy is the head of the Christian Militia, these are his bodyguards. We are here in secret. Take care'.

Susy and I nearly fell backwards with astonishment.

One day, the bombing and gunfire continued until gone lunchtime. It's impossible to ignore that sort of noise, knowing that people are being injured. And, yes, concerned it could soon come our way.

'If this is still going on tonight, I'm not going to work,' Susy said, producing a bottle of gin from her bag. By the time we were collected for work later, the bottle was empty. If it hadn't been, the effects of the next hour might have been worse.

As usual, the cab taking us to the club was the only car on the highway. The road drew narrower as we approached and turning a sharp bend I heard one of the Austrians scream. On the hard shoulder there was a car riddled with gunshots. By its side we could all make out a body lying face down. I'd never seen a corpse before but I knew the man was dead. We all responded in different ways. I was silent, seized up with shock. Another girl opened a window to throw up. It was a chilling photograph, blasted into my brain under the harsh streetlights.

Susy and I both wanted to pack our bags and leave but the boss assured us we were safe. 'No one will touch you in here.' A few nights later our minds were made up.

Two men started to argue and a fight broke out in the club. Fights escalated very quickly here but friends always intervened and calmed everyone down. This time the weaker man pulled out a gun and started shooting. Anyone onstage would have been killed in the crossfire. Terrified, I managed to crawl backstage where the rest of the girls were shaking in silent tears.

Eventually the commotion stopped and I heard a familiar voice.

'You can come out now. Everything's all right.'

It didn't look all right. The stench of hot metal mixed with body odour filled the air. We picked our way over the broken chairs and shattered glass and ran as fast as possible through the blood-spattered door.

That was my last night in Paradise.

Getting out of the country was a problem. The airport remained closed for two days and, when it opened, no taxi driver would entertain going beyond the safety of the green zone. Fortunately, there were two French journalists waiting to escape who joined Susy and me; we paid two hundred pounds each for a driver to take the risk.

I've never trembled as I did that morning, four of us rigid in the back, almost not breathing, driven by a terrified man praying under his breath. Soaked with perspiration, we got through and checked in with a plane-load of other brave or foolhardy – we would soon tell – passengers. We paced up and down, wishing every minute away until allowed to board. Even as we took off, we weren't safe. But it was better than waiting to be shot in that club.

As soon as we got to Athens we burst into Jack's office and I really lost my temper, which was out of character for me. Jack was outraged, but looked as guilty and baffled as his wife; she calmed us all down and he eventually apologised for leaving Susy and me in the dark as the situation had deteriorated in Beirut. But even as he was speaking I saw his eyes glaze. He was no different from a hundred other agents, prepared to lie through their teeth at the drop of a hat, and I knew that his undiscovered star, as far as he was concerned, had waned.

*****

Athens had confirmed that memories can distort. The showbiz world can change and the good venues and helpful contacts can disappear. But when the Russells called with a three-month stint in Finland I was grateful, where better than the home of some great successes?

On arrival, Doris looked strained, 'Things have changed a lot'.

New agents had hit the scene and every café or pub advertised shows. Whereas before Doris had been careful to line me up with bookings that suited my act, this time I found myself in a very different setting, in unsuitable venues with new girls willing to do anything and the clubs offering customers "rooms upstairs".

Instead of flying to destinations, we had to travel by bus or train, for hours at a time, arriving cold and hungry. No-one cared if we had eaten and I often had to find the chef and mime that I needed food. Finland will always remind me of kitchens.

I still won over some of the more sophisticated crowds but any illusions of being a hit were dismissed with vulgar efficiency. Then I had a wonderful surprise.

Artistes rarely met one another here, for we were usually booked as a solo slot, departing early and arriving somewhere just in time to unpack and prepare for the shows. It was a feat of juggling for Doris and some days we had a gap and did not work, and were put up in a hotel or guesthouse.

In Tampere, when I had the weekend off, there was a knock on my door and there stood Deborah. It took a few moments to register but no-one could forget Bertin's best dancer! It turned out that she was a Doris regular and had also done Taiwan and Hong Kong. She was just as natural and warm - such a good laugh and so good for me, especially as she never took herself too seriously! She had continued to do a lot of group work but had branched out into solo contracts so she had a well-rounded view.

We let rip and spent the day expressing all our pent-up feelings and what we thought of every place; our dread, disasters and depression. It was such a boost but hard to go on alone for the rest of my stay, although Deborah left me with a pile of Mills and Boon (the only books she could get in English) and a smile on my face. I realized I missed laughter and lightness on my travels and was determined to keep up-beat.

Lahti, famous for its ski jump, stands out as a repeat booking of my (our) worst nightmare. Shows were afternoon slots in front of old men, with lodgings upstairs in a mouldy room, reeking of stale sheets. It could fall as low as forty degrees outside. Even wrapped in all my clothes with Germolene smothered on my face, I would be in tears from the bitter cold trying to make calls from the coin box. Breathing in froze the nostrils, like having two twigs shoved up them, and made your eyes water. The only saving grace were the cinemas where I would watch any film I could to escape the cold.

Things definitely came to a head when I arrived at the address of my next employer in Helsinki. The English sign above the entrance said, in unmistakeably large letters, "The Scala Sex Cinema".

This is the bottom of the barrel – and I'm booked for eight days.

It was as bad as it looked. I had to walk through the auditorium, down to the stage, with a robe over my costume. Hardcore films played between the acts, men openly masturbated during the shows, and anyone who saw me enter assumed I was a prostitute. At the end of the contract Doris shook her head as she paid me. 'You're too artistic for Finland.'

She passed me a letter from Deborah which summed up our experiences.

Dear Tessababe,

Had a foul week but managed not to get depressed again. I got so down because of the flu but I think there's always the possibility of being driven to suicide at Parvoo! Arrived at Patijoki yesterday after 10 hours sitting on a bus, my bum didn't know what hit it.

Did you survive the horrors of the 'Scala'? Couldn't believe it when Doris mentioned she was sending you there. My last stint in Lahti – the absolute pits. Arrived for the 4.30 matinee with all that natural light coming through the windows, showing any cellulite to marvellous effect. One man said to me, "I see you've been making love on the gravel again". I think it's time to retire gracefully to Woolworths check-out desk! Sod 'em all!

Love Deborah.

I returned to London confused once again. My career was so insecure and yet at the same time charged with all sorts of possibilities. It lifted me one minute and dropped me the next. Part of me responded to that thrill of not knowing. But each blow was taking longer to recover from. I knew there were good contracts out there and not all venues were going down the seedy slope of soft porn. I desperately needed some focus in my life. When I began taking yoga classes from Frances, a retired ballerina, I realised I'd found what I'd been looking for. It was a fantastic way of stretching my body and focusing my mind. My energy had been all over the place and yoga grounded me.

Feeling recharged, after a decent break and some stability in London and quality time with Mum, I happily accepted the offer from a new agency, Libretto, based in Kent, for two months at a beach club in Nahariyaa, Israel. They were desperate for an attraction act since the contracted show had not turned up. I'd had good times in Old Acco – I looked forward to more of the same.

I was, in fact, about to endure the worst ten weeks of my life.

*****

I scraped together the airfare, to be reimbursed on arrival along with very good wages. Everything about the contract, at face value, was impressive.

The club was run by two couples. The husbands, one dark, one fair, met me at Tel Aviv and any enthusiasm I had for returning to Israel was killed almost immediately. They ignored me during the journey which was the worst sign of all. If people can't try to be the least bit civil at the start there's usually little room for thought and understanding down the line. We stopped at a modern estate where I met their wives, all hair and fingernails, common and hard, who greeted me with disappointed expressions, as if the wrong package had been delivered.

I couldn't wait to get to my accommodation and start work so that the icy response would start to melt once they saw my shows. But there was a problem. Nothing had been organised. I was abandoned while the four owners had a heated discussion. Then the blonde wife came over.

'You can stay in our spare room.'

I couldn't work them out. It was offered as if it was a huge inconvenience and was obviously an afterthought. In fact it proved only the first violation of our contract's agreement.

When the couples went to the club that night I stayed in my room and I heard them lock the front door. I fell into a troubled sleep, still in my clothes, and in the morning I was taken to rehearse after being offered just one cup of coffee. The DJ was a nice young man, as they usually are, impressed by my dancing, which was always a good sign. But it wasn't his opinion that mattered.

The dark boss had a grim look that refused to shift. The fair one just smiled with disdain, already screwing me in his mind. I'd seen that expression too many times. But no one criticised so I unpacked my costumes in the dressing room and was finally dropped off in town for two hours to eat something.

The club itself was a modern block with sea views, a massive stage and seating area, DJ box above and dressing rooms below. I had the luxury of watching the show before taking part that night— and I was horrified by what I saw. It confirmed that I'd made a terrible mistake in coming.

A heavy-set English dancer, obviously not trained for anything, came off the stage and plonked herself into men's laps, pouting and miming a blow job on a coke bottle. She was absolutely awful and not even attractive and yet the audience applauded loudly.

Fair boss appeared at my shoulder. 'We need your show more like this with disco music,' he said, his face too close for comfort.

They didn't want talent, they wanted sleaze. How on earth had an agent sent me here? I wanted to go home and I hadn't even done a single show: that was a new record.

The next day I was taken to an old apartment block and moved in with the headline attraction, a trio of talented musicians from Paraguay, all short, bronze-skinned, baby-cheeked and dressed in ponchos and panamas. Only when dark boss had left, did they talk, and even then, in hushed tones. They were gentle souls, totally professional, but obviously scared. Not a good sign.

No thought had been put into where I was to sleep. The room was already overcrowded with only two beds for the three musicians. With the guitarist taking the lounge, I was told to sleep in the larder. At least the stone floor was cool and the trio loaned me a sleeping bag. I could close the door and hang my clothes up to cover the glass and so I made my little home. It's amazing what you can tolerate if you have your privacy.

As soon as they went out I began practising my yoga in the lounge, determined not to miss a day's workout. But my mind was already on my debut that night. I was going to dance as never before. *I'll prove them all wrong.*

I put in the performance of my life on a surprisingly good stage and some of the crowd rose to their feet in response. But the owners weren't happy. Everything was wrong, they said. Even my disco number was "too show time".

'You need to sit on laps, get their cash,' Fair said.

'I don't do that.'

'Then we'll send you round other clubs. Can't have you here costing us money all night.'

'Speaking of money, I'm still owed for my air fare.'

'Later. You choose new music with the DJ tomorrow and be ready for extra shows.'

Dutifully I went in early and tried to second guess what they would prefer. Michael Jackson and *Caribbean Queen* from Billy Ocean seemed good bets so I began working out moves for them. We hadn't been going an hour when there was swearing and shouting from the doorway.

Fair burst in, shouting at the DJ.

'What's going on? What are these lights doing on? What's all this music? Who told you you could waste our electricity?'

The DJ didn't say anything and they switched their gaze to me.

'Wasting our time and money, Skola? This will come out of your wages.'

My engagements at the "other clubs" were terrifying. Not knowing where you're going is an unpleasant way to live. I was never told in advance so I could never leave a note for the Paraguayans. It was just a precaution but...

The husbands took it in turns to ferry me around. Each night would follow the same pattern. I'd get in the car and Fair or Dark would try to touch me. I'd shrug them off and we'd drive in silence, both aware that if they'd wanted to push the point there would be nothing I could do against their towering, brutal strength. The clubs in the area were numerous and small. The glossy disco bars had more civilised, well-to-do audiences who actually gave me good responses. Several were bars for getting those on military service to let off steam. I'd stood with soldiers on the bus, kitted out, a rifle up my nose – all very matter-of-fact. The training and fighting was a way of life to them.

The husbands were paid $40 a show and if I was lucky, they'd hand over $5 to me. They cheated me, they cheated the clubs and one night, I realised, they even cheated each other. A new venue paid Fair $60 because I'd been so popular but he told me to tell his brother-in-law it had been $40 – or else.

My fee didn't go up either. Their measly handouts could buy a meal in Acco or three days' supply of food. One week, for no reason, they gave me nothing. I survived on Matzos water biscuits.

The sense of violence that surrounded the husbands was almost tangible. I threw myself into yoga sessions, repeating the mantra about loving all, but these men more than proved a match for my beginner's chanting. Each day that went by brought new horrors and fresh restrictions. My clothes were taken from the dressing room, for example, and locked up.

'You stay in the club until three,' Dark told me. 'Then you get changed when we are finished with you.'

It was pointless but it was scary. I decided to break the habit of a lifetime and call my mother in my moment of distress. She would know what to do.

That was easier said than done. There were no mobiles in those days and pay phones in Israel required tokens for calls. I felt cut off and abandoned. When the DJ told me he'd seen Fair throw away post addressed to me, I only felt worse.

My movements during the day began to attract attention as well. One evening both bosses blocked the dressing room door as I came off stage. Fair had hands on hips; Dark, arms folded. Both were incredibly intimidating.

'We know where you go,' Fair said menacingly. 'We know who you talk to. It's not a nice idea.'

'Tomorrow we collect you at two,' Dark added.

I burst into tears in front of them for the first time. I was just about to plead when Fair held up his hand, calmly.

'Now, before you do anything rash, we've spoken to Libretto and informed them about events. If you take one more step out of line they will hear about it. You'll never work again. Understand?'

The idea of my agent, my new agent, hearing a pack of lies from these animals sickened me. More urgently than ever I had to get to a phone.

The DJ came to my aid. He had a friend who worked at the post office and who was prepared to help me make a call – something I was also forbidden from doing. The next day I pretended to mail a letter and so set off for the post office. The second I stepped inside, the DJ's friend grabbed my shoulders and ushered me into a back room. With him translating for me, I made a reverse charge call to Mum while the DJ stayed on the lookout out front.

I almost broke when I heard her voice but I had to keep to the point.

'Mum, I haven't got long. Please listen.'

'What is it? Are you hurt?'

'No, nothing like that. I need you to phone Libretto. Tell them that whatever my bosses here have told them is a lie.'

I rang off and waited. It seemed like an eternity and I tried to make conversation with my knight in shining armour, but my mind was elsewhere. Then the phone rang.

'Tessa, Libretto has heard nothing. In fact, they have been trying to get in touch with your bosses for an update. They have been worried'

Thank God for that. I gave Mum a précis of what was happening for her to pass on. But at the same time I didn't want to worry her. Only once I'd hung up did my emotions kick in. I was so grateful to learn that my bosses hadn't blacklisted me in the industry. But now I knew what I was dealing with. They would lie to scare me. What else would they do to keep me under control?

I don't know if they heard from Libretto but shortly afterwards the abuse from the husbands escalated. I was now expected to do eight shows a night: and the way they spoke to me would shock a sailor.

The only highlight of my week was the big Saturday show. This brought a completely different, more cultured audience to the beach club. It also attracted some very big acts. It was so refreshing to step out in front of well-dressed, interested crowds rather than the usual unshaven mob in a half empty club. My first experience of the Saturday show was amazing and the standard of appreciation never dropped, despite the bosses' interference.

With just two weeks to endure, I was getting ready backstage as that night's guest arrived, a comedian who looked like WC Fields. He was a natural clown and very friendly, as was his large entourage. After a chat with his manager and technicians, he entered into a conversation with a slim man of about thirty, tanned and fair-haired with the most spectacular blue eyes.

Footsteps clattered down the passage. I braced myself. Only two guesses to whom that tread belonged.

Over the commotion of the comedian's organisation, Dark yelled, 'Skola, you fucking do as you're told. Onstage – *now!*'

I didn't notice the room go quiet. The comedian, his manager, his staff and his friend just stared at Dark in disbelief: but the footsteps were already retreating up the corridor.

Blue Eyes came over and put his hand gently on my shoulder. 'What on earth is going on here?'

I was so used to being spoken to harshly that it took a second to understand the question. He saw that too.

'Look, tell me to mind my own business, but if you're so used to being treated like that that you don't even notice it anymore, then it's time to get out.'

His concern was music to my ears. I wasn't going mad. I wasn't imagining things.

'I just need to hold on for another week or so,' I sniffed. 'Then I'll get my wages and be able to go home.'

The man's name was Chy. He was from Tel Aviv and he wanted to take me out to eat the next day. I whispered that I was followed.

'I don't care. I will protect you. This cannot go on. No one can stop me seeing you.'

We spent hours talking in a café tucked away in a suburb. If anyone had followed me they'd have a long wait. Chy was going through a difficult divorce and ran his own car accessory business. I poured my heart out and he bought me a box of food from the supermarket and loaned me some money. He'd be returning with WC in ten days, he said, but I should be gone by then. I took his address so I could return the money and let him know I was safe.

It was an excruciating week, counting down each hour, trying to remain neutral but with renewed faith. Finally the moment arrived. I'd performed my last shows the night before and the DJ and I turned up for our wages and to say goodbye. He gave me my tapes and squeezed my hand.

If I thought my problems were over, then I was mistaken. When I went to the dressing room to pack up, I discovered someone had pulled out all the diamanté stones from their claws and unpicked the sequin flowers from my costumes. They hung there, limp, like I felt.

I was broken by the time I stood with my bags in the office, waiting for my £1500 wages, plus my return fare and my publicity photos. First Dark came into the room, then Fair. Eventually Dark spoke.

'You're not going,' he said.

'What?'

'You're not going. We need you here another two weeks and a friend with a club in Tiberius wants you for a month. You'll get your money then.'

'No,' I said. Then louder, 'No, you can't do this. I'm going home.'

Fair looked at me, sneered then looked down at some paperwork. As far as he was concerned the meeting was over.

I stood there, shaking, for ages. I kept thinking it was a nightmare or a trick. They would start laughing in a minute then hand over my money.

But they didn't. In fact, when they did start laughing I knew it was at my expense. Crushed, utterly beaten, I left the office with the DJ. He'd heard every word.

'They're never going to pay me,' I said.

He shook his head. Once we were out of earshot he said, 'I think you should go.'

He was right. They hadn't paid me for the last two months, why would they pay me for the next? But what choice did I have? I had no money. That was the whole point. That was their power over me. I was trapped, reliant on them for even my bed and the hope of money.

Two days later WC Fields walked back into the club. Chy was with him again. As soon as he saw me he knew I'd been double-crossed.

'You're leaving,' he said urgently. 'Tonight.'

I had to forget the money, he advised. But I already had. I would trade anything for my freedom and sanity. I left my costume bags hanging, stuffed with old towels. Chy procured my tapes from the DJ and relayed my farewell message. Fair dropped me home at two o'clock, as usual, then two hours later I heard another car outside. It was Chy, the car's headlights dipped. With the bosses' spies everywhere even the fact that it was four in the morning gave us no guarantees and my heart was thumping as Chy took my case and I slipped down under the dashboard. I didn't dare even break the silence to close the door, just holding it steady until we turned onto the main road. Then Chy put his foot down, I slammed the door shut, and we both began to breathe again.

'They said if I ever left, they'd find me. They have contacts everywhere.'

'It's all talk,' Chy insisted. 'They are only big fish in their little pond. There's nothing they can do.'

He dropped me in Tel Aviv with enough money for a hotel and the airfare home. He apologised for not doing more but he had to get back to sorting out his own life. I didn't mind. He'd done enough. He was the one who'd gone out on a limb for me. He was the one who, I'm convinced, saved my life.

CHAPTER FIFTEEN

IT'S ALL RIGHT, DARLINK

Just before I left Tel Aviv a stranger said to me, 'You look like a dancer.' He was right, of course, but it took me by surprise.

'What makes you say that?'

'The way you walk, the way you hold your head, your hair, your dress. Everything. You remind me of a sleek racehorse!'

Over the years I've received a multitude of benefits from people who have made the same deduction, from free entry to clubs all over the world by doormen with an expert eye for posture and poise, to interviews with journalists looking for a professional's opinion. Once, at La Scala opera house in Vienna, I was even called to the front of the toilet queue by a cloakroom attendant. 'Let the dancer have first pee!'

Stepping off the plane at Heathrow in 1985 I didn't feel like a dancer. I felt beaten, cowed and afraid. The trauma of Israel had scarred me more than being raped or bullied. When I saw Mum waiting I thought I'd crumple into floods of tears. But something very odd happened instead. Seeing her loving face waiting to smother me with kisses, I felt strong.

And instead of a breakdown, I had a breakthrough.

Returning to London was the first part of my rejection of the untreated poison festering inside me. The rapes - physical and mental – and the bosses who had threatened to break me, had, at times, come close to succeeding. Until I confronted my demons I realised I would always be under their spell. In London I began to tackle them head-on. Yet it was by going back to Cornwall that my healing really began.

I'd never thought of it before but Fowey was my anchor. The sudden surge of salt up the nostrils and the lapping of water and clank of boat chains were a cocoon for the senses. And in the middle of it all was Gran's conservatory, my sanctuary in those fragile weeks. On a hot afternoon I'd sit alone in the sun chair, drenched in comfort, the smell of strong tea and moist geraniums wrapped around me. Blissful, healing moments, when happy memories returned and, slowly, so did plans. The future didn't seem so futile anymore and the pain of the past was fading.

Someone once said that dancers have fast karma. Hadn't I paid my dues yet?!

I needed to draw a line under events and my twenty-fifth birthday gave me the perfect opportunity. That was the day I stopped drinking and became a vegetarian. That was the day I cleared out my wardrobe and possessions to simplify my life. That was the day I retook control.

I was excited by the change in me, and by what the future had to offer. If I'd been running before, as Audrey in Basel had accused me of, then I wasn't going to any longer. I would put the positives back into my job and not be weighed down by the negatives. Travel would be on my own terms. There was plenty of work for me in London, so I didn't need to go anywhere. And when I did venture abroad it would be because I wanted to, not because I had nothing else to hold me back.

A year later I would make my longest journey yet and for the best possible reason.

*****

The club scene in London had expanded beyond all recognition since my earliest job as a shy seventeen-year-old. But now, anxious not to travel just yet, I was pleased to discover a West End cabaret circuit that I didn't know existed. Within a three-mile radius, Soho, Piccadilly, Bond Street and Tottenham Court Road had quietly become the most important place in my life.

Some clubs were intimate venues with private membership. Others welcomed anyone looking for a drink at the end of the day. Business meetings, men in search of company, stag nights and tourists all filled the spaces. In return they found a bar, a few tables and a dance floor with a acts performing a show every half-hour.

Of course there was another side. The clubs were in business solely to make money from consummation via the hostesses – and most of these were prostitutes earning hundreds of pounds in the more high-class venues. Unlike a lot of the scared, hard hostesses I'd met on my travels, many of the London girls seemed empowered by their lives, to an extent, even if they weren't exactly open about it. On my first night at Bond Street's Kabaret club, I met Tracey, who had a husband and two children who never twigged that her evenings supposedly driving a taxi were actually spent with regulars at Claridges – where she made a point of swiping the room clear of goodies every time she checked out.

Kabaret was a basement cabaret between the haute couturiers of Mayfair, filled with hostesses of all nationalities and run by Tony Knight, a look-a-like Dev from *Coronation Street*. Unlike a lot of bosses he took an interest in the acts he hired and was happy to talk candidly about his time behind bars.

By contrast, the backgrounds of Tony and Mario, owners of my next venue, were immaculate. They'd both been waiters at the famous 1950s show clubs Churchills and Murrays and had been bringing the same style to Le Rafifi, off Berkeley Square, since 1968. From my first night to my last it was an absolute pleasure to work in an environment that respected its acts – regardless of how the place made most of its money.

I couldn't have wished for nicer bosses and I think they liked me. No other club ever bought me a Christmas present – a hairdryer! I'd been there a week when Mario said, 'Tessa, would you do us the honour of being interviewed by a journalist about the club?'

'Of course, but why me?'

'Because if someone who has played in clubs all over the world can't give an honest opinion, then who can?'

The piece was for London's *Time Out* magazine which then led to interviews for the Evening Standard. I'd done it for Mario but the knock-on effect on my own career was quite something. Bosses and agents began ringing *me* for once and I was soon doing spots in three or four different clubs a night to a rapturous reception from audiences, other acts and even the hostesses. One of my favourite compliments was being told, 'You're a breath of fresh air, Tess.' It sort of summed me up. I was happy to work in that world but I wasn't a real part of it – I was a dancer, pure and simple, and after the horrors of Israel, I finally felt whole again.

It was still an endurance test, with my daily routine geared to a life of the night, even if I had part-time work in a book shop or as a life model. Fitness and yoga training every day - main meal by four o'clock – bathe, shave, tan and grooming – a short siesta, then make-up and out of the door by ten. Home no later than three a.m. to relax and unwind once costumes had been hung to air.

By September I was ready to dip my toe back into international waters again. I looked at my choices and one contract immediately appealed: two month's contract in Oslo. Near, cultured and a place I'd never been.

I knew I was right the moment I set down. After Greece, Africa and Israel, recently, it was like chewing a refreshing mint. Clean, compact and orderly – all descriptions in marked contrast to the intense heat, emotions and chaos of the Middle East.

The skies were cloudless and the days full of pure enjoyment; walking around the harbour and museums, visiting the Kon Tiki and Vigeland Park. Everyone spoke good English. People seemed so wholesome and gentle.

The Rose Cellar club booked rock bands so my heavy metal and more futuristic shows fitted in well. It was so hassle-free that I returned several times to work there, once flying through the grey blanket of fallout from Chernyobl. It really was the perfect welcome back to my business abroad and gave me the confidence to continue.

To this day Oslo holds my most enduring memories, especially auditioning for the bosses of the grand Oslo Kabaret in front of Victor Borg's piano. He was their guest star that week. And, in contrast, being booked at a hall in the suburbs, lit by candles along the front of the stage, performing for the most unlikely but lovable gathering: bikers, in full leather gear, sporting long hair, beards and helmets!

'Where are you going next?' Mum asked, now so used to my packing up and disappearing to anywhere around the globe.

'I don't know – yet. But it will be somewhere lovely I hope.'

Thanks to my burgeoning London bookings I could afford to be picky. But being popular at home had its own downside and trying to squeeze as many shows in per night as possible was a common problem. Each night the West End streets would be filled with rushing girls, the striptease acts and artistes, flying off to their next venue. They were all identifiable by nocturnal uniforms of gym shoes, jeans, long coats and always lugging great holdalls. I would wear a long black shift dress that I could slip on and off quickly and still look elegant entering the clubs.

'Good luck at the Directors Lodge.'

'What are the crowds like?'

'Just how you like them.'

Then we'd be out of earshot: little snatches of conversation carried on the night breeze.

A lot of girls relied more on slow, seductive performances but that wasn't my style. I treated every performance like I was onstage at the Lido. I put my all into every one, but, as a result, I could only manage four spots a night without collapsing in exhaustion whilst trying to earn a decent living.

Burlesque in Bruton Place was a favourite venue with its spacious dance floor and taxis chugging in lines up to the door; it was always packed. The Rheingold Club, off Oxford Street, was another good venue for showcases where agents could come and watch new acts. And then there was Chatterleys on Albermarle Street which enticed tourists wandering into Mayfair from Piccadilly. The doorman was known as "Micky Shoulders" for obvious reasons when you saw his tight-fitting cashmere coat. 'A lot of "faces" meet here,' he told me with pride although when I thought of some of villains I'd met abroad I couldn't get too excited. But the boss and audiences were exemplary.

After a busy spring the offer I was waiting for came in. I couldn't think of anywhere better to spend summer than in Italy. It was a stay of two halves. I worked in the oppressive summer heat in Milan, at the famous William's le Roi nightclub. This was the only club I ever worked in that produced a full, glossy entertainment programme and employed an actual orchestra that changed every six months .

I stayed at a Pensione Ballerin on the third floor of an old building that housed many models and gay make-up artists – always a hive of activity. My pensione was full of well-behaved hostesses and strictly run by the landlady – no cooking or guests allowed in the rooms. Despite everything starched, spick-and-span, I was horrified, when leaving, to discover I had caught crabs. I thought it was the heat that was causing such terrible itching until I inspected the area with a mirror.

I slathered hair removal cream over my entire pubic area and had a bald pussy for weeks afterwards. Thank goodness I hadn't taken on a new lover, I thought!

I then transferred to the welcome breeze of the coast and a disco in San Remo, which went without a hitch, so I could celebrate my twenty-sixth birthday in style at the Royal Hotel on the esplanade. I was alone but content with my lot in life – more than I'd been for a long time.

I continued to work all over Northern Italy and returned for many years with my agent Luciano Migliorini. He cut an imposing figure; heavy set and always dressed immaculately in a suit and tie even in sweltering heat. His wife was an English ex-dancer, so they knew the ropes and how to treat their artistes. Contracts included performing in sumptuous transvestite shows. I was the surprise ending to the whole facade when I undressed fully at the finale to reveal that I was the only real woman in the show!

But Italy's bosses were as hard as ever. They had the option to sack the acts they didn't like three days after a contract started, so there was absolute chaos as artistes were moved around by fraught agents. I must say, Luciano stuck to his guns and stuck up for me, and we only encountered one change of plan.

In Venice one February, I would witness the most moving and exquisite "show" that I would ever see. Carnival.

This was a tapestry of moving theatre; of ponchinellos posing in doorways and hooded, white-masked monks gliding by. Camp monstrosities, divine and devilish, ravishing and mysterious. Wandering the streets, I'd turn a corner to see the train of a gown disappearing over a bridge or a golden hooked nose, glinting from an archway .

It made my imagination race – all the possibilities for a new show theme!

And whilst in Turin, this happened. A marvellous disco dancing duo, Michele and Alessandra – Kaos – had gone out of their way to compliment my act and, more importantly, to suggest ways of improving it. Michele was a marvel at choreography and costume design (and making the best ever tiramisu) so I put myself in his hands to create a completely different show at a cost of £300. It was a lot of money, which gives some idea of how much I trusted him. But the end result would become my signature dance for the next ten years.

Every dance act would have one number that they would be remembered for.

Moody, disturbing and physically demanding, Grace Jones' *Slave To The Rhythm* brought out a new creature in me, incorporating advanced yoga contortions and acrobatics with the most extreme dance moves. The first time I performed it I was met with gasps. As the music built and swelled, in black net balaclava, ripped skirt and boots, I finally let down my hair which added movement and effect. But the twist was that, whether topless or nude, I then dressed and put on a diamanté-studded leather jacket to finish. It broke the rules and it brought the house down and, most nights, won me nothing but praise.

Unfortunately, London would have to wait to see it. I needed to continue working but only Burlesque had a spot for me. I had been out of the country too long.

A burgeoning campaign to "clean up" Soho had reached a head while I was away. Nudity was being stamped down on. In the spirit of trying new things, I took a contract at a peep show with a difference, opposite the Prince Edward theatre. Ten slots over five hours a day I danced and posed on workout stations wearing fitness gear, but as good as we all were, I'm sure, I could hear the howls of "rip-off" from the other side of the wall.

A club further along which advertised "Bed Shows", was another rip-off, in that there were just hostesses plied with drink from customers, sitting fully clothed on a bed.

I was employed to do some short five minute dances which seemed to ease the tension and give the punters some value for their hugely overpriced cocktails. This venue was in fact filmed in all its reality, girls included, for the film *Mona Lisa* with Bob Hoskins. I was treated well and never encountered any trouble.

I was focused entirely on earning and saving as much money as possible and for one particular reason. I'd reached a decision in Italy that had been more than twenty years in the making. I'd decided I was going to go to Australia.

To Adelaide.

To find my father.

*****

'I can't believe I'm going to live here for six months.'

I'd only been in Adelaide for a few hours but I was sure of one thing. I had never seen a more beautiful country. The first revelation was the light. The sky somehow looked spherical as its intense blue infused the landscape with the richest hues. Parklands were a cornucopia of colour and even traffic islands seemed aflame with a profusion of plant life to dazzle the eyes. Even in the play area opposite my "unit" (studio flat) flocks of pink cockatoos would fly in and land on the swings.

Beneath the beauty I quickly discovered an approach to life more in keeping with my own than anywhere else in the world. Compared to Europe's climate and constant striving to make ends meet, people here relished their time away from work, putting an emphasis on health, freedom and friends, not dollars, bricks and mortar. I was entering a fitness fanatic's paradise.

Just imagining that I had been conceived in this outstanding environment sent a chill up my spine. The idea threw up so many other questions, none of which could be answered. What if I'd been born here instead of England? What if I'd gone to an Australian dance school, swum in Australian waters as a child and fallen in love with an Australian man? Every day I thought of new "what ifs" but there was one that kept recurring.

What if I'd known my father?

The time had come to make contact and meet my Father. I was on an eight month contract and so I had space to make myself comfortable and settle into work whilst I prepared myself.

*****

It wasn't just normal citizens who seemed happy in Adelaide. In clubland the city was known as "a fruitcake with icing on top". The Crazy Horse advertised "the best striptease cabaret in Australia" and was run by John Monaghan along the same lines as the Parisian club and Raymond's: and I had been booked to star there.

Crazy Horse was at the more respectable end of Hindley Street. Further along the strip were massage parlours, call girl salons and strip clubs which were out-and-out vulgar. But there was also a proliferation of gay clubs which excelled in *La Cage aux Folles* style shows with superb costumes and amazing queens of the desert.

Taking a tour of the club before the lighting rehearsal, I was impressed to see proper dressing tables with bulb-lit mirrors, showers, a mattress to crash on and a TV. Even better, the other acts couldn't have been more welcoming. I sat between Nicole and Rebel, two ex-members of Les Girls, an exceptionally talented and beautiful Australian touring troupe of model sex changes, and I swear if you didn't know their history you would never guess. Rebel was happily married and living like a normal housewife during the day.

One by one the rest of the cast came in, vivacious in the Adelaide setting. There was Charlene, the ex-Raymond girl; Lisa, the ice skater from California; Katy, who had polio and disguised it well with a classic seated burlesque number; and Monique Star, another American whom I had met before on the London circuit. Local resident dancers were April and Katie and one male striptease, Rob.

Everyone was there – or so I thought. Then I heard the door open again and a familiar voice.

'So you found me at last then, Tessa my darling?'

It couldn't be, could it?

I spun round and there in the doorway was the beautiful, dark-haired figure of Anne, my love from the Windmill.

'What are you doing here?' I gasped, running over to hug her.

'I helped set this whole place up. I've been waiting for you'.

I couldn't believe it, after all these years. This stunning Morticia with the most fabulous physique had just walked back into my life after nearly a decade. As I got ready to perform I couldn't help thinking of the times we'd shared. She'd been my first female love and although I'd had several since, some physical, some not, none of them had compared to her. None of them had made me feel as she did. She'd been the first woman I'd kissed – and the first woman I had wanted to kiss.

Would we pick up where we'd left off?

The whole night was full of surprises. The crowd turned out to be enthusiastic and not at all intimidating as I'd been warned Australian audiences could be. They were even supportive when my headdress got caught in my hair and I had to run offstage to find some scissors before I choked to death.

Afterwards we celebrated. Anne and I had so much time to make up and everyone else was buzzing from the show. Unusually, the entire staff of the Crazy Horse at that time was female – sexy waitresses, female bouncers and the excellent DJ technician, Tammy, pulled all the strings – a fact that went some way to offset the testosterone of the audiences.

'They were polite tonight,' Anne assured me. 'That never happens two nights in a row so brace yourself tomorrow!'

I opened the show with *Cabaret* while people were sober. The loud, aggressive numbers were best saved for last, I was advised. 'If they get out of control I just turn the music up,' Tammy said.

'Is it that bad?'

She laughed. 'Probably worse.'

It was actually not until the weekend that I really experienced the true red-blooded Ozzie audience – and I wasn't impressed. It was a fully nude show, although some revealed more than others, but on a Saturday it did seem to tease the perverts out of the shadows.

I knew it was a raucous night but only when the girl before me came running off in tears did I begin to appreciate what I was up against.

It was my last spot of the night and the crowd was unrecognisable from the boisterous faces I'd seen half an hour earlier. They were drunk and almost out of control. I was unreachable during my performance normally, but this mob managed to break the spell and get through to me. Barely thirty seconds in the baying started, 'That's the ugliest beaver I've ever seen.'

Huge laughter. In response I heard Tammy up the decibels a few notches.

'Show us what you had for breakfast then,' another wag called out.

I fixed my expression and danced harder. Two more minutes to go. But then they got me.

'Show us where you've had your abortions.'

That was the end. I'd spent my life performing for men, trying to entertain and impress, and I'd always done it with a clear conscience and a proud spirit. But whoever shouted that out, and all those guys who laughed at it, made me think about whom I was performing for, for the first time. They didn't deserve me. They didn't deserve any woman.

It was upsetting but I survived. I'd been through worse, after all, and it didn't happen every night. The best thing, in a weird way, was that it happened to all of us. I wasn't being singled out. These idiots just hated women by the look of it. But they were the ones paying to see us. They were the ones who were hurting more than us, for whatever reason.

The second male member of the Crazy Horse team was Joseph, the show's artistic director and choreographer. By night he performed in drag as "Josephine" both compère and an impressively strong dancer.

After a week of admiring my own shows he approached me with an idea.

'Why don't you use any props?'

'Because they're impossible to carry. I live out of a suitcase, don't forget.'

He thought for a second. 'Well, you're not going anywhere for five months, so why don't we make the most of that?'

Two weeks later, wearing a gold hat and voluminous cloak, gold bikini and gold body straps, and, naturally, to the accompaniment of Spandau Ballet's *Gold*, I opened, climbed up, balanced on, and crawled into, a giant gold safe taking up most of centre stage. It took the act in a fresh direction. In one way my dancing was reined in by it, but in another the safe opened up new channels.

It quickly became the centrepiece of my night and I never tired of the thrill of having an artistic director taking an interest in my work. It was such an honour compared to the choreographers who just wanted me to memorise steps that they'd thought of years earlier for completely different women.

I later adapted *Gold*, performing the acrobatics over a chair, which I sprayed gold and carried around to the London clubs. That caused quite a lot of comments as I strode along Regent Street!

One evening, to boot, during the Adelaide Arts Festival, the cast of *Cirque du Soleil* watched the show and sent a note backstage for me, saying congratulations!

Life at Crazy Horse was physically demanding, the temperature on stage often reached forty one degrees; but the world outside the club couldn't have been better. Running in guaranteed sunshine was a pleasure; doing yoga in vast open spaces, enjoying inexpensive good food, exotic fruits, the craft centres in the Adelaide hills and being surrounded by smiling, genuinely happy people, all made every day a treat. After a few months I felt like I truly belonged in my original "home town". Then one day, after a walk past the old Governor's House where Mum had worked all those years ago, I decided to call her.

I don't know if she'd been expecting the question or not but probably. She knew I was in Adelaide and she knew what I was like. When I said, 'Can you give me Daddy's address?' I think she was prepared.

'He doesn't live there anymore,' she said calmly.

'Oh. Well have you got his new address?'

'It's not in Adelaide.'

'Well where is he living then?'

She paused. 'He moved to America.'

Seconds of silence passed between us. I'd been building up to this moment secretly for months. The seed had been planted in Italy, I'd saved money for the trip in London, and now I was here: ready to meet my father in Adelaide.

I've never blamed Mum for her choices. I didn't then. But I felt such a blow of disappointment and, truth was, she knew. After an age she said, 'There's someone else you might like to meet, though.'

Someone else? Who?

'Someone who knew your father very well. Someone who knew me very well. His name's Adolf Sulcs, he was the most amazing pastry chef – and he was your Daddy's stepfather.'

I took the address and hung up. The show that night was harder work than usual but my mind blocked out any rowdiness from the crowd. My father had gone. That had floored me. All this way for…

I tried to be positive. *There's a reason for everything. And it's not a wasted journey because there's still my step-grandfather.*

The next afternoon the club handyman, Johnny "Yak Yak", a talkative, white-bearded man in his sixties, drove me out to the suburbs. I've never been more nervous in my life. I'd taken the precaution of writing to Adolf first and been very pleased to receive an invitation to the house he shared with his new partner, Martha. Even so, the trepidation I felt as I waved goodbye to Johnny and walked up that stranger's path was debilitating. When I reached the door I fell upon it for support. I didn't have the strength to knock. I was too frightened.

The nerves of waiting behind a curtain for the first time are nothing compared to this!

But then the door swung open and standing there was a man who, if circumstances had been different, I would once have called "granddad".

I fell into Adolf's arms as if reunited with an old friend. He hugged me firmly and kissed the top of my head as the tears flowed.

'It's all right, darlink,' he said. His accent was strong and even though I'd never heard it before it was unmistakeably Latvian to me. It was as though the voice was in my genes.

Martha cooked a delicious meal but I just remember the talking. Adolf and I spoke as though we'd known each other all our lives. I told him about myself and he chuckled with pride, wanting to know every detail of the exotic places I'd been to. But it was what he could tell me that I was dying to learn. Over the next two hours my father stopped being an unknown phantom in the back of my mind and became a reality.

Adolf had married Jo, my grandmother, a few years before I'd been born and was proud to become a stepfather to Daddy and his brother, Viktor.

'Your father had gumption as a boy, he really did. Spying on the Nazis, yet making a few pennies selling them whatever he could filch, then chased out of his country at such a young age. It was a terrible thing for any child.'

Dad had become a pilot and then met Mum and had been as happy as Adolf had ever seen him. But then the drinking had got out of control and Mum had left.

'He never recovered from that,' Adolf sighed. 'He lived in a stinking room, he was unwashed, always sleeping in his clothes, just living to have another drink.'

He fell out of the plane hire business and into grocery but that couldn't support his addiction. When Adolf and Jo separated and she moved to America, Daddy had been too drunk to agree to go. Eventually Jo persuaded him that life would be better over there and she sent him the money for a plane ticket.

'But your father just spent it on booze,' Adolf said. 'Jo did that twice and then she just sent a ticket itself and he finally went.' He shrugged sadly. 'And I haven't seen him since.'

Of course it had been a huge disappointment not to meet my father after so many months of private planning. But talking to Adolf was the next best thing. If anything I actually needed to have that conversation with him before I met the man himself. *It's for the best,* I convinced myself. *When I do meet Daddy I'll be ready.*

For the rest of my stay in Australia I visited Adolf and Martha, my two new family members, every week to eat a hearty Sunday lunch with them. It was an honour to see them and to go through the boxes of Adolf's late sister's belongings. Each heirloom had another memory of Latvia that brought my heritage closer to me. They stored everything and I realized that this was a trait from the war years – nothing was wasted or thrown away. The kitchen was for hospitality, the lounge, which was kept immaculate but untouched, for show.

My Australian adventure had to come to an end eventually and my heart was heavy. Nothing sexual had been rekindled between me and Anne but the bond we'd shared in London was as strong as ever. Emotionally she gave me everything I needed, though, and more than any man had managed. Saying goodbye to her was spiritually draining. The curse of my itinerant life had never seemed so real.

And even though I was burned out from the workload, I would have danced at the Crazy Horse till I dropped if my visa had only permitted it. John Monaghan had made me so welcome and even on my last night repeated, 'We need ten of you, Tess.' It was so kind because we both knew I wasn't what the average customer wanted to see – too arty.

My send-off was totally unexpected. I was called back on stage and, as everyone circled round, they handed me flowers, presents and champagne. Then a hat passed round the audience returned filled with money. What a perfect finale to my season there and yet another incredible memory of that country.

But I still had one more show to do and it would be my most memorable of all. There was a large festival at the Latvian Hall for Adelaide's vast Latvian population and Adolf had begged me to perform. I was strangely nervous because it was so personal and so special to dance for 'my community'. I performed the best *Cabaret* I could manage and retired to a standing ovation. But the best was yet to come. As I sat with Adolf and Martha to enjoy the rest of the show, I realised so many other people on our table had stories about Dainis and Doreen. The night passed in a blur of tears and laughter.

At the airport the next day Adolf and I hugged for what seemed like an hour. There were no words. Neither of us could speak. Eventually I let go and walked away as slowly as I dared. Every fibre of me wanted to look back but I knew if I turned round now I wouldn't get on that plane.

It was the hardest parting of my life. Australia had given me everything I could ever dream of; the softest cushion for all my losses, worries and missing pieces in my life. I wept until I fell asleep.

CHAPTER SIXTEEN

WHO'S THAT OLD ROUÉ?

Dancing was always the driving force of my life but I wonder how long I would have lasted if I'd been tied down to one place. Approaching thirty years old, I began to reflect on how I'd turned down so many lucrative year-long contracts at major venues. Had I made the right choices? I think so, even foregoing the security and the comfort of living something close to a "normal" life. It seems unreal to talk of a year in Paris or Tokyo as claustrophobic but I would have felt like a butterfly with its wings clipped. The thirst for travel was in my blood. I think the thrill of taking risks played a part as well. And there really was that niggling suspicion that something better was just around the corner. The feeling never left me: always, just around the next corner.

Dancing was my passport. Wherever I travelled in the world, on business or pleasure, as long as I had my holdall with music and costumes, I could usually find a venue to offer my show to and later add to my CV. I often enjoyed a startling response as the surprise act of the evening; in Jamaica, Bali, Cairo, Madeira, Malta and Mexico City. In fact, by the time I hung up my g-strings years later, I think that, of the major tourist destinations, only Singapore, Spain and Iceland had eluded me.

After the head-spinning events of Adelaide I took myself straight off for a break in Turkey. Naturally that turned into a contract in Istanbul. I had a lot to mull over and it was the perfect opportunity. I danced at Regine's Nightclub along with the most exotic belly dancers who made their own outfits. I paid them to embellish my costumes with sequins and beads, to stunning effect.

Adolf had painted an irresistible picture of Latvian life. Daddy hadn't come out of it in the best light, but after so many years at least I felt like I was beginning to know him and our homeland. I thought back to my own years of drinking.

Why did I do it? Was I trying to hide from my life or search for something that was missing?

What drove Daddy's alcoholism? A lot of people dispossessed by the war clutched the bottle for support. But a lot didn't as well. What if he drank because there was something missing from his life? What if I was that thing? And what if seeing me would help him stop?

It was too much to take in but I had a decision to make. *Shall I go to America to find him?*

Yes, I thought. *But not now.*

Something held me back. Maybe I didn't want to spoil the picture that Adolf had created. Or maybe I was just confused and scared by everything I had been through. Often life just took over: work, making money. I would get side-tracked.

I returned to London not entirely sure of my decision. I'd waited so many years to meet Daddy I could wait a little longer. I'd been mentally strong when I looked for him in Adelaide. I needed to feel that again. I thought about where to go, how to build my reserves back up. The whole world was open to me. If only I had someone in it to love.

It was such a surprise then to find what I was looking for on my doorstep.

*****

It was a great privilege being able to travel the world and come home to work in my own city. After more than ten years in the business I was proud to be as in demand as ever. On the corner opposite the Ritz stood the De Luxe, a superior pink-and-white designed cabaret with a six-piece band, popular with Asian groups. When the lease expired, I moved with them to Casanova on Edgware Road. The exterior looked like any building around the high street but inside it was like walking into a Hong Kong club with topless barmaids in the circular bar, a glitzy dance floor upstairs and, I guess, bedrooms above – I was never allowed up.

The New Georgian, another favourite, was the smallest venue on the circuit and although owned jointly by two bosses, it was Manolo, the Italian maitre d', who had the major say in booking the artistes that were popular. Short and swift, in dark suit and white bow tie, he pampered the guests with ease and we worked together at several venues for most of my career. To meet real characters, establish a good relationship and be treated well was a bonus working through the night.

Each club was its own little world and ran to its own rules. Only a few places were open on Saturdays for the simple reason that "married men go home for the weekend". Casanova was one of the few to open but with such thin crowds it was a real chore to do one spot, but I'd enjoy a Lebanese meze and mint tea afterwards at the next-door café, surrounded by men smoking their pipes. We'd watch the hostesses depart with their customers to rooms in the hotels that lined Sussex Gardens towards Paddington.

Any longer gaps between shows and there was Bar Italia on Dean Street, crammed with bizarre party-goers and Italian insomniacs, sipping cappuccinos and watching football on the TV.

The world of the nocturnal city dwellers felt surprisingly homely. Yet my own to-and-fro existence from Providence Court and the clubs was missing something. Then one day, on a bus going to Knightsbridge, a middle-aged man paused next to me and said, 'Excuse me, is this bus the number twenty-seven for Harrods?'

What an odd question. Of course it was. I expected the man to move to one of the many empty seats but he sat down next to me. I smiled politely and stared back out of the window, watching London slip by. Then I heard a slight cough.

What does he want now?

'I hope you don't mind, but you're not part of the Royal Ballet, are you?'

I didn't see that one coming. 'Not quite, but I trained with them many years ago.'

'Oh really? Yes, I thought you had the look.'

There was a time when I would have swapped seats to escape such an obvious chat-up attempt but something about this man's clumsy enthusiasm made me stay. Studying his rather lined, expressive face and sparkling hazel eyes, I smiled at the way his hand kept darting up to his longish, grey hair. He was a bundle of energy – like me.

'I'm Tessa,' I said.

His name was Colin and, he claimed, he had just been helping to devise the story line for a new ballet, *The Prince of the Pagodas*. I'm not sure I believed it but listening to him trying to make conversation was a diverting way of passing a bus journey. When he asked for my number I changed the subject. That, however, was before he mentioned that he was really a screenplay writer – a successful and quite famous one I later realised.

Someone with my passion for not standing still, for seeing new places? And he knows about ballet!

A few days later I was rushing around Providence Court getting ready for a lunch date. Mum knew I was going out but not with whom. As she sat at the window in the lounge I heard a derisive chuckle.

'Who's that old roué?' she laughed, pointing out a tall, gangly figure in a smart tailored suit that he'd somehow managed to make look crumpled.

'Mum, that's Colin,' I said, and skipped out to meet him before she could say anything else!

We ate at Dino's, an Italian restaurant on North Audley Street, where locals and Embassy staff from Grosvenor Square could linger, away from the Oxford Street din. Lunchtime turned into early evening and before I knew it we were being offered the supper menu as well. We spoke about all the places each of us had been, our passions for particular personalities, paintings and possibilities. Colin loved hearing about my adventures – well, the ones I was prepared to tell him! – and I could have listened all night to his bewitching voice enthuse about everything from the sunlight to the Sahara to the salt cellar on our table. By the time we said goodbye I knew I was falling in love but in a completely new way.

Colin mixed in higher circles of course and had many friends, from stage and television personalities to the Royal Family even. But when he said, 'Have you been to Florence?' there wasn't a piece of architecture he could name that I hadn't seen and loved.

He clapped his hands, eyes twinkling in delight. 'I've met my match in you!'

I don't know if he wanted to prove he really was a writer but for our second date Colin invited me to a function at Hatchards, the Piccadilly bookshop. I was introduced to everyone including PD James and Frank Muir who were very charming and funny. He was allowing me into his world. I felt slightly abashed and then came into my own. I was just myself and, in being so, I could mix well with any crowd.

Colin opened my mind. In return I opened up a side of Colin that had lain dormant, he said – his sense of mischief. When you've struggled alone in so many arduous circumstances, you learn to look for the fun in any occasion and I lost count of the times we'd be strolling somewhere, talking sombrely about a characteristic of a building or the light's reflection off a window, and I could have him collapse against a doorway with a quick observation or just by disappearing from view while his back was turned. *You're never too old for hide-and-seek.*

Colin had just written a TV drama about an uptight journalist who meets a showgirl from the other side of the tracks and falls in love with her. He had scripted me into his life.

The thirst for new experiences bound us tighter than either could have predicted. As soon as I could get a break from my London commitments we shared our first trip together, the first of many around the British Isles. It made a change to actually see things together rather than compare memories. I did notice, though, that while I was never more content than when drinking in the landscape, Colin spent as much time staring at me as sightseeing.

'It's so rare to see someone enjoy life this much. People are normally so worn down. You see everything with the wonder of a child.'

Was it childlike, I wondered, or the relief of having come through so many other experiences that made me grab each day's beauty with both hands? One day I would confide in Colin the times I was too scared to look anywhere other than at my feet as I walked through Senegal or even Switzerland. Maybe even the times I could only foresee darkness.

Life before you've had a knife at your throat and life afterwards can never be the same. But at least it was life. *And I'm determined to live mine to the fullest.*

Over the next six years Colin and I would travel all over the world – from Malaysia, Indonesia and Mauritius to the West Indies, Europe and America. But it was taking him to my spiritual home of Adelaide to introduce him to Adolf and Martha that really excited me. That was when I knew I was truly in love, when I realised how important it was for me to show him my roots.

A week before we were due to fly, however, my plans fell apart. Mum took the call from Martha.

'It's Adolf. He's passed away.'

Even though he wasn't a blood-relative he was Latvian and he felt like family.

'Are you going to cancel your trip?' Mum asked.

'Not at all. It seems more important than ever to go now.'

I also had a contract at the Crazy Horse to fulfil.

Flying into Sydney harbour still beats any other view and this time I had Colin to share it with. When we went on to Adelaide, I couldn't wait to show him my favourite haunts but first I had something else to do. As Colin watched, I found a local phone book at the airport and thumbed nervously through. There it was: "Skola".

'I think I've found a relative.'

Margaret Skola was my aunt, having married Viktor, Daddy's brother. Colin and I drove out to Murray Bridge. I wondered what she would be like. Viktor had been an alcoholic and delusional when he'd committed suicide. His last words were, "The soldiers are coming." What if Margaret somehow blamed my family connection for her suffering? None of my relatives were good at tracing their families. It seemed they had made a life and didn't rock the boat by churning up the painful past. That was my role!

I shouldn't have worried though. Just as Adolf and I had connected instantly, so did Margaret, her children and I, clutching hands with tears flowing.

'You look so much like your mother.'

'You remember my mother?'

'Of course I do,' she laughed. 'Although I haven't seen her for almost thirty years.'

From Margaret I learned that I also had a cousin, Irisa, the daughter of Daddy's cousin, who lived in a purpose-built house on Sylvania Waters in Sydney. She was married to a Latvian architect.

'One of the successful ones,' Margaret said.

I couldn't believe that I had more family to meet.

While I danced at the Crazy Horse, Colin worked on a screenplay set in the outback. Once the contract had finished we flew to Queensland and spent a week on a private island - as near Nirvana as I shall ever find. We walked around naked, I swam, he wrote. We scuba-dived with manta rays and sat in humble wonderment, watching by torchlight, as turtles laid their eggs and slowly struggled back to the sea. I was so happy and so in love.

Later our relationship really showed its strength when Colin disappeared to China to research for a new film and I, after a few months in London, took up the offer of a contract in Holland. It wasn't the best experience of my life, booked in clubs in Amsterdam and Rotterdam with cabaret downstairs featuring live sex shows and bedrooms upstairs. No pushing for drinks or more – just my dancing, but in an environment for men, led along by Asian and Brazilian girls to take a shared Jacuzzi or a trip to the corridor of beds beyond.

On many occasions Colin would rescue me on my days off and flit over to wherever I was working in Europe, book a luxury hotel, feed me to the gills but cry pity when he had to leave me to endure the rest of an awful contract. The sense of love and assurance and comfort almost made it more difficult to see a contract through. But I always did.

I felt so lucky, to be able to take a chance on a country, knowing that if it didn't work out there was work waiting for me at home, and somewhere - Colin.

*****

Even in the 1990s the Eve Club, 189 Regent Street, was a living image of the 1950s and 1960s, still holding on by a thread to the glamour of those golden cabaret days. This was once *the* club in London where the jet set and politicians used to dine and enjoy the sumptuous shows.

Gran's neighbour, Raggie, who was seventy-plus and whom I loved because of her wit, naughty humour, elegance and charm, used to pour out treble vodkas and talk about her nights there with her husband in the oil trade. How she dressed up, how glamorous were the showgirls: she'd describe the whole event for this was the place to be seen, with a guest list including Errol Flynn, Judy Garland, Frank Sinatra, Onassis, Maharajahs - even the KGB.

This was the only club in London where I had a proper audition. It was like opening a door into another era. The entrance hall was carpeted wall-to-ceiling, lined with gold statues and photos of previous productions which at one time included thirty-five showgirls. The club still had ninety minutes of top variety at one o'clock and to be accepted was a rare chance to work in a showbiz atmosphere and meet other acts.

In keeping with Adam and Eve, plastic leaves entwined above arches and draped over pillars. The red-clothed tables had apple-shaped lamps and fig leaf mats. The perspex stage was raised three feet for show time and lit from beneath. The club was managed by Marina, the daughter of the Eve's famous owner, Helen O'Brien.

Helen, then in her mid-sixties, wore her dyed blonde hair loose, full stage eyelashes and dressed in see-through chiffon evening gowns in peach and turquoise. It was said that she had at least peripheral knowledge of almost every well-known intrigue of the last three decades, having supposedly worked undercover for British Intelligence.

Helen didn't like my heavy metal, tough girl image but requested all my classical/cabaret numbers.

'You've got the old-fashioned showgirl appeal,' she enthused. 'Just my type.'

Adele Warren was Helen's protégé, a soloist and ex-Windmill tableau girl, with long legs, beautiful feet and perfect insteps, famous for twirling her nipple tassels in different directions. I discovered that the tassels stayed on due to pieces of ordinary sticking plaster. Adele turned them sticky-side out to form a loop which stuck to her flesh and the nipple cup. A painful end to the night if pulled off too quickly!

The dance acts Helen booked were not the striptease girls we worked with elsewhere, these were duos or groups, who had been through ballet training or stage schools but had rejected the conformity of the corps de ballet. Only the duos travelled as I did, performing on the world circuit. The London-based dancers had day jobs but we all did it for our passion, our chance to dance our own way. Even pinned down to a contract for three or six months at a time didn't seem so daunting in such rarefied company.

Variety acts would perform at Eve between foreign contracts, to earn a crust and perfect new shows. It was a stopping-off point and ideal to get the latest gossip on agents: Jac and Jaz, a comedy duo who were the image of Frankie Howerd and Buster Keaton respectively; Frederic with his marionettes; magician Larrott with his black panther; and singers from cruise ships – all with a tale and tons of experience.

One month when I was abroad, Hugo and Barbara, the act from Majorca were booked. Hugo slipped during the show and broke his neck, dying in Barbara's arms on the Eve stage. A tragedy, but a fitting place for him to take his leave.

In many ways the Eve was the best London had to offer – and I was part of it. As I entered my thirties I realised that I was a decade older than many of the other performers who appeared here. Age didn't concern me; I felt young and energetic, I was on a roll, I was polished, experienced and really enjoying the dancing. The desperation of the younger self to succeed at any cost had given way to a more measured enthusiasm which, in turn, meant I was as happy to perform charity Christmas shows for Crisis as I was to step out in front of my usual paying audience. I couldn't have had a more special and appreciative audience than the members of the Star and Garter home in Richmond, who were wheeled out front to watch me on their VE Day celebrations.

The auditioning never stopped though. I seemed to be constantly posting my CV to new contacts and now included a video of my acts.

I had a new costumier, Bernard, who had been a dancer at the Lido. He dressed me in more vibrant colours, creating sensational outfits. Through him I met Shirley Davis who made hats for TV (including Hyacinth Bouquet in *Keeping Up Appearances*) and dance productions. She designed some unusual headdresses for my grander shows. This meant that personal packing was reduced to the absolute minimum – the coat, dress and shoes I was wearing plus one dress for the club and my gym gear. Nothing else: my case was full of costumes and I carried the hat boxes.

The shows were first class but having to pay for accommodation meant I stayed at the cheapest guesthouses, often without a kitchen. I usually ate my food sitting on my bed and used my hands instead of cutlery and the plastic bag from my purchases as a plate. Window sills became my "fridge" for cheese and salad although my supplies were often diminished when items disappeared over the edge. I didn't own up at one pensione when the owner yelled, *"Mama mia!"* on discovering a pile of rancid food in his private courtyard!

*****

I saw lots of fellow thirty-somethings drift away from the business – and many more who threw the towel in while still in their late twenties. Some girls got married and stopped and plenty were bullied into leaving by the media. I lost count of the number of girls who told me, 'I think I'm too old,' on the strength of adverts in *The Stage* always requiring dancers aged eighteen to twenty-five, the misplaced logic being that beyond that, girls couldn't be as fit or beautiful. Others quit because they had suffered injuries or could not bear the sacrifices anymore, because of missing a "normal" life, because they had grown tired of travelling or earning a pittance. If you have never been possessed of that burning drive to be on the move, if you haven't dreamed all your life of seeing all four corners of the world, then I can imagine the constant planes, trains, dodgy cabs and dreadful digs would soon become wearing. I could never imagine that happening to me – even less so now that, in Colin, I had found a fellow traveller.

As we celebrated our first year together – as together as a pair separated on occasion by thousands of miles can be – I mulled over Colin's other qualities. He was my best friend, my companion and keeper. In many ways he was also my backbone, for he above everyone understood, at gut level, the drive to dance, the suffering for the jewel to shine, the craving to create, the necessary solitude, but also the need for stimulating company and adventure. He wanted to keep me, look after me and let me be free at the same time. What a contrast to Matt and the men like him – the ones who wanted to control me. Colin didn't want to stop me dancing. He loved that I was a dancer.

With the confidence that only happiness and a supportive relationship can bring I came to another decision. Enough time had passed since I'd ventured to Adelaide that first time. I'd regrouped emotionally and, now that Adolf was no longer around, my next step was clear.

'Where do you fancy going next?' Colin asked me one night. 'Madagascar, Moscow?'

'I'm going to America, Colin,' I announced, suddenly firm in my decision. 'I'm going to find Daddy.'

Tony Knight from Kabaret had contacts at Camelot's Club in Washington DC and if I arranged my flight and hotel they would hire me.

'You just have to let us know when you're coming.'

That was a relief to hear. Even as I packed my costumes I wasn't one hundred per cent convinced I was doing the right thing. I'd steeled myself for weeks in Adelaide, only to find disappointment. Meeting Adolf was incredible, of course. But the flatness I felt at missing my father had been hard to bear. What if it happened again?

Or worse?

What if he doesn't want to know me?

I pictured the man I had never met refusing to talk to me. I dreamed of a figure hiding behind a door, saying, 'Go away. I don't know you. Leave me alone.'

I don't think I could recover from that.

I compromised. Just as in Adelaide I would get my feet on the ground, build up my courage and then make my move.

America is a big country. It will take as long as it takes.

I'd never had a strong urge to visit the USA but the second I touched down alone at Dulles Airport I instantly felt at home and knew I would return many times. I sensed I could be myself here. People talked, they were open and interested. I loved their enthusiasm and positive attitude. They weren't too dissimilar from the Dutch in that respect. It would take days, if not weeks, to come to terms with the sheer mind-boggling scale of everything but I could taste in the air the sense that anything was possible in this country.

'Hold onto your dreams,' a busboy told me on my first night. Like everyone else, he believed that if you worked hard enough you could achieve what you wanted. It was just like being in a movie.

Attitudes were certainly different – unfortunately, so were the clubs. The American equivalent of cabaret appeared to be pole dancing – as I discovered as soon as I stepped into Camelot's and was presented with a square foot to perform in, between two poles.

'Don't you have places where soloists can dance?' I asked one of the other girls.

'Sure we do,' she said. 'It's called Broadway.'

She wasn't kidding. Very few places offered a costumed, choreographed show, which they called a "feature". This wasn't advantageous for me. There was no middle ground between these clubs and the major ticketed shows. Cruise lines and casinos featured European showgirls but like Paris they were coveted for their height and mostly auditioned in London through strict rules and regulations.

I didn't let it get me down and gave as much as I could in the limited space. More exciting for me was exploring a new city and Washington's vast stretch of museums. Around the White House you could almost smell the power of politics. I just walked and walked until I was in danger of becoming too tired to dance that night. I'd have so much to tell Colin. I missed him.

I wish he were here.

After Washington and armed with a multi-flight ticket, I had a choice. My father and his family lived north, in Albany, the capital of New York State. But I wasn't ready. *No, not yet.* On the other hand, I didn't fancy dancing on another tiny podium. *I'll think of something.* I flew to California and arrived among the beautiful vistas of Santa Barbara. There were ranches, sacred Indian land and, of course, health supermarkets, New Age centres galore and a Mecca for yoga enthusiasts. I was in my element. I got a job in a yoga studio and met like-minded people, including a Canadian teacher called Pam. It's surprising how quickly life rushes by when you've found a blissful niche and weeks turned into months before I eventually continued on to San Francisco. Surely there would be a cabaret scene there?

There was but most of it was tacky and unwelcoming. I really felt a 1960s vibe in the Haight area and I was desperate to stay. Eventually I found a decent venue, just a few doors down from Finnochios, a famous transvestite revue that I went to watch several times. If I needed inspiration a *La Cage aux Folles* type show did the trick, it triggered something within me; that I had to entertain. All the glow, glitter, mystery and make-believe.

I was advised not to walk around on my own late at night but I had no other choice and I never encountered any crime in the States. The days of being stalked by sinister couples were well and truly behind me, I was sure of that. Walking back to my guest house after work, China Town was like a film set at two in the morning, with its rising steam, streamers, swaying lanterns and twenty-four-hour coffee kiosks. I really did leave a piece of my heart in San Francisco .

Las Vegas, on the other hand, was a whole different world. Mouth-dropping acts like Siegfried and Roy opened my eyes to another level of performance. Most dance contracts in the big shows were for one year - the "tits and feathers" productions. I visited them all to glean ideas.

I could only find casual work at the end of the strip, at the Palamino, a pole and lap dancing venue with features. I fantasised about a long-term stay but only lasted a few weeks. I couldn't cope with the toxic atmosphere. This was the other end of the scene, a cut-throat business verging on porn, where I was competing with brash, big-bosomed fillies, who were tough as nails.

'Who do you think you are with those costumes?'

'You're in the wrong show in the wrong town.'

I had to agree. But where to go next?

It's time, I thought. *I can't put it off any longer.*

The flight into New York's JFK airport was one of the most nerve-wracking of my life. I planned and I plotted and I revised and I changed every detail about what I was about to do. By the time I was in a cab on the way to Manhattan I'd settled on a compromise: get a base, build-up my confidence after the mauling in Vegas. Then get my family back together.

The first thing that struck me in downtown Manhattan was its gritty, exciting energy. Nationalities mixed and mingled more than anywhere I'd ever seen in my life and the sheer *joie de vivre* of everyone came across loud – very loud – and clear. I booked into the Chelsea hotel, notorious for so many of its illustrious past guests, from Sid and Nancy to Dylan Thomas and Bob Dylan. But work was hard to find. The plan to become stable and secure before making the trip that I knew would change my life was faltering.

Just when I was about to give up, an invitation to perform in the Hamptons arrived, out of the blue, from old contacts who organized private shows in the exclusive hideaway. The event followed on from the original "BLT" party (bow tie, lingerie and toga), started by the infamous Mayflower Madam herself, Heidi Fleiss.

The tranquillity of the mansions with swimming pools and lawns stretching to the water was a welcome change from the Big Apple. There was space enough on the enormous verandas to make an ideal stage and all with sound systems installed. I could almost smell the money in the air. But there was no lace underwear or sandals worn by the audiences, only dinner suits and long dresses and uptight crowds who politely applauded and carried on eating canapés. I wish Heidi Fleiss had still been in charge!

I didn't go back to New York. And I didn't go to Albany.

I don't know why, but I just couldn't do it. I know now I was just making excuses to myself. But I wanted everything about my visit to be right. I spoke to Colin on the phone and he was trying to be supportive, but I could tell he wished I'd make the call, speak to my relatives, reach my father and get it over with.

'What have you got to lose, Tess?'

'Everything. If it doesn't happen as I imagine it then I will lose everything. And I'm not sure I can take that risk.'

I had walked into the airport and asked for the first available seat to Canada.

'There's an American Airlines flight leaving for Vancouver in ninety minutes, Ma'am.'

'I'll take it.'

Vancouver was a breathtaking setting. Included in my world package was a week in a mega-sized hotel room at the Pan Pacific, with two sitting rooms overlooking the marina. I revelled in the decadence and actually found it hard to motivate myself to leave. When I did I was shocked to discover work extremely thin on the ground. Eight days after arriving I downgraded into the YWCA, full of battered women with screaming children. But I found work in their fitness studio and as always had to satisfy my search for any dancing work before moving on.

After a dozen appointments with theatrical agents ended with the same answer – "we don't handle cabaret acts" – and more pole dancing venues in rougher parts of the city, I took my leave. I embarked on a spectacular train journey through Whistler, lit up like a Christmas card, with its ravines, waterfalls and lakes reflecting the sunsets, finally pulling into Prince George, British Columbia, where I was shocked to see it was sunbathing weather. On the face of it the journey was a random one, but Pam, whom I'd met in Santa Barbara, lived here.

'If you're ever passing through, we can always put you up somewhere, do please visit,' she'd said.

Well, I thought, *I'm going to pass through.*

Thanks to Pam's generosity I didn't really pass through at all – well, not for a few months. Every time I offered to find a hotel she said, 'Don't be silly, no one else is using our spare room.' Normally, I would never accept an invitation. I preferred to be independent and rarely stayed with anyone.

Pam was a feisty mix of homemaker (she had two sons), yoga teacher, waitress and proud owner of a Harley Davidson. With long blonde hair and brown eyes, she looked the business wearing her bike leathers.

Pam talked me through the club scene in the area and said I'd have no trouble finding work in the "C" venues – entertainers in Canada were booked on the A, B or C circuit, with C standing for "crap" as they put it.

'Unless promoters know you it will be harder to get the other venues,' she said, 'but some of the C's are pretty nice.'

She was right. Most bars and clubs had dancers and considerably fewer poles than in America which was a blessing. The first place she suggested signed me up that day. The conditions were reasonable, with quiet afternoon slots, nothing sleazy and cash in hand. What more could I ask for?

'Come along tonight and see what we're about,' the manager said. 'You can start tomorrow.'

If I'd had to guess the audience based on my stereotypical knowledge of Canadians in the smaller areas, I would have imagined lumberjacks and the standard country music uniform of stetsons, boots and fringed jackets.

And I would have been absolutely right!

Pam laughed at me as I scoured the bar's clientele for someone who didn't look like he'd stepped out of a film casting. But I was happy with the atmosphere. The bar's customers, mainly men, all seemed amiable enough although I was interested to see how that would change when the entertainment started.

The first girl came out to whooping applause and immediately I knew the sort of venue I'd signed up for. Like everyone else I saw that night, she had a fulsome, sexy figure with enormous silicone bosoms stretching the nipples to bursting, a back-combed fringe and thick make-up. She walked slowly around her stage area, posed and pouted. She did anything but dance.

Each show lasted twenty minutes which was far too long, and every act titillated the crowd until taking their clothes off and lying down on a rug, revealing everything, for the last five minutes. Nothing was left to the imagination.

'I don't think I'm going to go down very well, Pam,' I worried afterwards, but she wouldn't hear of it.

'Don't be silly. They won't know what has hit them.'

The next evening, I performed my *Slave To The Rhythm* routine to a sea of stunned faces. When I ended, arms triumphantly aloft, a wall of silence greeted me. Two seconds later the bar erupted. Hats were thrown into the air, beer glasses slammed down onto the table and cheers rang out.

'They've never seen anything like it!' Pam called over. 'You've won them over!'

Word of this strange English girl with her elaborate costumes, unusual music and finely choreographed act soon got around the town. Not only did my afternoon slots get better turn-outs but I stepped up to the B circuit for some of the evening shows. Before long I was running around town performing two or three times a night.

It was with sadness that I left Pam and Prince George but I had a mission to accomplish. Albany was calling and I was very nearly ready to reply. Once again, though, the thought of ticking off a few other cities before I headed back south was too great. Next stop Toronto, followed by Ontario and, by July, Montreal.

Despite having names like Chateau du Sexe, a lot of Montreal's table clubs were actually clean and professional, with no hostesses and a variety of good acts. At the Chateau Champlais hotel, in the city centre, I was surprised to find a little theatre attached which had an eight-girl Paris revue. How different from Vancouver!

I joined the team at Wanda's, an all-day club serving snacks and cocktails to a healthy, mixed crowd. Even though I was hired as a main feature and not a table dancer the pay was low, just covering a room at the YMCA. I happened to mention my predicament one night to two strapping regulars at the club, and my luck suddenly changed.

Denis and Greg worked in the fur trade and, with their pony-tails and long leather coats, looked like extras in a Davy Crockett film. But Denis owned a flat which was only used for parties.

'If you want to clean it up for me, you can stay there rent-free as long as you like,' he offered. I snatched his hand off. It took three days to get straight but after that I had six glorious weeks of working in a delightful venue, to enthusiastic crowds, before coming home to a smart little apartment.

After one of my many walks through the city's amazing parks, I sat on a bench one evening under a full moon, at one with the Canadian wilderness just a few miles away. A family of racoons rustled in and out of the bushes by my feet and, as I watched the trees sway high above my head, the forest felt alive. I don't know where it came from but for a second I was touched by something powerful, euphoric and strong. I knew it was time.

A few hours later I rang home. Colin had just returned from a trip. He was delighted to hear my news and promised to come out soon to join me. How refreshing to know that, unlike Thierry, these promises would be honoured. Then I called Mum.

'It's like just being here has cleared all the clutter out of my head. I'm ready now. I'm going to finish the week then I'm going to do it. I'm going back to New York and I'm going to find Daddy.'

There was a pause on the line. Then Mum's voice spoke slowly and quietly.

'I didn't know whether to tell you before,' she began.

'Tell me what?'

'You're too late.'

My heart was sinking.

'Too late? Where's he moved to now?'

'He hasn't moved anywhere darling,' she said. 'He's dead.'

CHAPTER SEVENTEEN

HE NEVER FORGOT YOU

'Dead?'

The word hung in the air. I repeated it over and over in my head so many times it lost any meaning.

'Tess?'

'I'm still here, Mum.'

'I'm sorry,' she said. 'It happened a couple of months ago. I didn't know whether to tell you or not.'

What else haven't you told me? Angry thoughts flashed through my mind.

'I was going to find him,' I said, desperately trying to stay calm. 'I was finally ready.'

'I know.'

'And now it's too late.'

There was nothing else to say. I hung up and Mum said she'd call back later. When she did, I was prepared.

'I'm going anyway,' I told her. 'I want to see where he lived. I want to see where he' – I felt the tears well again – 'I want to see where he died.'

Mum gave me a number. Jo, my grandmother, had died in 1985 but her two sisters and one daughter were still living at the same address.

'You could try to contact them if you want.'

Of course I want to contact them. And this time I'm not going to put it off.

I felt my world falling in. It was my fault. There was no getting away from it. I should have gone to Albany as soon as I'd reached America. Why hadn't I? Why had I put it off? Because I wanted to get settled first? Was that really the answer? How settled do you need to be to meet your own father?

I picked up the phone and dialled the number Mum had given me.

By sheer fluke, Denis and Greg mentioned they were driving to New York State a few days later to make deliveries. If I didn't mind travelling in their van they'd be happy to drop me off.

The journey across the Canadian border was one of the most sad and unsettling moments of my life. We crossed the line into New York State and I knew then there was no turning back. The boys dropped me at a motel in Albany and we made our farewells.

'Thanks for everything,' I sobbed.

'I hope you find what you're looking for,' Denis said.

'Be strong and be happy, Tessa,' Greg added. 'You deserve it.'

I called my relatives as soon as I got into my room. They would drive over in the morning and collect me. I couldn't sleep and just stared at the ceiling, not focused on anything, dazed; eyes and body swimming with emotion. I must have dropped off because my alarm clock shocked me straight into action, to shower and dress. Then there was a buzz on my room phone.

They're here!

I ran down to reception where three women stood nervously; Maria and Ena, my great-aunts and Elga, Maria's daughter. They looked up as I entered.

'Hello, Tessa.'

Those were the last words I remember. We all trembled as we hugged, choking back tears between smiles and stepping away at arms' length to look at each other. Not many words came out, none were necessary. They had the Latvian features and the familiar heavy accent. I felt like I was looking at my own past and future at the same time. It had been so long time since I'd felt such love. I was with my family. I felt like I was home.

As soon as we were able, they drove me to the bungalow they all shared. In many ways it was exactly like Adolf's. It still had that unmistakeable European feel in simple, good taste. Life centred around the kitchen and as dish after dish of delectable Latvian recipes were being served my new family and I poured out our hearts. They were handsome women with short, wavy hair wearing winged fifties style glasses, smart slacks and jackets.

When we'd finished and sat deep in thought over coffee, Maria said, 'I have something for you.'

For me?

She disappeared for a few minutes then returned carrying a battered old suitcase. It looked just like the old one Mum had lent me years ago.

'This was your father's. These are his things.'

Maria put the case on the table and let me open it. I had no idea what to expect. I didn't have great hopes – from everything I knew of Daddy he hadn't been the materialistic type. But as soon as I lifted the lid I froze. The case was almost bare.

This was his life.

I pulled out some scraps of paper. To anyone else they were just shopping lists and notes to himself. But to me they were pieces of him. I stared at the heavy penned scrawl. I'd never seen that before. I'd never seen my own father's handwriting.

It was getting harder to stand. I felt my legs quiver and I let Maria get me a chair. It was becoming too much. They were only possessions but they were *his* possessions. I was getting a glimpse of the man I never knew.

The silent ceremony continued as I picked up a watch and a tatty leather wallet. I fondled each one lovingly, caressing them with my fingertips then holding them to my cheek. I wanted to smell him, to feel him through his things. I knew I couldn't take in much more when Maria came back into the room.

'And finally,' she said, 'Dainis's most treasured possession.'

What could it be?

She handed me a poster size card. It was familiar, but it couldn't be, could it? I stared at the photograph of me, aged sixteen, wearing a barrow boy's cap from my modelling days. Tears filled my eyes and I had to look away.

'Why is this here?'

'You meant everything to him, Tessa,' Ena said softly. 'He never forgot you.'

It was like a punch in the stomach. The wind left my lungs and I fell forward, collapsing on the suitcase, hugging it as I would have my Father. I was suddenly dizzy, faint with emotion and shock.

'He never forgot me? But he never knew me.'

'But he wanted to. He wanted to meet you more than anything in the world.'

The next day we drove out to Daddy's grave. It was an anonymous plot, just a hole in a field with a flowerpot on top. But it was natural and untouched, in an open space that meant much more than a row of plaques in concrete.

'He's there,' Maria pointed, 'and Jo, his mother, is next to him there.'

I looked down to the man who had dominated my life without ever showing himself to me, and said a silent prayer.

I'm sorry I never knew you. I never thought you wanted to see me. I thought you had forgotten all about me. But now I know I was wrong.

'I will see you one day,' I promised.

That night I walked along a beautiful mountain path, the heat of the sun dancing on my back. I saw a log cabin in the distance and marched purposefully towards it. I watched as the door opened and a well-built man with dark, good looks and vivid blue eyes stepped out. He wrapped strong arms around me and whispered, 'I love you' into my ear. Then he went back inside the cabin.

When I woke up I knew I'd met my father at last.

*****

I was so lonely on the flight back to London. Even with Colin beside me I would still have felt empty, as though a piece of me were missing. Parting from Maria, Ena and Elga had been difficult. It felt like we'd known each other for decades, not days.

'I will be back,' I promised. 'Thank you for everything.'

But it wasn't the past that was troubling me. It was the future. In particular it was the immediate future and the conversation I now knew I had to have with my mother. I'd grown up thinking Daddy had cut me out of his life. But he'd never forgotten me, his own family – *my own family* – had said. He had always carried a picture of me. Where had that come from? Mum. She must have sent it.

Mum has the answers.

I wasn't looking forward to asking the questions at all.

*****

'He sent these?'

I looked at the pile of letters on the kitchen table, bound by a piece of frayed string. Mum nodded as she undid the string and began sifting through the pile. She found one and handed it over.

I gasped at the writing. It was identical to the scrawl on the shopping lists Maria had given me. But this time it was really Daddy talking.

I scanned the page, eager to drink in the words, my eyes full with tears. *I can't do this.* But I read on. The words were like little stabs in my own heart. Daddy was alone, he was distraught, he was beating himself up over his behaviour, promising to change. And he was beseeching, absolutely begging Mum to come back. But not just her.

My eyes halted on one line.

'I beg you, Doreen, come back with our little girl.'

Our little girl.

Me!

I read the line aloud again and again.

'Do you know what this means, Mum?'

Again she nodded.

'He wanted me. He hadn't forgotten me. I wasn't abandoned.'

'No,' she cried. 'I sent pictures to Jo every so often. He always knew what you looked like. He always asked after you.'

I stared at the letter then back at Mum. It was one thing for her not to keep in touch with Dad but another to prevent me from knowing him. But that's what she'd done. I knew why she'd done it – to protect herself and to protect us. Nobody in the 1950s leaves the father of their unborn child lightly. Nobody flees to the other side of the world rather than expose their daughter to a parent she thinks unfit. Everything was done for the right reasons. But I'd stopped needing protection years ago. Now I needed the truth.

'I know you had to leave, Mum, I'm not blaming you for that. God knows I've been with enough troubled men. But,' and here I broke down again, 'but not to know he cared about me and was writing to you... To grow up believing I'd been forgotten...'

I couldn't go on. The pile of letters was calling me. There were notes there addressed to me, little comments on cards to Mum, best wishes and kisses.

But I had never had a clue that these existed.

The next few days were uncomfortable. I avoided Colin's calls and tried to keep out of Mum's way as well. I wasn't blaming her. I just needed time to think. My whole life had been turned upside down in the last week. There was so much mess to be picked through.

I watched Mum busy about her work at Providence Court. She really had given me a tremendous life. She'd done the best she possibly could for me. Made every sacrifice, worked to exhaustion, put herself out time and time again.

And I knew why. She did for me what her own parents had done for her. How hard must it have been for them to give up their daughter even with her best interests in mind? Well, that's why Mum had walked away from Dad. What sort of home life would he have given a new baby in 1960? Hadn't she always told me what a wrench it had been to leave, to board that ship, when she'd loved him more than anyone else in the world?

'You can't imagine, Tess. It felt like everyone on the ship was staring at me. As though they knew I was pregnant, and running away. And everywhere I looked I saw your father. The waiters, the cabin boys, the guests – even the captain himself. They all reminded me of him. They were all trying to tell me I'd made a mistake, I had to go back. But I knew I hadn't. I knew I had to come home to England. And then you were born and you were my salvation. I focused everything on you.'

I understood. I wasn't happy, but I understood.

And I was suddenly clear on something else. The years of denying that having a father was important were over. To all those women who say that having a child's dad around doesn't matter I say, "You're wrong." It took me thirty years to realise because I never really felt I was missing anything. But when that day came the damage had already been done. My life had already chosen its path. It was a life without balance. A life spent, I now realised, craving male company, boys and men, to fill the subconscious void.

A life book-ended by not knowing my father and, now, never being able to know him.

*****

Life can be divided into all sorts of sections and mine is no exception. Age is often the separator, or it could be location or a relationship or a job. My largest point of reference is more esoteric: there's my life when I thought my father didn't care about me and then there's my life knowing he did.

But we have to go on, even after a watershed moment. Back in Colin's arms once more, I started to feel alive again, open to the opportunities all around me. He was loving and supportive through my personal crisis, which I'll never be able to thank him enough for. And in Colin I had a kindred spirit. We laughed at the same things and were prepared to push each other to the limits. Who else had ever encouraged him to spend an entire day wearing a beauty mask and pretending to be from some tribal order? Or arranged a sombre ceremony to commemorate the burning of his rancid trainers?

I knew then that Colin was the man I needed to marry. He would bring my life full circle. Unlike so many other men I'd known, he had no agenda other than living his life. He wanted nothing from me other than me. He didn't want to shape me or control me.

Which is exactly the reason he could never marry, I realised.

But I hoped. I always live in hope.

*****

After a few months back on the London circuit I ventured abroad once more. Again I had choices but my experience of Latvian hospitality in Albany still lingered strongly. *It has to be Europe,* I decided. *I need to feel at home.* This included returning to Greece. It was a stupid mistake.

I corresponded with an ex-Moulin Rouge dancer promoting her agency in *The Stage* and was signed up, sent a contract and even asked for copies of my ballet certificates. I thought that if anyone appreciated standards, it would be this lady.

Since the Berlin wall came down, Eastern bloc beauties had flooded onto the club scene to earn a living. Many were bought and sold and were so desperate they would do almost anything for a cigarette. The few who were terrific dancers were often haughty and cold and difficult to work with, as they wanted top billing. Mainland Greece forged the worst reputation for treating dancers badly. I heard rumours of girls smuggled in, their passports and their lives taken away. In Thessaloniki I saw this for myself. I danced my four shows a night but did not sit in the club for consummation. The surly Greek owner only spoke to me once and I later discovered that he was the agent's husband!

There were ten young Dutch girls who were distraught at being split up from their friends whom, they told me, were being held captive at an apartment block somewhere inland. One victim had managed to make a call out on a customer's mobile. They were locked in, sold for sex and had no idea where they were.

Unwittingly, I saved the day when the agent appeared at closing time. I was summoned and told to pack my costumes and leave immediately. Was she really an ex-dancer with morals and standards? There was a commotion as she began to choose some of the girls to take away whilst arguing furiously with her husband. I was so incensed that I jumped up as if stabbed and slid across the bar by sheer instinct .and grabbed a plastic bag she was fumbling with behind the counter. It all happened in a flash and everyone just stood open-mouthed, completely stunned by my actions. Inside the bag were twenty passports including mine! The girls piled outside with me, kissed and cried as they clutched their passports and those of their friends, and ran off to their freedom. I was quite proud of myself.

Agents and club owners were now so corrupt that Equity started a blacklist of these villains when they were reported, even via non-Equity contracts. Artine, my Cypriot agent, was found strangled in his office.

It was getting more difficult to find anyone that I could trust. All the great agents like Bajot in Paris and Pires in Portugal were stepping down and in their place came a fragmented, more open and dangerous set of entrepreneurs who advertised club work. Many were pimps or shady owners of some rough establishment and some were even the mothers of dancers whose boyfriends managed some club abroad.

Fortunately, I received safe offers for Belgium, France, Luxembourg, the Moulin Rouge in Stuttgart and then Berlin, thanks to my agent, Carla Schnitzler. Germany meant hard contracts but good money and job satisfaction. I don't know if it came across in my persona or performance but I definitely felt a different person. The absence of a father no longer hung over me like a curse. On the contrary, everywhere I went I had the sensation of him close to me, like my guardian angel. I liked it.

Berlin was the city where cabaret was born: "crazy, debauched - cesspool and paradise in one" as Brunningen wrote in 1913.

Das Kleine Nacht Revue had originally been a famous drag revue called Dollywood. Drag acts still appeared here to compère and sing haunting war songs next to slick, bi-sexual acts and raucous comedy.

Sylvie, a supreme showgirl and contortionist, ran the club and performed nightly. "Sandra" sat next to me in the dressing room, arriving as a little chap in jeans, to become a blonde powerhouse in a diamanté gown. It was bad luck for anyone to see the transformation and "tucking away". But when I heard a feminine cough behind me and *'mein schatz'*, I could turn and face he, as she, and blow a kiss.

"Claire" was another hilarious drag act whose naughty antics caused mayhem. His finale was to choose a member of the audience to come up on stage and sit on a throne. After adorning them with a cloak and crown, he would suggestively peel a banana and present it to the lucky customer.

Stefan and Gaynor from Essex, were an acrobatic apache act called Pastiche. We had met at the Eve Club and by luck, toured most of Germany together. I admired them, for they had plugged away for years to polish their act and had done well to attain top theatre bookings in Europe.

Whilst in Berlin we were able to get tickets to see other shows including the famous Friedrichstadt Palast variety theatre which used performing white horses from Austria in the dance routines. This was show business at its best.

My four solo spots at Das Kleine Nacht were the peak of my career so far. Drenched in sweat for the quick change finale, we presented ourselves in a line to say farewell in ten languages. I felt on top of the world.

One regular face in the audience was Rupert, a clown in the Italian circus which I had practically followed around Europe. One night he invited me to his performance at the circus in Potsdamer Platz. After winding down with a glass of wine in his van, when all was sultry and still he led me between tent pegs and trailers. 'You see that mound over there? That's Hitler's bunker'. We reached another huge tent that blotted out the moon.

'I'll show you something wonderful' he whispered as he pulled back the flap. 'Be very quiet'.

The sight I saw stopped any words. Standing in a row were twelve enormous elephants. Every other elephant was standing, watchful, over his mate who lay sleeping; noble, serene, gentle giants, awkward yet delicate, silent except for the sway of a trunk, a sigh of breath.

Eavesdropping on this extraordinary and moving scene was unforgettable. I knew that someone was watching over me too.

From Germany to London and to a cabaret market in the West End besieged by problems. With the new music copyright laws requiring clubs to have a licence to play recordings, I could no longer turn up at any venue with my tapes and expect to perform. One manager laid it on the line. 'Sorry, Tess, we're not paying for a licence. You can either dance to the band or give it a miss.'

What a choice. My new routine to Tina Turner's *Private Dancer* (the lyrics epitomise the cabaret scene) was entirely built around the musical edit. Taking away the accompaniment was like taking away the choreography, especially after I'd paid so much for the tapes in the first place. (The outlay for new shows was increasing. My yearly expenses were now over £3,000.)

Licences weren't the only problem. The venues themselves were disappearing. I had received a call one afternoon in 1992 to say the Eve was closing – that night.

'You'd better come and collect your costumes or they'll be binned with everything else.'

'But I was only there last night. Everything seemed fine.'

'Well, it's not fine today. I'm sorry.'

When I went in there was no sign of Helen. I can't imagine how it felt for her but for acts like me it seemed like the end of an era.

A few years later and the death knell had sounded. Investment in my sort of show was disappearing fast. Once Peter Stringfellow persuaded magistrates to grant his lap-dancing venue Cabaret of Angels the first licence in 1996, others were quick to follow. Despite its name, the Cabaret of Angels was the beginning of the end for variety artistes.

At least I still had my international contacts. Most girls I knew in London never left the country. They were the ones hardest hit – especially once they'd reached a certain age. The new clubs' obsession with strippers over performers focused on youth. After years of service dancers were discovering just how much loyalty there was in the business – absolutely none. I was present at the New Georgian club the night Janie, a popular act in the West End, broke down. She wasn't even performing – she'd come to ask – *beg* – for a spot.

I found her sobbing in the stairwell. 'They won't even let me try out. They've taken away my life. Dancing is all I am, all I do. All my confidence is on stage. Off it, I'm nobody, until I perform again.'

As much as I tried to console her, I knew she was speaking the truth – for all of us.

'The clubs have trashed me. They've just thrown me away.'

Her crime? She was forty-one.

I felt for Janie but the truth hit home to me as well. She had five years on me but here was proof that I wasn't indestructible, I wasn't indispensable. In Janie's despair I felt my own horror. But unlike her and so many other girls, all my eggs weren't in the one basket. *I've still got a life abroad.*

*****

One of Colin's greatest pleasures in the world was finding new ways to educate me. He enjoyed the fantasy of shaping a rather raw disciple, transforming me from village girl to a worldly-wise woman and, as ridiculous as it was, I indulged him. We were on a beach one day and I said mockingly, 'Oh, how Proustian.'

Colin immediately seized on my mispronunciation.

'Not Prow-st, my dear, *Proooo-st!*'

The next day he bought me a copy of *Remembrance Of Things Past* and to this day Proust, however you say his name, is one of my favourite authors. In fact, it's a quote from the French writer that sums up my attitude to travelling: "The real voyage of discovery consists not in seeking new landscapes but in having new eyes."

With that in mind, I booked tickets to Nairobi for my return to Africa.

'It's as though I have unfinished business with that continent,' I told Colin. 'I have to go back.'

I'm so glad I did. The Nairobi Casino offered a contract for their intimate Club Galileo during the week of Diwali, the Indian Festival of Lights: there was as large an Indian population as British. I have rarely been treated so well.

I was met immediately from the plane at Nairobi Airport and from there fast-tracked straight through to my awaiting chauffeur-driven car – we even bypassed customs like a proper VIP! When I pulled up at the Casino I gasped. There, ten feet high, was a billboard advertising my show and featuring a poster-sized headshot of me. I couldn't wait to take a picture of it.

Mum will never believe this.

I didn't believe what happened next: a porter showed me into the foyer and the second I stepped inside I was presented with a bouquet of flowers. Galileo's staff lined up against the wall, broad smiles on their faces as they clapped heartily. It all seemed surreal.

My apartment in the hotel was equally impressive, as was the meal in the dining room. To think, as well, that I was being paid £300 for a fortnight's work plus all expenses– I felt like I should have been paying them!

The longer the day went on the more pressure I felt under to deliver an unforgettable show.

What if they hate me? What if they think it's all been a waste of time?

I needn't have worried. When I performed Cabaret that evening I thought the applause would never stop. Lunging into a backbend on the blue carpeted stage that felt like mink on the skin, I gazed up through the glass ceiling to see the night sky full of stars.

This is perfection. Life doesn't get any better than this.

What the Nairobi Casino offered in luxury, Cape Town matched in the beauty of its natural resources. I arrived on spec in South Africa, as the top entertainment venue - the leisure palace, Sun City - only booked showgirl troupes. Deborah had worked there and the only way she could bring home her earnings was in the form of diamonds that she purchased.

I was blown away by the breathtaking landscape: I could stare at Table Mountain all day, intoxicated by the way its peak swept down to the ocean. Unfortunately the area's cabaret scene left a lot to be desired. I danced at another Moulin Rouge but didn't stay long. Although the streets were quiet and the club was a block away, my hotel insisted that I be escorted to and from the venue. Sure enough, one night someone was shot dead right outside the stage door and I realized that the silence was ominous. Even during the day, as I got to know the city, there were places where I felt uncomfortable and I sensed an increasing menace.

I took a train journey along the Garden Route before I departed so as to return home with positive memories – the side that the tourists see.

But arriving at my next destination, New Zealand, and thinking of it as the home of hills and sheep, I found the most beautiful place on Earth!

Wicked Willies club in Christchurch had paid for my ticket, set up an apartment and even arranged the use of a car, for me to appear as their guest star on opening night, for a four month contract.

Voyna, a Kiwi dancer I met on the London scene had recommended me to the boss. She was a dynamo, with masses of thick blonde hair, strong features and a trim figure. Her signature number was dancing to *Burlington Bertie* disguised as a man, then revealing a leopard g-string and writhing around like a temptress. She was a great fan of my shows and said I was the right top class act to front the new venue.

The wages were low but the chance was too good to miss. The sights I discovered each day in the wild were worth any amount of dollars. But with the case of Janie still fresh in my mind I did begin to think about the future. Where was my income going to come from in five years' time? Should I be chasing more money?

After being interviewed on TV to promote the club, I was invited by the network for a stay in Queenstown and to take a flight over Milford Sound.

It was indeed rare to be given such gifts in my profession.

Within ten weeks though, the image that the club was trying to portray couldn't hold. The boss ran escort and massage parlours and filtered his girls as hostesses through the club. There was a brutal side to him that wanted total control. He had a sidekick, a dwarf called Alfred, who ran around doing his dirty business. Fights broke out, even amongst the female guests. They were nasty to witness and many times I had to leave by the fire escape. Everything was played out in the club.

I was eventually moved to a smaller unit, the car was taken back and, although I performed until the end of the contract, I nearly lost my courage. One evening after the show, as I unlocked my door, I was accosted by a man in a balaclava waiting in the shadows. He shoved me up against the wall and grazed my cheek as he slammed into me and squeezed my throat.

'This is a warning' he growled, sweating and spitting into my ear. He jerked, but only to release me, to slip back into the night. I just knew it had to have been the boss's idea to create fear so I would not step out of line and report what I'd seen going on in the club. I hadn't been harmed physically but I barricaded the door with furniture that night and slept upright, with a dumbbell in my hand.

The day I left there was an article in *The Press* newspaper about my career, my successful stint at Wicked Willies, and a photo of my smiling face.........

My life had been one of extremes; highs and lows, Cornwall or the furthest destination, full of love or full of loathing. New Zealand had been the most bizarre combination of utter beauty and ugliness. But finally as an attraction show with no more consummation dramas, I was on a winning streak. The highest reward that the profession could afford me was consistent work, though albeit still treacherous.

Denmark couldn't be further away from New Zealand, either in geography or in climate – or in the quality of the clubs. I arrived from the southern hemisphere's summer to a freezing Danish spring.

I was excited to be premiering my latest – and what would be my final – show. This combination of *Lawrence of Arabia* and the Bond theme, *GoldenEye*, was one of my most theatrical routines yet, with an elaborate Cleopatra headdress, gold lamé dress and veiled bikini, performing a mix of ballet and acrobatics.

There were four main clubs in Copenhagen all owned by a very fair and unassuming boss, Erik. I worked at the well-run Waterloo and Wonderbar cabarets advertising, "You have not visited Denmark if you haven't spent an unforgettable evening here, presenting a big bouquet of beautiful ladies and international shows."

Erik preferred to employ buxom Caribbean girls with generous figures and double D's, who seemed almost motherly when entertaining the majority of bashful, moustached, pale Danes who salivated over them. Although the system was as hard as anywhere, I was respected and offered a clean apartment and a private dressing room.

I don't think I've ever seen more aggressive hostess work – or more lucrative results. One of the local girls, a pretty and young brunette called Marie, was brutally frank about her motives for working there.

'I've been here for three years, working every night, drinking and fucking,' she admitted. 'But I'm thirty, I've got a house, a Porsche – everything I want.'

I was impressed. I couldn't help it. But I wasn't jealous, not even one per cent. I saw Marie every night. I saw her down her own bottle of Dutch courage in the dressing room before stepping out into the melée of roaring customers. I saw the emptiness in her eyes and the scars on her body. And, when we stood next to each other at the mirror, I saw that she looked ten years my senior, not the other way round.

No job is worth doing for the money, I thought, *however much. You have to do it because you love it.*

Marie seemed to have everything but happiness. Was I kidding myself if I said I had it? *All things considered*, I thought, *No I'm not. I love what I do.*

But for how long can I continue to do it?

By 1998 the rest of the world was beginning to catch up with London. Opportunities for solo cabaret artistes were becoming fewer and further apart. I found work in Japan and Norway again, on some excellent contracts but there were gaps of months, not days, in between each trip. But eventually even the good clubs themselves started to turn.

I returned to Australia to meet my cousin in Sydney and went back to the Crazy Horse in Adelaide, scene of so many exhilarating nights. This time I only managed one week there. Attraction shows didn't work anymore. John Monaghan had to move with the times and give customers what they wanted. The club had changed beyond all recognition. Where once I'd felt at home I was now a stranger. The theatre was dotted with poles and even backstage had been converted to a private lounge for lap dancers, where anything went.

Anne had retired and the girls taking her place were a different breed. *This isn't me*, I thought as I drove away, but it didn't matter. A new maturity and acceptance washed over the sadness. I smiled with fond memories and gratitude. I didn't need or want what was behind me except for Anne, who had a new apartment by the ocean and had gone back to nursing. She had held on almost too long through the changes. The greatest star of Adelaide is still remembered now, although on her final night the girls at the club gave her no memorable farewell, no reward or acknowledgement. Pure jealousy and ignorance – a sign of the drop in standards all round.

However phlegmatically I took the news, there was no getting away from the truth that the world was changing – *my* world was changing. And if things were bad on the global circuit that could only mean London would be worse.

Friends, too, were moving on. Voyna in New Zealand retired to run her father's camp site; Stefan and Gaynor had hung up their whips in order to buy a home in Southend; and Shelley from the Windmill had married again and made me Godmother to her daughter.

As I picked my way through bookings in late 1999 and early 2000 I knew the writing was on the wall. The age of the DJ running a state-of-the-art show was over. They just played CD's now and acts, if there were any, were responsible for their own lights and music.

Gone, too, was the sense of a feature performance. Lap dancers overwhelmed all the venues that had previously welcomed magicians, jugglers and fire-eaters. Those places that still pretended to host cabaret relegated their attractions to the post-midnight slot. It was death by billing. What audience wants to see card tricks after four hours of drinking and watching naked women simulate sex?

I should have stopped a year before I did, but dancing had been my drug all my life and you cannot just quit something that powerful. But the last year, on the whole, was not pleasant. On the occasions I could get a booking I had to peek through the curtain to check that the lap dancers had finished before pressing "play" on the sound system and taking my starting position. And who was I dancing for? Punters who'd paid to see women mime their every sexual fantasy – not this vision in gold with her leaps, splits and arches. What audience like that wants to see a highly skilled dancer incorporate the sense of the Sahara in her production of *Lawrence of Arabia*?

On a good night it was tolerable; on a bad night abjectly humiliating.

I just needed a sign to stop and in July 2000 I received it. Kabaret was one of the few clubs still hiring attractions. I walked in one evening ready for the one a.m. show and Tony Knight happened to be standing on the pavement talking to a friend. He greeted me with the usual kiss on the cheek but stopped me going downstairs.

'Don't bother tonight, Tess. It's finished for the shows. The lap dancers are enough.'

'You can't be serious?' I said, shocked.

'That's how it is. But here, take your wages for tonight'. And pushing fifteen pounds into my bag, with a shrug of his shoulders, he turned back to his friend. After fifteen years' service that was my thanks.

A few weeks later I celebrated my fortieth birthday. It's a significant milestone in anyone's life and I celebrated in the only way I knew how: by flying to Berlin for one last true showbiz stint at the Kleine Nacht. There was plenty of work left for me there but I could see the tide turning.

If I'm getting out, I'm getting out on my terms, I promised myself. *I'm not going to be chewed up like Janie or ignored like Anne.*

By coincidence, the very venue that had broken Janie's heart, the New Georgian Club in Mill Street, was more than happy to offer me a final contract until the end of the year. In contrast to my experiences in so many other venues it went well for the simple reason that the owners invested in their shows. In fact, it would have been easy to have convinced myself that there was nothing at all wrong with the industry. But I knew that wasn't true. And in any case I had made plans. There was no stopping now.

But am I doing the right thing?

The morning of December 19th 2000 was one of the most overpowering of my life. I could barely eat anything and the afternoon passed in a blur. At eleven o'clock I kissed Mum goodbye and walked up to Regent Street, enjoying my twilight city for the last time. Two hours later I stared at the curtain at the New Georgian and smiled as it stared back. That old sensation of "what lies behind?" had never left me and I immersed myself in the view, in the scene, for the very last time.

I recalled for the umpteenth time Martha Graham's quote which summed it all up, "Wherever a dancer stands ready, that place is holy ground."

Suddenly the music played, the curtain peeled back, and I was on.

As I stepped back down into the wings afterwards, breathless, a familiar hand reached out.

'Thank you for coming,' I said.

'I wouldn't have missed it for the world,' Colin replied. 'It was amazing. You are always amazing.'

As I zipped up my costume bags for the final time, I looked around the packed dressing room, swamped by champagne from the bosses, bouquets from the hostesses and dozens of cards gathered from well-wishers, I smiled to myself.

It was amazing, wasn't it?